A Deeper Learning Companion for CLIL

If education is to prepare learners for lifelong learning, there needs to be a shift toward deeper learning: a focus on transferable knowledge and problem-solving skills alongside the development of a positive or growth mind-set. Deeper learning is inextricably linked with subject-specific processes of constructing and communicating knowledge. Therefore, disciplinary literacies need to take center stage in every classroom.

Designed as a companion to the influential volume *Beyond CLIL*, this highly practical book offers step-by-step instructions for designing and implementing innovative tasks and materials for pluriliteracies development in Content and Language Integrated Learning (CLIL) – a transformative teaching approach where students study subjects in a different language.

It contains annotated case studies of deeper learning episodes (DLEs) across a wide range of school subjects, using an innovative and proven template, to help teachers explore the potential of Pluriliteracies Teaching for Deeper Learning (PTDL) inside their own classrooms. Theoretically grounded, this book offers a road map for schools, ranging from exploratory first steps, to transdisciplinary projects, to whole school moves for curriculum development and transformative pedagogies.

Do Coyle is Chair in Languages Education and Classroom Pedagogy at the University of Edinburgh.

Oliver Meyer is Head of the Department of Teaching English as a Foreign Language at the Johannes Gutenberg University of Mainz.

Susanne Staschen-Dielmann works in the Preparatory Service for Teachers at the Berlin Senate Department for Education, Youth and Family.

Together they have been working on ways to implement their shared vision for deeper learning across subjects and languages.

T0349604

A Deeper Learning Companion for CLIL

Putting Pluriliteracies into Practice

Edited by

Do Coyle
University of Edinburgh

Oliver Meyer
Johannes Gutenberg University of Mainz

Susanne Staschen-Dielmann
Berlin Senate Department for Education, Youth and Family

CAMBRIDGE
UNIVERSITY PRESS

Shaftesbury Road, Cambridge CB2 8EA, United Kingdom

One Liberty Plaza, 20th Floor, New York, NY 10006, USA

477 Williamstown Road, Port Melbourne, VIC 3207, Australia

314–321, 3rd Floor, Plot 3, Splendor Forum, Jasola District Centre, New Delhi – 110025, India

103 Penang Road, #05–06/07, Visioncrest Commercial, Singapore 238467

Cambridge University Press is part of Cambridge University Press & Assessment,
a department of the University of Cambridge.

We share the University's mission to contribute to society through the pursuit of
education, learning and research at the highest international levels of excellence.

www.cambridge.org
Information on this title: www.cambridge.org/9781316517284

DOI: 10.1017/9781009043755

First published 2023

Printed in the United Kingdom by TJ Books Limited, Padstow Cornwall

A catalogue record for this publication is available from the British Library.

Library of Congress Cataloging-in-Publication Data
Names: Coyle, Do, 1952– editor. | Meyer, Oliver (Professor of English), editor. | Staschen-
    Dielmann, Susanne, editor. | Coyle, Do, 1952– Beyond CLIL.
Title: A deeper learning companion for CLIL : putting pluriliteracies into practice / edited by Do
    Coyle, Oliver Meyer, Susanne Staschen-Dielmann.
Other titles: Deeper learning companion for content and language integrated learning
Description: Cambridge, United Kingdom ; New York, NY : Cambridge University Press, 2023. |
    Follow-up to Beyond CLIL (2022). | Includes bibliographical references and index.
Identifiers: LCCN 2022026499 (print) | LCCN 2022026500 (ebook) | ISBN 9781316517284
    (hardback) | ISBN 9781009044523 (paperback) | ISBN 9781009043755 (epub)
Subjects: LCSH: Language arts–Correlation with content subjects. | Language and languages–
    Study and teaching. | LCGFT: Essays.
Classification: LCC P53.293 .D44 2023 (print) | LCC P53.293 (ebook) | DDC 418.0071–dc23/eng/
    20220817
LC record available at https://lccn.loc.gov/2022026499
LC ebook record available at https://lccn.loc.gov/2022026500

ISBN 978-1-316-51728-4 Hardback
ISBN 978-1-009-04452-3 Paperback

Contents

Tables

Figures

Contributors

Editors
PROFESSOR DR DO COYLE
University of Edinburgh

PROFESSOR DR OLIVER MEYER
Johannes Gutenberg University of Mainz

DR SUSANNE STASCHEN-DIELMANN
Berlin Senate Department for Education, Youth and Family

Chemistry
DR TERESA CONNOLLY
Stefan-George-Gymnasium Bingen

Physics
JOHANNES LHOTZKY
Johannes Gutenberg University of Mainz

ANDREAS PYSIK
Johannes Gutenberg University of Mainz

PROFESSOR DR KLAUS WENDT
Johannes Gutenberg University of Mainz

Geography
DR NICOLE BERG
Neues Gymnasium Rüsselsheim

History
DR SUSANNE STASCHEN-DIELMANN
Berlin Senate Department for Education, Youth and Family – Preparatory Service
for Teachers

Political Science

DR SUSANNE STASCHEN-DIELMANN

Berlin Senate Department for Education, Youth and Family – Preparatory Service for Teachers

SASKIA HELM

Heinrich von Stephan Secondary School, Berlin

Modern Languages

FREDERIC TAVEAU

International School of Geneva (Ecolint)

Religious Education

PROFESSOR DR STEFAN ALTMEYER

Johannes Gutenberg University of Mainz

JOHANNES KERBECK

Johannes Gutenberg University of Mainz

Music

PROFESSOR DR VALERIE KRUPP

Johannes Gutenberg University of Mainz

Mathematics

PROFESSOR DR SUSANNE PREDIGER

TU Dortmund University/IPN Leibnitz Institute for Science and Mathematics Education

DR ANNA-KATHARINA ROOS

TU Dortmund University

Preface

This book was written for all those teachers who suggested we offer more practical guidance in taking the first steps toward putting pluriliteracies teaching for deeper learning (PTDL) into practice in their subject classrooms. This is a big ask: PTDL as a pedagogic approach to deeper learning is complex and demanding because it challenges practitioners to rethink their role as subject teachers in several ways. Primarily, PTDL asks practitioners to revisit their understanding of subject teaching and learning and how it might contribute to the development of transferable knowledge and lifelong learning skills. This requires not only an in-depth understanding of deeper learning and disciplinary literacies and what they mean for the subjects they teach but also the knowledge and skills to put that understanding into practice. Classroom learning using PTDL principles is about joining the dots – making transparent the necessary connections needed to construct deeper learning episodes. This requires aligning disciplinary core constructs, the *mechanics* and *drivers* of deeper learning, in order for teachers to design *trajectories* for pluriliteracies development within their subjects/fields of expertise.

Therefore, we reached out to invite subject specialists not only to delineate the relevance of those concepts within their disciplines and subjects but to design sample *deeper learning episodes* in order to illustrate the process of alignment for their specific subject. In addition, we asked them to reflect on key principles and ideas of PTDL to make the thinking behind their planning visible, hoping that this might offer additional insights for interested educators.

Teresa Connolly argues that a profound understanding of key **chemistry** concepts and processes is as fundamental to scientific literacy as mastering complex procedures and skills, such as performing experiments, interpreting data or communicating one's findings using specific text types. However, she points out that such an understanding of chemical concepts is inhibited not only by learners' poor command of academic language but also by the fact that chemical processes can be observed at different levels of abstraction. This poses a specific challenge in chemistry because learners often report having difficulties distinguishing clearly between processes at the sub-microscopic, the microscopic and the macroscopic levels, which will lead to misconceptions and prevent deeper understanding. To address that issue, Connolly's deeper learning episode on redox reactions offers engaging ways of promoting scientific reasoning through a series of student-led experiments and inquiries. Systematic guidance in academic language use will enable learners to express their findings and observations precisely and adequately and thus help them distinguish the processes occurring at various levels of abstraction with increasing ease and confidence.

The **physics** chapter by Klaus Wendt, Andreas Pysik and Johannes Lothzky aims at promoting deeper understanding of the complex phenomenon of the rainbow and encourages learners to demonstrate and share their understanding through an article for a Wikipedia page. In this deeper learning episode, learners carry out a number of experiments on spectral colours and colour sequences. They organise the information gathered and explain the physics concepts and processes underlying the phenomenon. The authors use innovative ways of scaffolding academic language development to increase the meaning-making potential of younger learners.

Nicole Berg's deeper learning episode aims at improving learners' ability to orally explain **geography**. To do that, learners will listen to podcasts on global heating to analyse expert explanations. In this way, they will learn about the nature and structure of scientific explanations in context. In addition, learners will decode, analyse and practise prosodic features of spoken language (in terms of intonation, stress, pausing and phonological chunking). This will support storage and retrieval of academic language elements from long-term memory. Ultimately, learners will structure and formulate their own oral explanations of subject-specific content. This highly innovative approach to promoting oral language skills uses insights into the mechanics of language acquisition and speech production to facilitate subject learning.

Susanne Staschen-Dielmann's **history** episode is designed to offer learners deep understanding and command of a specific historical genre. Criteria-centred evaluation is one of the most challenging text types to master in history. It requires the ability to analyse and evaluate historical events from different perspectives in a nuanced way through a set of criteria. A series of tasks leads to students creating instructional videos for other students. In those videos, students explore aspects of society in the German Empire guided by the research question: 'After unifying the German Reich with "blood and iron" in 1871, did Bismarck manage to unify German society as a nation?' After sharing their findings on different social and political factions and analysing similarities and differences according to social, political, economic and ideological positions, learners collaboratively assess the degree of national unity or disunity in Germany under Bismarck following the principles of the criteria-centred evaluation.

For their **politics** lessons Saskia Helm and Susanne Staschen-Dielmann create a digital learnscape based on the well-known simulation *Model United Nations* (MUN) – usually based on the organisation of an international conference. The idea of a digital MUN emerged during the first lockdown in Great Britain and was refined using pluriliteracies principles during the second one. Within the authentic setting of a United Nations conference, learners are guided through more and more sophisticated text-production tasks. These include writing a conflict analysis, a draft resolution and an opening speech. Learners take part in a highly formalised debate, which requires the use of a highly elaborate register. The digital learning space is used to ensure formal and informal communication and information exchange within groups of varying sizes as well as providing meaningful feedback.

Frederic Taveau makes a strong argument for reconceptualising **modern languages** as a subject discipline – in this case French – with knowledge domains and pathways that explore alternative ways of learning and using language with beginner or near-beginner students. By foregrounding textual fluency, he challenges more traditional approaches to language learning that emphasise linguistic systems. Instead, he focuses on the use of multi-modal literary texts to promote meaning-making and language learning through deepening critical and cultural awareness of relevant, motivating real-world phenomena. Taveau outlines the processes involved in enabling novice learners of French to become more self-confident and self-directed creative literary writers using language in unprecedented ways. Through a series of scaffolded text-centred learning episodes, learners are guided through pluriliteracies-based steps, increasingly using cognitive discourse functions creatively and confidently (explaining, describing, classifying, arguing and evaluating) to construct their own descriptive literary texts on a gothic theme. These texts are 'owned' by students, demonstrating language learning as a creative, motivating means to understanding their world and that of others.

Stefan Altmeyer and Johannes Kerbeck explore **religious education** as a means for enabling learners to build life-relevant knowledge and critical understanding. They argue that religious literacies are underpinned by an awareness of interreligious views shifting from the neutral to critical and ultimately leading to positioning individual decisions and identities within religion-aware thinking. Learners are guided along a pathway from understanding 'religious language' to actively engaging in religious dialogue using the 'language of religion' in appropriate, critical and reflective ways. Investigating the differences between subjective and objective positionality involves learners in facing changing perspectives that build on developing basic religious knowledge, applying their understanding to lived experiences and constructing critical yet relevant evaluations of arguments and counterarguments. When these evaluations demonstrate appropriate use of the 'correlative' or 'dialogic' principle of religious learning, students exhibit deeper understanding. The learning episode focuses on a national initiative on global development, featuring a video-streamed interreligious panel discussion with experts from different creeds. Drawing on issues of diversity, empathy, solidarity and responsibility, learners were invited to prepare for (using digital media), actively participate in and connect personally with issues through deep reflection informed by religious literacies development.

Conceptualising **music** education not only as 'music-making' but as 'musical meaning-making', Valerie Krupp's learning episode provides a fascinating example of developing learner musical literacy skills – involving intrapersonal and interpersonal negotiation and reflection, drawing on subject-specific knowledge, skills and processes. She argues that for learners to engage meaningfully in music analysis, recensions, aesthetic arguments and so on, they need to practise and use the language of musical genres and musical inquiry alongside language for critical and aesthetic evaluation. This, she proposes, promotes learner agency encompassing musical literacies, competences and critical cultural consciousness. Situating the learning event as praxial, student-relevant and real-world, it concerns the posting of a sea shanty, 'The Wellerman', on TikTok. Against all odds, the song 'went viral,' leading to 'in the moment' global interest in sea shanties. Learners investigate why such a musical phenomenon took place. This opens up critical inquiry into the socio-cultural context of the shanty genre, classifying, analysing and critiquing musical and social media and analysing user comments. This example could be transferred to exploring other musical genres and interpretations.

Susanne Prediger's and Anna-Katharina Roos' chapter offers profound insights into the nature of literacy in **mathematics**. It documents a precise account of the way the knowledge and activity domains of *doing, organising, explaining* and *arguing* translate into algebraic activities and procedures. Using the example of transformation and transformation rules, they argue that algebraic rules that are not underpinned with meaning will become arbitrary and lead to typical student errors. They make the case for algebraic reasoning as a way of developing conceptual understanding and promoting deeper learning in the math classroom. Based on their empirical classroom research, the authors propose three principles to inform the design of deeper learning episodes in mathematics: connecting multiple representations and languages, engaging learners in rich discourse practice and employing macro-level scaffolding that integrates mathematics and language learning.

We are very grateful to our colleagues who have shared their insights and explorations in PDTL across disciplines and subject classrooms. We hope that these will contribute to furthering our collective understanding of the conceptual and practical realities, challenges and successes of developing PTDL to enhance the quality of learning experiences anywhere.

PART I
Key Ideas and Principles of Pluriliteracies Teaching for Deeper Learning

The rationale behind *A Pluriliteracies Approach to Teaching for Deeper Learning* (PTDL) has been deceptively simple: based on empirical data, our own experiences in the classroom and conversations with experts, practitioners and colleagues from all over the world, we felt the need to develop a pedagogic approach to *Content and Language Integrated Learning* (CLIL) that would empower teachers and learners to go beyond superficial levels of learning. We wanted it to focus on helping learners 'connect the dots' to develop and internalise conceptual knowledge while practising relevant skills and strategies in such a way that they can be successfully transferred to other contexts and problems. This is deeper learning. It is of fundamental importance because deeper learning is key to lifelong learning.

There is a growing consensus that deeper learning is directly linked to domain- or subject-specific ways of constructing and communicating knowledge. There is now growing evidence that transfer of learning can no longer be considered as a set of generic or transversal skills. Research shows that generic problem-solving skills on which our learners can rely to successfully complete novel tasks do not exist. Instead, transferrable knowledge requires deep understanding of subject content and deliberate practice of subject skills and strategies – in a nutshell, the development of subject literacy.

As a pedagogic approach, PTDL aims to facilitate deeper learning through an explicit focus on subject literacies. The use of the prefix 'pluri-' stresses our goal of extending the concept of subject literacies across languages and all subjects of schooling. Therefore, the term 'pluriliteracies' refers to:

1. **An explicit focus on disciplinary literacies in all subjects of schooling.** Since deeper learning is a domain-specific process, education needs to find ways of promoting subject literacies in all subjects of schooling by focusing on subject-specific ways of constructing and communicating knowledge so that learners can become pluriliterate in the sense of acquiring subject literacies in several subjects of schooling.
2. **Pluriliterate language use.** In a global world, learners need to be able to successfully and adequately communicate knowledge across cultures and languages. Therefore, an equally important facet of the 'pluri-' in pluriliteracies embraces and extends to being literate in several subjects and languages.
3. **Textual fluency.** Communication is increasingly plurimodal or hybrid in nature and reliant on multiple analogue and digital communication channels and semiotic systems. Being able to critically evaluate sources is key to global citizenship and will prepare young learners for the world they will inhabit through understanding the need for social justice and democratic cultural competence. Therefore, being pluriliterate also entails the ability to critically navigate, evaluate and produce a wide variety of plurimodal texts and text types.

In *Beyond CLIL: Pluriliteracies Teaching for Deeper Learning* we offer an in-depth look at the various components of our model and explain in great detail how they affect each other. In seeking to understand better the nature of deeper learning and its implications for learning and teaching, we have discovered useful perspectives on deeper learning: the **mechanics** or cognitive-linguistic processes through which deeper learning evolves and the **drivers** of and for deeper learning. We have defined drivers as those factors that promote or inhibit the processes or mechanics of deeper learning, such as student and teacher engagement, their sense of self-efficacy, mastery-orientation or the ability to critically reflect on their own learning. The drivers focus on the learners and, subsequently, the role of teachers in mentoring learning. The careful and deliberate alignment of drivers and mechanics allows the **trajectories** or knowledge pathways to emerge. These trajectories are at the core of PTDL because they will enable teachers to map learning progressions into all subjects of schooling by designing complex tasks and practice activities that will systematically increase their learners' subject literacies. Increased subject literacies will be reflected in the learners' growing ability to engage in the four prototypical activity domains of subject learning: doing, organising, explaining and arguing.

Deeper learning develops within deeper learning ecologies or learnscapes. Learnscapes are 3D spaces that are non-linear and sequential and only come into being when all four dimensions of the PTDL model are active at the same time. Teachers can transform traditional classrooms into deeper learning ecologies by designing (through planning) and sustaining (through dynamic and interactive scaffolding) tasks and activities that focus on deep understanding and deliberate or deep practice, which requires a *growth mindset* in both learners and teachers. Growth mindsets are key to the formation of learning partnerships between learners and teachers. Learners need to actively engage in deeper learning processes with teachers who mentor learning for personal growth. This involves generating and sustaining the conditions for learner engagement, achievement and the development of growth mindsets.

A central idea to PTDL is **alignment**. It is a unique and indispensable feature of deeper learning tasks and activities (see Chapter 4). We suggest that alignment brings together the core features of disciplinary literacy with classroom tasks and activities, which are fundamental conditions for deeper learning, as well as learner strengths, needs and interests. It is this process of alignment that distinguishes tasks for deeper learning from the more traditional tasks and activities. To emphasise the difference, we have coined the term **deeper learning episodes** (DLEs) for tasks and supporting activities that promote pluriliteracies development. These episodes consist of a number of interconnected phases where teachers and learners jointly engage in complementary activities to stimulate and sustain deeper learning processes.

To help educators assess the quality of DLEs, we introduced the construct of **task fidelity**, which allows us to evaluate the degree to which DLEs promote deeper learning through ten design principles (see Chapter 4).

Working with a group of international teachers and teacher educators, we developed a set of **guiding questions** to help teachers design, mentor and evaluate DLEs. Building on the concept of *task fidelity* and its design principles, these questions address all four dimensions of the PTDL model.

This book is meant as a companion volume to *Beyond CLIL: Pluriliteracies Teaching for Deeper Learning*. Building on the key principles and ideas of PTDL, we aim to offer practitioners more practical insights into PTDL by illustrating how that approach can be put into practice in various contexts of schooling. To that aim, we invited experts and practitioners to design DLEs for a wide range of school subjects.

Taken together, these DLEs demonstrate how the concept of deeper learning may translate into classroom practices and offer insights into how *alignment* can be achieved to increase *task fidelity* and quality of learning. Also, we wanted to make the thinking that goes into the planning and the designing of those DLEs visible in order to offer teachers further useful insights into what we call a *deeper teaching mindset*. The ultimate goal of this book is to inspire teachers to move into deeper teaching and to show how to take the first steps on the journey to transform classrooms into deeper learning ecologies.

We are fully aware that our positioning and understanding of deeper learning run contrary to the way that most education systems assess learning. Therefore, many episodes contain very concrete and practical suggestions about how to assess deeper understanding. The DLEs presented in this book illustrate how some of the key ideas of PTDL can be put into practice.

Walking through the Model

Now that we have briefly summarised key ideas of PTDL, we would like to present our model, explore its various components and illustrate how they work together to promote deeper learning.

1 Exploring the Mechanics of Deeper Learning

1.1 How Does Conceptual Understanding Develop?

For knowledge to become transferable, it needs to be stored in long-term memory in such a way that learners can successfully retrieve it. However, 'merely' committing information to long-term memory does not equal deeper learning. Teaching that focuses mostly on facts and does not provide learners with ample opportunities to use and apply their knowledge will lead to so-called *inert knowledge*, which cannot be accessed to solve problems. To really understand content, our learners need to establish connections between new information and prior knowledge, relate new information to larger contexts and understand its relevance inside and outside the classroom.

In *Beyond CLIL: Pluriliteracies Teaching for Deeper Learning* we argue that transferable knowledge evolves from conceptual understanding. Concepts are the building blocks of organised knowledge. Concepts are formed when learners discover regularities in events or objects (see Figure 1.1).

All learning starts at the surface level when learners encounter new information or content. To make sense of that content, learners need to find and connect the dots to determine how events, facts and observations are connected. This information is then 'packed' into meaningful patterns, schemata or concepts. To consolidate understanding and to gain control over a concept, learners need to language or communicate and share their growing conceptual understanding. This is fundamental because it is through languaging that concepts become more and more abstract. Abstraction is required to fully internalise conceptual understanding. Once concepts are fully internalised, learners can use these concepts appropriately and creatively in various contexts. Progression in understanding occurs when the original concept is expanded, extended or deepened.

Transfer of knowledge is only possible when concepts have been fully internalised. It is hard to overstate the role of language in the process of concept formation: language holds concepts together; when learners language their understanding, patterns emerge and thinking becomes visible. This allows teachers to mediate their learners' thinking and understanding through scaffolding. In other words, when

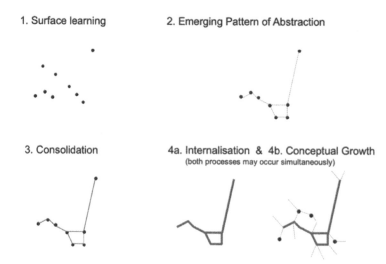

Figure 1.1 Visualising internalisation of conceptual knowledge

teachers teach their learners how to explain increasingly complex concepts adequately, they actually teach them how to understand and think better.

1.2 What Is Deep Practice?

One of the reasons that teaching for deeper learning is so challenging stems from the fact that different types of knowledge are stored in different parts of long-term memory and that successful storage, retention and use require different types of learning and practice activities: whereas concepts are stored in the part of declarative memory that is called *semantic memory*, procedural knowledge or skills are stored in *procedural memory*. Any skill can be automatised through the right kind of practice.

In *Beyond CLIL: Pluriliteracies Teaching for Deeper Learning* we explore thoroughly the role of practice, introduce relevant concepts and frameworks and examine how practice relates to deeper learning. One of the most exciting ideas that we discovered is the concept of deliberate or 'deep practice'. Based on recent breakthrough discoveries in the neurosciences, its proponents offer a radical new perspective on the issue: they define skill as the cellular insulation that coats neural circuits, which responds and grows in reaction to certain signals. The thicker the myelin layer, the faster signals can travel. The idea is that higher signal speed inside a neural circuit will lead to increased performance. However, myelin growth requires very specific practice activities: complex tasks need to be broken down into smaller components, which can then be practised and automatised. Deep practice is a highly focused and reflective activity, it requires deep engagement and long-term commitment and motivation. Deep practice also involves slowing down the pace of learning and demands plenty of repetition. Successful performance of complex tasks requires both deep understanding and deep practice: it depends on complex conceptual knowledge stored in long-term memory AND the ability to smoothly activate skills as a result of practice.

The way these ideas relate to deeper learning is this: deep understanding, or the internalisation of conceptual knowledge, will lead to the formation of neural networks in the brain. The same is true for new skills or skillsets. The more often these networks are activated through deep practice, the thicker the myelin layer and the faster signals can travel. This will affect understanding and performance. In other words, if learning creates new networks in the brain, deeper understanding will increase the complexity of these networks while deep practice will increase the speed at which these networks operate effectively.

2 Exploring the Drivers of Deeper Learning

While understanding the mechanics of deeper learning is fundamental, deeper learning can only become a reality in our classrooms when we pay close attention to the drivers of deeper learning. This will allow learners to embrace a deeper learning mindset, which is required to develop academic tenacity or resilience, to work consistently over sustained periods of time, to engage in and master challenging tasks, to successfully interact with their peers and to self-regulate their learning.

This also goes for teachers: adopting PTDL requires the mindsets and skills needed to turn classrooms into learnscapes, where mentors and mentees form **learning partnerships**. Teachers can generate and sustain learner engagement and achievement and mentor personal growth based on how they design learning and through scaffolding, feedback and assessment for deeper learning (see Figure 2.1).

Our revised model stresses that pluriliteracies development will only take off and can only be sustained when all of its four dimensions are continuously integrated and active. It depicts the intricate, complex and dynamic relationships between the mechanics and the drivers that will allow teachers to guide learners along the knowledge pathways.

Figure 2.1 The revised pluriliteracies model for deeper learning

3 Exploring Progression in Deeper Learning

In *Beyond CLIL: Pluriliteracies Teaching for Deeper Learning* we demonstrate that learning progressions typically evolve around big ideas in a discipline or a subject. Disciplinary core constructs show how disciplines or subjects use different approaches to collecting, analysing, evaluating and communicating information. This is why, in PTDL, those core constructs are used to inform and guide the development of learning progressions into/for individual subjects. Progress in subject learning is not linear but multi-dimensional and multi-directional. It involves specific ways of thinking and typical forms of representing information and specific text types or genres to share information. Progress in subject learning can be conceptualised as enhancing meaning-making potential. It entails growing conceptual understanding of content knowledge as well as a growing command of subject-specific procedures and strategies. It results from engaging in the specific major activity domains of a subject (*doing, organising, explaining* and *arguing*). This idea is captured in Figure 3.1.

Since learning cannot be separated from language, progress becomes manifest in the learner's ability to communicate knowledge and demonstrate understanding purposefully and adequately. This understanding becomes visible in

- a growing command of subject-specific text types and genres
- the ability to critically evaluate and extract information from increasingly complex texts in all relevant modes (oral, written, digital analogue, etc.).

Cognitive discourse functions (CDFs), such as *classify, define, describe, evaluate, explain, explore* or *report*, are fundamental buildings blocks of deeper learning. This is because they lie at the interface between knowledge construction and knowledge communication. Our Lego model (Figure 3.2) shows that, depending on the context, they can stand alone (as micro-genres) or be embedded in larger text types (i.e. macro-genres). The practice of PTDL is based on a dynamic and multidimensional perspective on CDFs. This will allow teachers to design highly individualised learning experiences by way of adjusting CDFs with regard to both the cognitive pattern underlying a phenomenon and the language used by the students to express their understanding of content.

STRATEGIES,
PROCEDURES,
CONCEPTS,
FACTS
CONCEPTUALISING CONTINUUM
DOING ORGANISING EXPLAINING ARGUING
Expert
DOING ORGANISING EXPLAINING ARGUING
Intermediate
Deeper Learning
DOING ORGANISING EXPLAINING ARGUING
Novice
COMMUNICATING CONTINUUM
PURPOSE, MODE, GENRE, STYLE

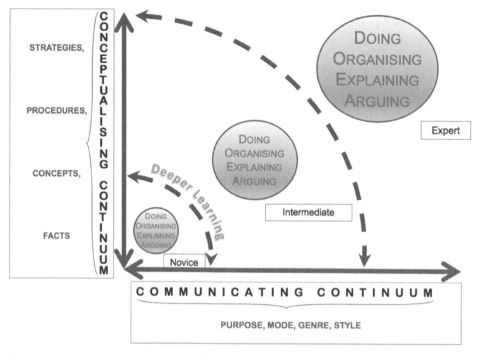

Figure 3.1 Connecting two axes of the model for deeper learning (Graz group)

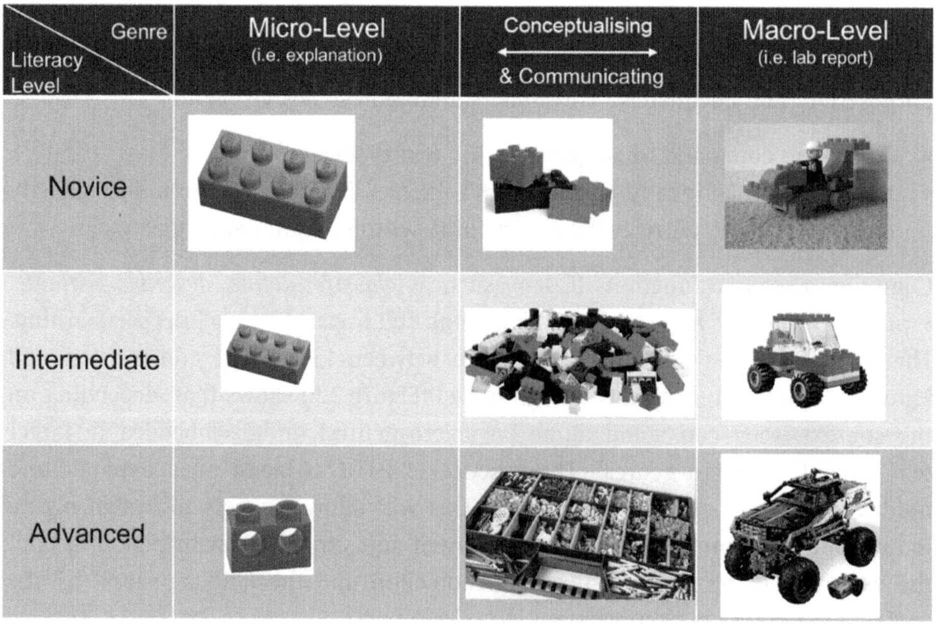

Genre
Literacy Level
Micro-Level (i.e. explanation)
Conceptualising & Communicating
Macro-Level (i.e. lab report)
Novice
Intermediate
Advanced

Figure 3.2 Visualising the role of CDFs in pluriliteracies development

Putting All the Pieces Together

Our revised model of PTDL attempts to capture the intricate relationships and complexities between *learner commitment and achievement, mentoring learning for personal growth*, demonstrating and communicating meaning-making, and *constructing new knowledge and deepening understanding.* As teachers and learners interact within and across these dimensions, they extend the space and create a dynamic momentum that fosters growth, thus evolving the basis into a 3D space. This space must be designed to maximise interactivity between the dimensions in order to grow deeper learning ecologies. In other words, all dimensions must be activated and integrated for deeper learning to occur. Since deeper learning is dependent on disciplinary cultures, adopting a pluriliteracies approach provides learning pathways into the subjects of schooling.

When all four dimensions together form a transparent base for designing and mapping learning pathways operationalised through a wide range of teacher strategies, the resulting tasks and sequences have the potential to promote learner confidence and learner agency. The goal for PTDL is ecological in the sense that it focuses on designing and 'growing' a learning environment that is flexible and responsive to the specific needs of learners. This fosters commitment and resilience, nurtures progression and growth and encourages choice and confidence in navigating learning pathways. It also provides learners with the tools and experiences needed for personal growth and lifelong learning (see Figure 3.3).

Figure 3.3 Fully animated 3D model of deeper learning environments

We have coined the term *deeper learning episode* (DLE) to emphasise the idea that PTDL's overriding objective is to offer opportunities for deeper learning through a focus on subject-specific literacies. Also, we felt the need to introduce a new term that is not limited to specific timetabled lessons. A DLE extends over a series of lessons, depending not only on the intentions, purposes and outcomes of learning but, more importantly, on whether or not those intentions, purposes and outcomes translate into deeper learning. A DLE organically flows into the next one when learners can demonstrate deep understanding of the specific content or sufficient mastery of the targeted skills. Otherwise, it is time for us teachers to go back to the drawing board to design and offer more opportunities for learners to understand and practise. Each DLE consists of a number of interconnected phases where teachers and learners jointly engage in complimentary activities to incite and sustain deeper learning processes (see Figure 4.1).

Each DLE begins with an *activation phase* to generate learner engagement, activate prior knowledge, establish relevance and set the ground for transfer of learning. Its focus is on facilitating learning by setting clear goals – for example, by using advanced organisers. During the *surface phase* learners explore new ideas, facts, concepts and skills to acquire a basic understanding of the content, which they demonstrate through a first learning outcome or product. The teacher provides feedback, feed-up and feed-forward at different levels as appropriate (e.g. task, process, individual and collective) to help learners reflect on their learning experience, to open pathways for further learning and to sustain their engagement. In the *consolidation phase* learners are provided with opportunities to deepen their content understanding (to support the process of internalisation) and to deep-practise specific skillsets (to support the process of automatisation). As before, learners demonstrate improved understanding and a growing mastery of skills through learning outcomes or learning products that reflect their progress. Individual or joint reflection along with specific feedback and subsequent revision activities pave the way for deeper learning. During the *transfer phase* learners are challenged to apply their knowledge to different contexts and situations. Such application involves utilising their knowledge and skills through investigating, experimenting, problem solving or decision-making. Demonstration of understanding, reflection,

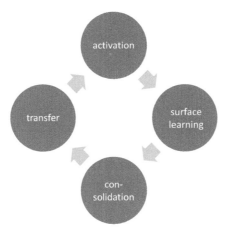

Figure 4.1 The four elements of a deeper learning episode

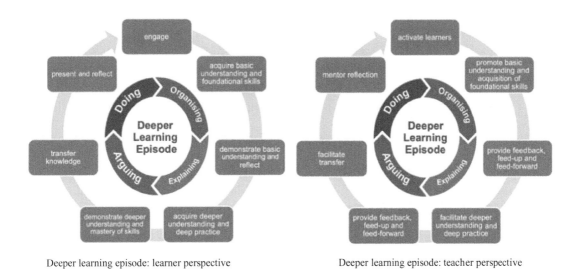

Deeper learning episode: learner perspective   Deeper learning episode: teacher perspective

Figure 4.2 Deeper learning episodes – learner and teacher perspective

feedback and revision are indispensable parts of this phase. Deeper learning requires teachers and learners to form learning partnerships with shared responsibilities. The visual in Figure 4.2 illustrates the responsibilities for learners and teachers during the four stages of DLEs.

To help practitioners assess the quality of DLEs, we have introduced the construct of *task fidelity*. This is meant as a tool or a set of evidence-based criteria to evaluate the degree to which DLEs promote deeper learning through design principles. High task fidelity is fundamental to deeper learning ecologies, or learnscapes, because it provides learners with opportunities for deeper learning through experiencing

- relevance (personal and practical)
- **practical knowledge building and knowledge using, the doing or application** (inquiry, problem solving, etc.) according to subject-specific practices
- development of **subject-specific literacies**, discourses and practices (literacies)
- **languaging** and **demonstrating** learning across subjects and languages
- co-construction of transparent **transfer** pathways (abstraction, contextualisation, relational transfer and schema building)
- **mentoring** learning and personal growth (dynamic scaffolding, feedback and assessment)
- **increasing awareness, engagement and progression** across all four activity domains
- **critical reflection, revision** and **self-improvement through deep practice**
- **assessment for deeper learning** cycles and praxis
- **partnership** working in a collaborative learnscape

(See *Beyond CLIL: Pluriliteracies Teaching for Deeper Learning* pp. 131–132).

High task fidelity is achieved through the process of alignment (see Figure 4.3).

Aligning disciplinary core constructs, knowledge activity domains of schooling and the mechanics of deeper learning with learner strengths, needs and interests is the key to designing DLEs. Alignment is how to achieve high task fidelity, and this is what distinguishes tasks for deeper learning from traditional tasks and activities.

Guiding Questions for Deeper Learning Episodes

The four guiding questions of PTDL are:

1. **What do I want my learners to know or be able to do?**
   Starting with this question will immediately shift the focus away from more teacher- or curriculum-centred approaches and will put the learner, their strengths, needs and interests front and centre. This question refers to the various aspects of knowledge (factual, conceptual, procedural, strategic/meta-cognitive) we want our students to acquire in the course of an extended DLE and will help define the learning outcomes. The follow-up questions (a–c) are meant to further support teachers in the process of aligning the knowledge dimension with the disciplinary core constructs to promote the development of subject-specific literacies.
   a. Inquiry practices and forms of reasoning:
      - What subject-specific procedures and strategies will my students use to construct knowledge?
      - Is inquiry deductive or inductive?

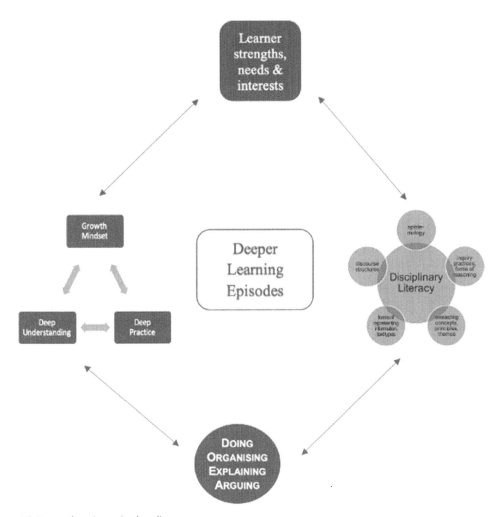

Figure 4.3 Deeper learning episodes alignment

- What problems can be posed and solved?
- What factual and conceptual questions need to be asked and answered?
- Where can I provide opportunities for critical thinking?

b. Overarching concepts, principles and themes:
- What subject-specific conceptual lens do I want my students to use in order to understand the content (big ideas, key concepts)?
- What connections can be drawn between new and familiar concepts?

c. Epistemology:
- How do I enable my students to understand the ways in which knowledge is constructed and interpreted in my discipline?
- How do I enable my students to distinguish between justified beliefs and opinions?

2. **How will my learners demonstrate increasingly deeper understanding at the surface, consolidation and transfer levels?**

Following up with the second question is crucial because the only way for teachers to determine if their teaching and student learning has been successful is by reading, listening to or closely observing demonstrations of learners' understanding. This typically involves the demonstration of specific skills or the presentation of a learning product as a result of investigating and responding to an authentic, challenging and complex problem or task:

a. What are the specific products I wish my learners to develop and evaluate?
   – How do I ensure that individual learners have a shared understanding of the goals of their own learning outcomes, the tasks and ways of 'validating' the outcomes? How will learners begin to use (initially with guidance) the following questions to guide their own learning?
     ◦ What is the purpose of the communication? Who is the audience?
     ◦ What mode is possible/adequate/ideal/best suited for our purposes?
     ◦ What are the characteristics of the respective text type?
     ◦ What are the language demands of the respective text type?
     ◦ Which specific strategies encourage my learners to understand, practise and compose text?

b. Discourse structures:
   – What discourse functions do the students need in order to produce the desired text type? At what level?
   – What style/register is adequate for the communicative purpose?
   – What specific language patterns/features are required?

3. **What is the best way for my learners to actively co-construct knowledge?**

This question aims at aligning subject-specific ways of knowledge construction and knowledge communication with learner strengths, needs and interests. Indeed, we have already underlined the importance of aligning both the mechanics and drivers of deeper learning in order to generate and sustain learner commitment and achievement.

a. Which process of knowledge construction will inform task design: inquiry-based learning, problem-based learning, experimenting, project-based learning, and so on?

b. Which of these processes is best suited (i) for surface learning, (ii) to consolidate learning and (iii) for transfer leading to deeper learning? (iv) And which type of materials will students use in the process?

c. What kind of social interaction patterns can I use to support co-construction of knowledge and learning partnerships (e.g. solo, pair and group work; jigsaw activities, think-pair-share)?

    d. Where do I position student voice and choice with regard to a–c so that it is visible and acted upon?

    e. How can I use digital media to support these processes?

4. **How can I support my learners *every* step of the way?**

This question is all about providing support and making sure that we as teachers help learners achieve a level of mastery and experience such that their investment in their learning process pays off, which in turn will nurture a growth mindset.

    a. How can I trigger, engage and increase student engagement?

      – How can I make topics relevant and meaningful?

      – Can I offer choice in terms of process and product and support autonomy and agency?

      – Can I support learners' use of creative and alternative ways of problem solving?

      – Can I incorporate opportunities that draw on my students' past experience, prior knowledge and cultural identities?

      – How can I personalise the learning experience?

    b. How can I help learners reach the next level?

      – How can I support and guide their learning in terms of process and product?

      – How do I provide ample time, space and opportunity for deep practice?

      – How do I promote/assess transfer of learning?

        ∘ How can I help my learners notice the deeper structure of a problem?

        ∘ How can I support analogy learning?

          ▪ Which generalisations can be constructed from the content of my lesson?

          ▪ How can I help my learners see how examples and generalisations are related?

          ▪ Which examples should be compared to support analogical reasoning?

        ∘ What do efficiency and innovation mean in my context and how do I balance them?

      – How do I encourage my students to reflect meaningfully on their own learning?

      – How do I facilitate constructive peer feedback?

      – Is my assessment based on clear and shard criteria for deeper learning?

    c. How can I support personal growth?

      – How do I nurture well-being and provide a safe and inclusive environment?

      – How do I engender resilience, grit and curiosity?

    d. How can I use digital media to support it all?

In order to simplify and streamline the challenging process of designing DLEs, we have developed a template for practitioners (Table 4.1).

Table 4.1 Designing deeper learning episodes – How can I increase task fidelity through alignment?

Designing Deeper Learning Episodes

How Can I Increase Task Fidelity through Alignment?

	What do I want my learners to know or be able to do?	How will my learners demonstrate increasingly deeper understanding at the surface, consolidation and transfer levels?	How can I support active knowledge co-construction for my learners?	How can I support my learners every step of the way?	How can I generate and sustain learner commitment and achievement?
Basic understanding/ knowledge and foundational skills:		Preliminary outcome products:	(Co-)Construction of Knowledge: • Inquiry-based learning • Problem-based learning • Experimenting • Project-based learning	Scaffolding:	Engagement: • Personal meaningfulness/ relevance: • Opportunities for autonomous learning:
Deeper understanding:		Main outcome products: • Genre: • Mode: • Style:	Social Interaction: • solo work • pair work • group work	Feedback: Feed-up: Feed-forward:	
Deep practice:					
Transfer:		Transfer Task:	Use of (digital) media:	Assessment:	Reflection and Revision:

PART II
Deeper Learning Episodes: First Steps towards Transforming Classrooms

5 Chemistry: Exploring Pluriliteracies through a Deeper Learning Episode on Redox Reactions

TERESA CONNOLLY

5.1 Inquiry and Literacy in Chemistry

As a natural science, chemistry deals with the composition, structure and properties of matter and the changes substances undergo during a reaction with others. Within this problem-solving discipline, knowledge typically evolves from evidence-based investigations like experiments. Thus, common activities in the field of chemistry are experimenting; questioning; hypothesising; reasoning; calculating; gathering, organising and evaluating data; noticing regularity; and relating findings to various representations and generalising them.

Chemical inquiry typically starts with a research question, which can be open (e.g. *What happens if substance A and B react together?*) or closed (e.g. *Is substance C flammable?*). As the underlying reasoning process can either be inductive or deductive, students need to be able to generalise their findings on the one hand, but also be able to apply a general law or principle to explain specific results on the other hand. Generally speaking, they must become scientifically literate. This is important not only for those who want to become future scientists or engineers but also for all students, because chemical literacy helps to solve real-world problems. According to Thummathong and Thathong (2018), 'chemical literacy refers to a person's ability to comprehend and apply the knowledge of chemistry in everyday life in terms of understanding three major aspects of knowledge, awareness and the application of chemistry in daily life appropriately and effectively' (p. 480). Besides chemical content knowledge and overarching higher-order thinking skills, moral awareness, a sense of responsibility and attitude towards chemistry also play a crucial role.

To accomplish all the aspects of chemical literacy mentioned above, key chemistry concepts like the law of conversion, chemical bonding and reactions, structure–property and substance–particle concepts, states of matter or the conversion of energy must be internalised and applied freely. Secondly, students need to be taught how to perform experiments, interpret data, evaluate the quality of their data, locate possible sources of error, compare their data to other research and critically reflect on products, advertisements and their own behaviour based on their scientific knowledge. Thirdly, learners need to be able to decode information in and encode information from discontinuous text types, such as lab reports or protocols. Those complex macro-genres are built up from several microgenres, like descriptions, explanations, definitions or evaluations, as well as tables, diagrams, models and graphical data. Besides those genres, students need to know about different degrees of causation, perspectives and technical terms and be able to differentiate between everyday meanings of words and their scientific meaning. In order to promote chemical literacy during class, linguistic and cognitive patterns can be used to foster the desired text types (i.e. a scientific explanation).

The subject of chemistry is often described as full of difficult and abstract concepts that are too far away from learners' everyday life. However, researchers claim that this is not due to the challenging content but rather rooted in a poor command of scientific language (Baumert et al., 2001) resulting in misunderstandings and learning deficits (Nashan & Parchmann, 2008; Parchmann & Venke, 2008; Vollmer, 1980). But what exactly is it that makes scientific language so hard to understand?

Firstly, the subject-specific language of chemistry has some unique syntactic and morphologic features, like discontinuous texts, nominalisations, passive constructions or the symbolic language of chemical equations. Even though some terms are borrowed from everyday speech, they might have a broader, narrower or totally different meaning compared to the original.

Secondly, subject-specific language is also not learnt automatically (Byrnes, 2013) but can only be acquired through active engagement within the particular subject. This is why Gillis (2014) describes the subject teacher as a 'teacher of *discipline appropriate literacy practices*' (p. 621). To support students becoming literate, various scaffolds during the phases of planning, formulating and revising texts are necessary. Also, underlying cognitive processes have to be made explicit by the use of meta-language (Lemke, 1993; Polias, 2016; Rose & Martin, 2012), breaking down complex cognitive processes into manageable steps. Once students move from the novice to an expert stage, these processes become automatised and scaffolds can be reduced.

Thirdly, chemistry's subject-specific language involves different kinds of representational forms that vary in degrees of abstraction. Being unaware of and unable to distinguish these levels inhibits the understanding and learning of chemical concepts. Thus, to participate in scientific discourse, all those representation levels must be mastered and used adequately in the particular situation. More practically speaking, if students want to thoroughly explain their findings made on the macroscopic level (substances), they must apply models and concepts based on the microscopic (particles) or sub-microscopic level (electrons) as backup. Besides this kind of deductive reasoning, hypotheses can also be formulated postulating possible characteristics of a substance based on its sub-microscopic structure (inductive reasoning).

macroscopic level	microscopic level	sub-microscopic level
Metals can be used as wires …	because they are electrical conductors.	This is due to the fact that they consist of delocalised valence electrons that transport charges in the direction of electric current.

Figure 5.1 Observations made on the macroscopic substance level explained on the sub-microscopic electron level

Unfortunately, if learners are not able to clearly distinguish those levels, this may lead to misconceptions and learning difficulties (see Figure 5.1).

5.2   Progress in Meaning-Making

Progress in meaning-making in chemistry entails an increase in competence in the activity domains of *doing, organising, explaining* and *arguing* chemistry, which can be observed in the students' presentation of chemical information and the quality of their production of chemical text types. If one compares a novice learner to an expert scientist, it becomes clear that progress equals a mastery of more genres, text types and cognitive discourse functions (CDFs). Thus, metaphorically speaking, it equals a higher quantity of meaning-making tools in the toolbox of scientific literacy. Just as tools can be more or less precise, language also increases in quality as learners progress. Content is then presented in a more elaborate and sophisticated way. For example, explanations do not only contain more scientific terms, but observations made on the macroscopic substance level are explained with principles on the microscopic particle or sub-microscopic electron level (Figure 5.2).

Furthermore, expert explanations show complex or multi-causal structures and contain increasingly precise causal connections (Figure 5.3). Implicit connections between several concepts are explicitly verbalised, resulting in greater depth (connection of multiple representational levels) and breadth (generalisations) in the content. Lastly, being able to participate in scientific discourse includes the ability to reflect and negotiate meaning, as well as to define and defend one's own position in the field.

To illustrate this progress in meaning-making, three explanations will be presented written by sixth-, eighth- and tenth-grade students using the provided scaffolding (see Figures 5.4 and 5.5). Even though beginners in science do not yet

The Combustion of Wood Explained on Three Different Representational Levels

Explanation based on macroscopic substance level (used by beginners):

If fuel and oxygen get in contact and the ignition temperature is reached, **(then)** a combustion reaction takes place, **because** all necessary substances are present.

fuel + oxygen + heat = fire

Explanation based on microscopic particle level (used by intermediate learners):

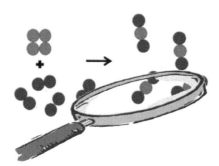

Carbon and oxygen react in an exothermic reaction **to form** carbon dioxide. **This is due to the fact that** carbon easily gets oxidised, **which means** that it accepts oxygen.

carbon + oxygen = carbon dioxide

Explanation based on sub-microscopic electron level (used by experts):

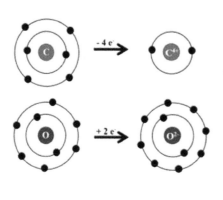

During a combustion reaction, an electron transfer between two reaction partners takes place. **In this case**, carbon atoms get oxidised as they donate four electrons. Simultaneously, two oxygen atoms accept those electrons during reduction reaction. **The effect is that** gaseous molecules of carbon dioxide are formed and heat is released.

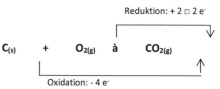

Figure 5.2 The combustion of wood explained on three different representational levels (Connolly, 2019)

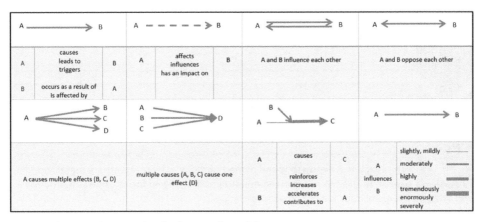

Figure 5.3 Causal connections varying in degree of precision

Figure 5.4 Visual scaffolding structuring causal explanations

b.) candle – oxygen – beaker (Becherglas)

If I put a beaker over a candle, then the candle goes out, because the beaker takes away the Oxygen, but fire needs Oxygen to burn.

Figure 5.5 Example explanation of a sixth-grade student (Connolly, 2019)

know about particles and electrons, they can still logically reason their findings on the substance level using the scheme laid out in Figure 5.3.

Eighth-grade students are introduced to the particle model, which means that they can leave the surface level of chemical matter and 'zoom in' to the next representational level. Observations are connected to principles, laws and theories, and causal connections like verbs expressing causality become more elaborate. Also, students are able to use the principle-reasoning-observation (PRO)-model by Putra and Tang (2016), as the example in Figure 5.6 shows.

The last example, of a tenth-grade student (Figure 5.7), shows how multiple kinds of explanations can be combined to explain the functionality of the Daniell cell on the sub-microscopic level with the respective scientific terms.

The way in which activity domains and activities in chemistry can be related to CDFs and student products that are typical in chemistry is shown in Table 5.1.

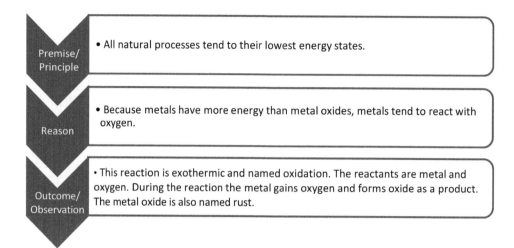

Figure 5.6 Example explanation of an eighth-grade student following the PRO-model (Connolly, 2019)

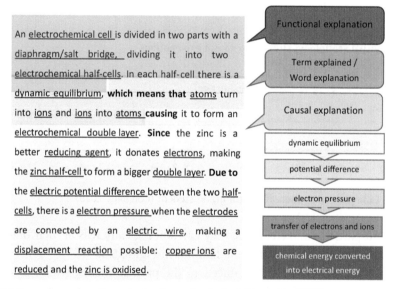

Figure 5.7 Example explanation of a tenth-grade student (Connolly, 2019)

5.3   Deeper Learning in Chemistry

Deeper understanding in chemistry includes the ability to reason experimental findings based on principles, laws and theories, as well as to transfer this gained knowledge to other circumstances, forming overarching concepts. Those cognitive processes of understanding, explaining and transferring content are initiated and solidified by scientific language.

Table 5.1 Activity domains, language functions and student products in chemistry

Activity Domains in Chemistry	Sample Activities in Chemistry	CDFs and Learner Progression in Chemistry (How these CDFs might be languaged by learners at different stages)	Complex Student Products in Chemistry
Doing chemical research: CDFs • **Report** (inform, recount, present, summarise, relate)	Presenting research results Collecting data through measurements Taking notes of observations Researching procedures Creating models Planning and performing an experiment	**Novice:** 'During the experiment gas bubbles rose in the test tube. Oxygen turned into carbon dioxide.' **Expert:** 'Carbon and oxygen (reactants) react to form carbon dioxide (product) during an exothermic reaction (energy conversion). $C_{(s)} + O_{2(g)} \Rightarrow CO_{2(g)}$'	**Preliminary:** • Protocols • Graphics and photographs • (Data) lists • Structured notes • Mind maps
Organising chemical data: CDFs • **Describe** (describe, label, identify, name) • **Classify** (classify, compare, contrast, match, structure, categorise, subsume)	Organising experimental data chronologically or thematically Describing observations Organising and structuring data in charts or diagrams Categorising data Calculating yield, concentration, etc. Summarising main trends and results	**Novice:** 'The copper letter turned black during the reaction.' **Expert:** 'At the beginning (*first*) of the experiment, the copper sheet was hard and shiny. In the course of the reaction (*second*), the outside of the copper letter changed colour from red to black. In the end (*third*), the sheet was brittle and matt.'	• Characteristics • Concept maps **Oral:** • Presentations • Gallery walk • Discussions • Talk shows **Written:**
Explaining chemistry: CDFs • **Explain** (explain, reason, express, draw conclusions, deduce) • **Define** (define, identify, characterise, compare, contrast)	Explaining cause and effect Explaining observations and measurements by applying general rules, laws or theories (deductive reasoning) Drawing a conclusion Defining scientific terms	**Novice:** 'Iron nails corrode because iron reacts with water and oxygen.' **Expert:** 'If an iron nail comes in contact with water and oxygen (*cause*), a chemical reaction called oxidation takes place (*effect*) because both necessary reactants are present (*reason*). The effect is that the iron nail changes its colour from silver to reddish brown (*consequence*).'	• Lab report and protocol • Definition • Evaluation • Data analysis and comparison with prior research • Comment • Explanation

Table 5.1 (*cont.*)

Activity Domains in Chemistry	Sample Activities in Chemistry	CDFs and Learner Progression in Chemistry (How these CDFs might be languaged by learners at different stages)	Complex Student Products in Chemistry
Arguing chemistry: **CDFs** • Explore (explore, hypothesise, speculate, predict, guess, estimate, simulate, take other perspectives) • Evaluate (evaluate, judge, argue, justify, take a stance, state, critique, recommend, comment, reflect, appreciate)	Answering research questions Deriving new hypotheses and research questions based on gained results Generalising findings to formulate overarching concepts or theories (inductive reasoning) Generating theoretical or physical models Relating results to former research Evaluating experimental data concerning yield, quality or sources of error Discussing pros and cons of methods and procedures Justifying new procedures or experimental setups Taking a stance on 'real-life issues' Critically reflecting on one's own impact on the environment and society Presenting results Verifying or falsifying hypotheses	**Novice:** 'The tested drug would worsen heartburn.' **Expert:** 'The experiment revealed that the advertised drug cannot be used as a remedy for heartburn (*statement tested/ contradiction detected*) since its pH-value is below 1, leading to an increase of symptoms if taken (*justification/ evaluation based on facts or inner logic*).'	**Digital:** • Experimental documentary • Animation of reaction mechanisms • Model of chemical reaction and processes • Instructional video of procedure

Even though deeper understanding is the desired goal of the learning process, there are numerous hurdles along the way. Concerning content, rapidly changing atom models and a lack of explicit connections between the macro- and microlevel can have negative effects on the learning outcome. Regarding language, if too many terms are introduced simultaneously without properly ascribing meaning to them and practising them, scientific language no longer functions as a meaning-making tool but becomes an obstacle in the learning process. Especially, symbolic language can cause feelings of incompetence and fear if not understood properly. Lacking such emotional engagement can also arise if students do not see a personal relevance in the subject and think they have little or no prior knowledge. This, again, makes it harder to integrate new knowledge into existing mental models, preventing deeper understanding based on more complex concepts.

To overcome the above-mentioned hurdles, the following deeper learning strategies can be applied.

Textual understanding can be **deepened** and the quality of student texts improved if meta-language and working examples are combined within the following three steps. First, authentic and typical text types in the field of chemistry need to be introduced. Then, the significance and purpose of those text types have to be discussed so that students understand when and why certain text types are used. Finally, strategies need to be acquired on how to decode primary sources and encode newly gained information in one's own text.

Especially for the subject of chemistry, **increasing content relevance** is of importance as many students claim that they do not know anything about chemistry and will never make use of the learned concepts again as they are too far away from everyday life. Because this is not the case, chemical content needs to be made more accessible to students by creating parallels and presenting examples from everyday life. During lesson introductions, authentic texts and material can be used to formulate hypotheses for real-life problems (e.g. how can we build/produce . . .). Also, teachers should choose experiments that lead to clear observations and are interesting and contemporary (e.g. choosing the recent explosion in Beirut instead of the Zeppelin disaster of 100 years ago).

Critical cultural consciousness is developed when learners are confronted with recent topics and asked to take a stance. Those could, for example, be climate change, waste recycling, the use of hazardous and cancer-causing substances or microplastics. As educated chemists on the one hand and responsible consumers on the other, they should be able to take both advantages and disadvantages into consideration and truly evaluate the benefit of a product critically and multi-dimensionally.

Agency and accountability are increased if students become responsible for their work and results. As soon as they are asked to plan an experiment and only receive the chemicals and material they included in their experiment supply list, the amount of accountability becomes visible if some essential items are missing and can only be received by trading points from their grade. Another possible scenario could be that students incorrectly request/use different chemicals or chemicals differing in their concentration during analysis, forcing them to produce their own results.

Similar to other subjects, **learning pathways can be differentiated** with help cards and tasks differing in their complexity or format.

The **individualisation of learning pathways** can be achieved as soon as students chose the topic they want to work on and the kind of sources they want to use. Another way to trigger individual problem-solving approaches is to only give students a basket of materials without further instructions other than tasking them with building a battery, for example. Results can be presented using different modes of representation, like tables, texts or movies, to provide further individualisation.

Deeper understanding also needs **deep practice,** contrary to tasks which show little variation. In this respect, asking for the underlying thought process that led to a result can be beneficial in the learning process. Additionally, concept cartoons trigger students to argue why a statement is right or wrong, and they have to use appropriate concepts and scientific terms for their explanation. Translating information from one text format into another also asks students to transfer their knowledge and demonstrate their understanding.

Scaffolds are temporary forms of support that gradually need to be reduced throughout the learning process. Concerning scientific language, detailed writing frames can, for example, turn into sporadic hints, and joint construction merges into group and individual construction. This means that the responsibility of the writing process is transferred from the teacher or the group to the individual student.

5.4   A Model Deeper Learning Episode in Chemistry: '(How) Did Ötzi Produce Copper?' (Year 8)

The main objective of this deeper learning episode (DLE) in chemistry is an understanding of redox reactions of metals. Eighth-grade students perform experiments concerning reactivity series and reducing agents and examine different production processes of metals. Redox reactions are not only relevant within the subject but can also be found in students' everyday life when a log burns or a bike corrodes. As this DLE consists of different subtopics, numerous learning products ranging from lab reports to explanatory videos, presentations and posters can be found. Students have various options for presenting their findings, which increases their creativity, motivation and engagement. Those affective components are indispensable factors for deeper learning processes.

Concerning subject-specific literacies, students get introduced to the recurring patterns of causal explanations and practise them within different situations. This CDF has been chosen since '[t]he ability to reason from evidence, along with understanding the central role evidence plays in science, is a core element in the development of scientifically literate students' (Brown et al., 2010, p. 126). Unfortunately, researchers report that students lack strategies to reason based on principles (McNeill et al., 2006; Putra & Tang, 2016). To tackle those deficits, students must receive explicit scaffolding in the form of working examples, definitions, cause-and-effect diagrams and the like.

Before the individual steps of the DLE are explained in detail, an overview will be given of how to align crucial aspects of the pluriliteracies approach to deeper learning following five guiding questions (see Table 5.2).

5.5   Alignment of Deeper Learning Episode

To achieve high task fidelity, a DLE has been designed creating a personal yet productive learning experience within an authentic context. Based on a practical experiment, students have to find out whether Ötzi was able to produce elemental copper 3,000 years ago and present their findings in a creative yet subject-appropriate way. To create a DLE that is tailored to the learners' needs and competences, the following four aspects had to be aligned.

Learner Strengths, Needs and Interests: especially for the subject of chemistry, it is important to keep learners' strengths, needs and interests in mind. Not all students are intrinsically motivated and interested in the matter but rather regard themselves as incompetent and think they do not have any productive prior knowledge at hand. However, if engaging and challenging learning environments are created, within which learners are taken seriously and treated as experts, those obstacles can be overcome. The chosen task shows a real information gap, asking students to build new knowledge based on existing concepts. Even though learners are responsible for the outcome, they can still cope with the task as they have a clearly formulated learning goal and can visualise the learning pathway.

Disciplinary Literacy and its Core Constructs.

- **Epistemology and inquiry practices.** Students need to extract information from a text and formulate a research question. Based on their hypotheses, they plan and carry out experiments in small groups. Afterwards, findings are analysed to answer the research question. The newly gained information is then encoded in various text types and presented in class.
- **Overarching principles, key concepts and themes.** The theme of reduction reactions has been put into a realistic context as a curious girl wants to know

Table 5.2 Planning grid for a deeper learning episode in chemistry

Designing Deeper Learning Episodes

Planning Grid for a Deeper Learning Episode in Chemistry

What do I want my learners to know or be able to do?	How will my learners demonstrate increasingly deeper understanding at the surface, consolidation and transfer levels?	How can I support active knowledge co-construction for my learners?	How can I support my learners every step of the way?	How can I generate and sustain learner commitment and achievement?
Basic Understanding: • Definition of redox reaction • Carbon as a good reducing agent • Metals can be extracted from their ore through oxidation **Foundational Skills:** • Formulate a research question and a hypothesis • Plan and perform an experiment • Organise information chronologically (observations) • Explain experimental data based on general key concepts **Deeper Understanding:** • Application of redox series of metals to reduce other metal oxides	**Preliminary Product Outcomes:** • Research question and hypothesis formulated correctly • Experiment performed correctly • Notes taken during the experiment **Main Learning Product:** Purpose: answering the research question and educating other people Genre: causal explanation Mode: optional (written/spoken/digital/analogue) Style: academic and	**(Co-)Construction of Knowledge:** • Inquiry-based learning • Problem-based learning • Experimenting **Social Interaction:** • Joint performance of experiment and construction of learner products within the group • Peer feedback **Use of (Digital) Media:** • Movie/PowerPoint presentation/explanatory video	**Scaffolding:** • Language frame and help sheet for scientific explanation • Language help (word railing) to scaffold observation • Cognitive scaffolds to plan the experiment and use the correct detection method for reaction products **Feedback:** • Individual teacher feedback based on the assessment grid	**Engagement:** **Personal Meaningfulness/Relevance:** • Authentic and challenging research question • All learners are physically and mentally active throughout the entire learning process • Learning products created based on personal interest and preference **Opportunities for Autonomous Learning:**

Deep Practice:
- Using causal connections and scientific terms to make a text more academic and concise
- Evaluating a scientific explanation (of peer students) based on the given criteria

Transfer:
- Colloquial vs academic language (video for museum visitors)
- Key concept of redox reactions

contemporary colloquial style (depending on purpose)

Possible Transfer:
- Explain why some metals can only be found as ore and others as metal via concept of noble and ignoble metals, reactivity series of metals
- Changing the form of representation (written explanation to chemical equation to particle model to . . .)
- transforming a text, making it more academic and concise (if the audience changed)

- Leaflet can also be written, revised and designed digitally

- Peer feedback using the help sheet 'A good scientific explanation'
- Peer feedback with tokens for presentation

Feed-up:
- Language frame and assessment grid 'Scientific Explanation'

Feed-forward:
- Individual teacher feedback on explanation, letter and movie/leaflet
- Peer feed-forward using the help sheet 'A good scientific explanation'

Assessment:
- Assessment grid 'Scientific Explanation'

- Creative writing of letter to Anna and recording of the movie (individual length)
- Independent research on good reducing agents
- Flexible use of help cards and word boxes

Reflection and Revision:
- Guided revision of scientific explanation and reflection of movie, keeping a possible audience in mind

whether the story she just heard in a museum is true or false. Authentic, or at least true-to-life, contexts allow students to identify with the subject matter, activate their prior knowledge and become emotionally engaged. Within this DLE, key chemistry concepts of energy, structure–property and substance–particle relationships, as well as the reactivity series of metals, need to be applied to explain how Ötzi was able to produce elemental copper out of its ore.

- **Forms of representation.** Creative final learner products, such as letters, explanatory videos and oral presentations, have been chosen since students tend to be more interested in and engaged by these forms of learner products than chemical equations and lab reports. Then, as students encode the gained information into various text types (i.e. diagrams, charts of continuous texts, etc.) and translate content from one text type into another, their ability to transfer knowledge is fostered and their understanding deepened. When students are asked to reply to Anna's letter, they can easily visualise the audience and thus decide which style and register to use for this communicative purpose. Whereas it is appropriate to use colloquial language within the letter to Anna, the supplementary explanatory video for the museum visitors requires a register change because such videos must contain subject-specific terms and academic language.

- **Discourse structures.** Within this DLE, typical discourse structures of the subject can be found. These are, among others: formulating research questions, hypotheses and chemical equations; describing, analysing and explaining observations; defining terms; and generalising knowledge to form overarching concepts. As mentioned earlier, a special focus is thereby placed on written causal explanations.

Activity Domains: learners are *doing* chemistry when they plan and perform an experiment during which they take notes about the physical property and appearance of chemicals used. They are *organising* chemistry when they describe the observations made in the experiment in a precise and chronologically correct manner. Next, students are *explaining* chemistry when they explain all observations based on the reactivity series of metals, define the terms reducing agent and reduction, and formulate a chemical equation. Within the final step of the deeper learning process, also called *arguing* chemistry, students answer the research question based on their experimental findings. A critical reflection of different reducing agents and procedures is also part of the last phase.

Growth Mindset, Deep Practice and Deep Understanding: if students perform an experiment they have planned themselves, the learning experience is more personal than if students simply follow an experimental procedure like a cooking recipe. Also, with their own experimental procedure, students know better what to do and what to observe during the experiment. Otherwise, it is possible that they forget to observe relevant aspects of the reaction, preventing them from formulating a thorough explanation afterwards. Since the experiment is performed and analysed in small groups, learning takes place in social interaction and within a safe environment. Students are free to decide on the format of their presentation, which gives them another chance to increase their self-regulative competence and self-efficacy throughout the learning process. Since the final presentation takes place in front of the class, students demonstrate their revised understanding at its best. During those presentations, learner products are evaluated and function as a common ground for feedback, discussion and reflection.

5.6 Move from Surface Learning to Consolidation to Transfer Stage

In this DLE, the transition from surface learning to the consolidation and transfer stage is achieved by causal explanations. With its recurring patterns, this CDF guides students to combine multiple levels of representation and to reason observations based on general principles. To start with, surface learning is achieved as soon as students can describe their observations on a phenomenological level and answer the first part of the research question: '*Yes, Ötzi was able to produce elemental copper out of its ore since the black powder was transformed into shiny reddish-brown grains.*' During the consolidation stage, students need to explain the reaction on the particle level using key concepts and subject-specific terms. '*Copper oxide and carbon react in an exothermic reaction forming copper and carbon dioxide. The reason for that is that carbon particles have a higher tendency to react with oxygen than copper particles. Consequently, copper oxide donates oxygen during reduction while carbon functions as a reducing agent, simultaneously accepting oxygen during oxidation. In general, a more reactive metal can displace a less reactive metal from its compounds.*' Finally, this knowledge needs to be abstracted and generalised to allow transfer. '*Ötzi could have used any other substance that is more reactive than copper as a reducing agent. For example, within a displacement reaction, aluminium can be used to displace iron out of its ore since aluminium is higher on the reactivity series than iron.*' In addition to being able to transfer knowledge from one situation to another, another activity during the transfer stage can also be that students argue why a statement is true or false and decide with which principle their answer could be backed up. All this could be done using concept cartoons (Figure 5.8).

Engage the Learner

To get the students activated, a letter from a young girl named Anna is read aloud. She has been to an Ötzi exhibition and is now wondering whether the man in the ice

❹ Paul, Tom and Louise still have trouble understanding why their favourite statue made out of copper turned black. Now you are the expert and can discuss their problem in class.

The statue disintegrated (hat sich zersetzt)

The exhaust fumes of the cars coloured it black

It got sunburned

What do you think?

I think ... is right/wrong because ...
I agree/disagree with ... because ...
In my opinion the statue turned black because ...

Figure 5.8 Concept cartoon to trigger deeper practice during the transfer stage of the deeper learning episode

was able to produce elemental copper 3,000 years ago. This context has been chosen as learners have prior knowledge that they can activate to formulate a research question and hypothesis. It is also an exciting yet challenging task bridging the perceived gap between theoretical concepts in chemistry and their practical application in everyday life.

Promote/Acquire Basic Understanding and Acquisition of Foundational Skills

Basic understanding is acquired by means of an experiment. Instructional snippets force students to get engaged in this active phase as they have to discuss and decide on the best procedure. This method also allows students to know what to do during the experiment without overwhelming them since reduction reactions are new to them. To formulate their observations afterwards, learners can make use of provided word railings.

Provide Feedback, Feed-Up and Feed-Forward/Demonstrate Basic Understanding and Reflect

Basic understanding is existent as soon as students can answer the first part of the research question ('Did Ötzi produce copper?') on a phenomenological level. Comparing observations of different groups in class can serve as a backup or, if differing, lead to an in-depth discussion and reflection of one's own results. Thus, feedback is attained through the interaction with other students rather than the teacher's expertise. However, he or she serves as a mentor throughout the entire learning process, providing individual feedback on the task completion and reminding students of the next steps. Language-wise, the help sheet on how to write a good explanation and the cloze activity feed students forward.

Facilitate/Acquire Deeper Understanding and Deep Practice

In the next step, students explain their observations using chemical key concepts and a flexible writing frame[1] to answer the second part of the research question (How did Ötzi produce copper?). Deeper understanding of the matter is acquired as soon as clear causal connection between general principles and specific observations can be made. As explicitly verbalising those invisible connections is challenging for students, conceptual and verbal scaffolds need to be given by means of diagrams connecting causes and effects, word boxes providing causal connectors, as well as visualisations on the particle level. Additionally, chemical equations and the definition of subject-specific terms help students to condense information, build overarching concepts and finally abstract this newly gained knowledge to facilitate transfer.

Provide Feedback, Feed-Up and Feed-Forward/Demonstrate Deeper Understanding and Reflect

Deeper understanding of the subject matter is demonstrated by answering the second half of the research question in class. With their checklist on how to write a good causal explanation at hand, students give each other feedback on the quality of their explanations and provide feed-forward on how to improve their work. After a second writing phase, the letters to Anna are read aloud.

Facilitate Transfer/Transfer Knowledge

Once students know how to obtain elemental copper, they are asked to develop possible procedures for iron or aluminium using other reducing agents than carbon. As they compare methods and discuss their advantages and disadvantages, complex cognitive processes are triggered and concepts internalised and abstracted.

---

[1] The writing frame is an adaptation of the PRO-model by Putra und Tang (2016) and the claim-evidence-reason (CER)-model by McNeill und Krajcik (2006).

Transferring knowledge also means applying this knowledge to topics like waste recycling or students' impact on the environment as they critically evaluate the (over)-use of aluminium cans or foil. As the so-called thermite reaction is also used to weld railroad tracks, students see an authentic connection between the subject of chemistry and everyday life.

Mentor Reflection/Present and Reflect

Anna really liked the students' sound research and asked students to demonstrate their deeper understanding via explanatory videos, oral presentations or leaflets sharing their knowledge with further visitors of the Ötzi exhibition. Depending on the kind of visitor the students have in mind, they move along the mode continuum to provide an explanation that is understood by children, adults or scientists. This deep practice or translation activity leads to a better understanding of the content and improves subject-specific language skills.

To motivate students to do their best, the remaining students in the audience give out toy money or tokens to the most appealing and understandable presentation. A critical reflection phase of the learning process and product follows as teacher and students discuss why groups 'earned' different amounts of money with their presentations and how they could possibly increase their 'income'. Coins or tokens are concrete objects that make a comparison easier for students than the abstract construct of explanatory quality, which is, however, still assessed and improved by giving feedback and feed-forward based on the help sheets 'How to write a good explanation' and 'A good scientific explanation has . . .'.

5.7   Conclusion and Outlook

Explanations are a fundamental element of the subject of chemistry as they allow for knowledge construction and knowledge communication. However, to utilise their full meaning-making potential, the underlying structure needs to be made explicit and practised deeply. Among others, this can be done by means of the presented conceptual and verbal scaffolding within the pluriliteracies teaching for deeper learning approach. Even though a special focus has been placed on causal explanations in this DLE, further research on other relevant CDFs in the field of chemistry is needed to develop more DLEs that can help students to improve their subject-specific language skills.

5.8   Learning Materials

Lesson Plan

Embedded in the DLE of redox reactions, the depicted sub-episode of copper oxide reduction can be structured with the lesson plan in Table 5.3, with assessment of the resulting explanations shown in Table 5.4.

Table 5.3 Lesson plan of the deeper learning episode 'Producing copper out of its ore'

Lesson	Tasks	Timeframe
1	Introduction: – Read Anna's letter and formulate a research question Doing Phase: – Plan and perform experiment Organising Phase: – Describe observations First Explaining Phase: – Fill out PRO-model writing frame – Answer research question in class	90 minutes
2	Second Explaining Phase: – Reply to Anna's letter with scientific explanation – Provide feedback based on checklist – Improve explanation – Present explanatory letters in class	90 minutes
3	Arguing Phase: – Apply principles of reduction and reducing agent to other reactions – Create explanatory videos, presentations and leaflets for imaginary museum visitors	90 minutes
4	Presentation and evaluation: – Present explanatory videos in class – Evaluation of videos	90 minutes

WORKSHEET 1.1 Redox Reactions – Ötzi the Iceman

REDOX REACTIONS	ÖTZI THE ICEMAN

Hello, my name is Anna
and I went to the Ötzi exhibition last week.
The museum guide said that Ötzi already knew how to produce copper.
I don't I think this is possible because Ötzi   lived in the year 3000 BC
(before Christ) which is a long long time   ago. Maybe the tourists
who found him in the alpine ice in 1991 just placed the axe next to him
to make their discovery sound more exciting. The only resources he could
have possibly used back then were   charcoal (carbon), fire,
and copper ores like tenorite containing   copper oxide.
Can you help me find out whether this story is true or false?

❶ Write down your research question and hypothesis.

❓ Research question:

_____

☁. Hypothesis:

_____

_____

❷ Order the snippets below and carry out the experiment.

	With a funnel, the powder is poured into a test tube.
	2 g copper oxide and 0,2 g charcoal are put into a mortar and mixed to a fine powder
	Once the test tube has cooled down, the product is put into a watch glass.
	The test tube is heated in the blue Bunsen burner flame.

Info box: The lime water test
If you want to know which substances are formed in a reaction, you have to make tests. The lime water test is used to test for **carbon dioxide**. For the test, you take clear lime water and put the gas you want to test into the test tube with the lime water.
- If the water turns cloudy, the test is positive: carbon dioxide is produced.
- If the water stays clear, the test is negative.

❸ **Write down your observations. Use the word railing.**

> 1. Before – reaction – reactants – mixture – black – powder – lime water – transparent – colourless solution
> 2. During – reaction – heat – powder – glow – colour change from … to … – gas development – lime water – milky/blurry

_____

_____

_____

_____

❹ **Write a scientific explanation to answer your research question. Use the following words:**

> black • oxygen • oxidised • reducing agent • red • endothermic • lowest energy states •
> more • copper oxide • copper oxide • energy • shiny • oxygen • oxygen • higher energy •
> oxygen • dull • copper • copper • coal (carbon)

Principle: _Give a general law/theory/model._

All natural processes tend towards their _____ _____ _____.

To reverse (umkehren) natural processes, you have to add _____ because in the reaction

you have to reach a state of _____ _____. To reduce metal oxides (to take

away their _____) you need a good reducing agent. Good reducing agents are substances

which are very reactive with _____.

Reason: _Logically connect the law(s) from your principles with your experiment._

To produce elemental copper from _____, Ötzi could have used every substance which

is _____ reactive than copper. **Due to the fact** (Weil) all substances at the top of the reactivity

ladder connect well with oxygen, they can be used as reducing agents. This means they reduce copper

oxide by taking the _____ away. **The effect is** that the reducing agent is _____

as it takes on _____. Ötzi knew that carbon is a good _____.

Observation: *Explain the main points of your observations by connecting them to your reasons.*

During the reaction, the powder changed its colour and appearance from _____ and _____ to _____ and _____. It also changed its properties **as** it is no longer powdery but consists of small but hard pieces of _____. An _____ chemical reaction took place because there was enough heat and carbon.

Conclusions: *Answer your research question from above.*

The experiment showed that elemental _____ can be produced by reducing _____ with _____.

❺ Define the word 'reductions' and 'reducing agent' using the following words:

reduction, reducing agent, endothermic reaction, oxygen, oxygen, metal/non-metal, product, metal oxide/ non-metal oxide, substance

_____

_____

❻ Fill out the word equation for the reduction of copper oxide. Label the reduction, oxidation, reducing agent and oxidising agent.

Tip: When you heat the copper oxide and coal mixture, a gas is produced. If this gas comes into contact with lime water, the lime water turns cloudy.

7 Write a letter answering Anna's question. Describe how Ötzi produced copper and explain the underlying chemical reaction using scientific terms.

_____

_____

_____

_____

_____

_____

_____

_____

_____

_____

8 Invent a possible procedure for the production of iron and aluminum out of their ores. Use metals as reducing agents and reason your choice based on chemical key principles.

_____

_____

_____

_____

_____

9 Create an explanatory video and a leaflet for further visitors of the Ötzi exhibition. Decide whom you want to make this video for (children, adults, scientists, …) and adjust your language accordingly.

WORKSHEET 1.2 How to Write a Good Explanation

HOW TO WRITE A GOOD EXPLANATION

An explanation is an answer to a scientific question based on facts, concepts, or rules. It explains why things happen, what they are made up of or how they work.

In general, a **causal explanation** has the following structure:

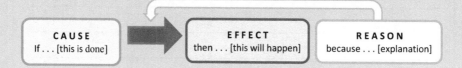

CAUSE	EFFECT	REASON
If . . . [this is done]	then . . . [this will happen]	because . . . [explanation]

Example: **If** I eat too much chocolate, **then** I will get fat **because** chocolate contains lots of unhealthy ingredients responsible for weight gain.

For a longer explanation, use the PRO Model and you will never forget anything!

Principle: State the general rule/law/theory/model your explanation is based on.

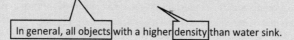

In general, all objects with a higher density than water sink.

Reason: Draw a logical connection between the general law and your observation.

Why does the general rule apply to your data?

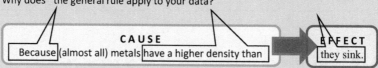

CAUSE — Because (almost all) metals have a higher density than → EFFECT they sink.

Observation: Describe and reason your observations. Use the following causal constructions:

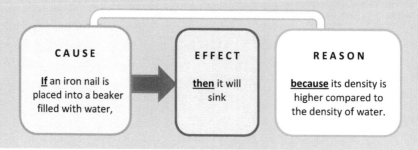

CAUSE	EFFECT	REASON
If an iron nail is placed into a beaker filled with water,	**then** it will sink	**because** its density is higher compared to the density of water.

You can also turn the PRO Model around. Therefore, start with your particular experiment and transfer your findings to a bigger group of substances.

Claim: Write one sentence about something that you want to explain later.
                Iron nails sink.

Evidence/   Back up your claim with facts/observations

Observation: *If … and … react together, then … is formed/caused*
                The effect is that…

Reason: Say why your observations explain your claim.
                Because/since/as/due to the fact that… This means that…

Principle: Can you transfer your claim to something bigger (all metals in general?)
                In general,… /As the law/rule/ theory of…says…

A GOOD CAUSAL EXPLANATION HAS:

❶ ideas connected with causal links

Incorrect	Correct
If I get in the pool, <u>then</u> I will get wet and <u>then</u> I will get cold. ☹ This is just a chronological order of steps.	If I get in the pool, I will get cold **because** water has a higher thermal conductivity than air. **As a result,** I lose heat much quicker and **consequently** feel cold.

❷ ideas ordered chronologically and linked by sequential connectives

Incorrect	Correct
<u>At the end,</u> I got in the pool <u>before</u> I got cold.	**First,** I got in the pool, **then** I got wet, **after that** I got cooler, **in the end** I was freezing.

❸ reasons based on relevant rules, concepts and definitions

Incorrect	Correct
If water is heated up to 100°C, it boils <u>because I say so.</u>	If water is heated up to 100°C, it boils **because** it has reached its boiling point.

❹ experimental data like observations and measurements as back up

Incorrect	Correct
… because <u>my father once told me so</u>	**The experiment showed that** water boils at exactly 100°C.

❺ present tense

Incorrect	Correct
Heat <u>caused</u> the water to boil.	Heat <u>causes</u> water to boil.

❻ scientific terms

Incorrect	Correct
bubbling point, burning, glass mug	boiling point, combustion, beaker

Assessment of Explanations

Table 5.4 Assessment of explanations in chemistry

Explanation in Chemistry	Perfect!	OK, but . . .	Not quite right yet. . .
Stating a Claim	You state an accurate and complete claim.	You state an accurate but incomplete claim.	You don't state a claim, or your claim is inaccurate.
Giving Evidence	You give appropriate and sufficient evidence for your claim.	You give appropriate but insufficient evidence for your claim.	You give no or incorrect evidence to your claim, or your evidence does not support your claim.
Reasoning Scientifically	Your reasoning links evidence to your claim and includes appropriate and sufficient scientific principles.	Your reasoning links evidence to your claim but does not include appropriate and/or sufficient scientific principles.	Your reasoning does not link evidence to your claim.
Using Causal Conjunctions like 'because' or 'therefore'	You use appropriate causal conjunctions.	You use inappropriate or not enough causal conjunctions.	You don't use any causal conjunctions.
Using Scientific Terms	You use appropriate scientific terms.	You use inappropriate or not enough scientific terms.	You don't use any scientific terms.

REFERENCES

Baumert, J., Klieme, E., Neubrand, M., et al. (Eds.). (2001). *PISA 2000: Basiskompetenzen von Schülerinnen und Schülern im internationalen Vergleich*. Leske + Budrich.

Brown, N. J. S., Furtak, E. M., Timms, M., Nagashima, S. O., & Wilson, M. (2010). The Evidence-Based Reasoning Framework: Assessing Scientific Reasoning. *Educational Assessment, 15*(3–4), 123–141. https://doi.org/10.1080/10627197.2010.530551

Byrnes, H. (2013). Positioning Writing as Meaning-Making in Writing Research: An Introduction. *Journal of Second Language Writing, 22*(2), 95–106.

Connolly, T. (2019*). Die Förderung vertiefter Lernprozesse durch Sachfachliteralität: Eine vergleichende Studie zum expliziten Scaffolding kognitiver Diskursfunktionen im bilingualen Chemieunterricht am Beispiel des Erklärens* [Unpublished doctoral dissertation, Johannes Gutenberg University Mainz]. http://doi.org/10.25358/open science-4833

Gillis, V. (2014). Disciplinary Literacy: *Adapt* not Adopt. *Journal of Adolescent & Adult Literacy, 57*(8), 614–623. https://doi.org/10.1002/jaal.301

Lemke, J. L. (1993). *Talking Science: Language, Learning, and Values* (2nd ed.). Ablex.

McNeill, K. L., Lizotte, D. J., Krajcik, J., & Marx, R. W. (2006). Supporting Students' Construction of Scientific Explanations by Fading Scaffolds in Instructional Materials. *Journal of the Learning Sciences, 15*(2), 153–191. https://doi.org/10.1207/s15327809jls1502_1

Nashan, M., & Parchmann, I. (2008). Fachtext versus Geschichte. Kommunikation in den Naturwissenschaften als Zugang zu einem Verständnis für die Natur der Naturwissenschaften. Unterricht *Chemie, 19*(3), 57–61.

Parchmann, I., & Venke, S. (2008). Eindeutig – Zweideutig?! Chemische Fachsprache im Unterricht. *Unterricht Chemie, 19,* 10–15.

Polias, J. (2016). *Apprenticing Students into Science: Doing, Talking & Writing Scientifically.* Lexis Education.

Putra, G. B. S., & Tang, K.-S. (2016). Disciplinary Literacy Instructions on Writing Scientific Explanations: A Case Study from a Chemistry Classroom in an All-Girls School. *Chemistry Education Research and Practice, 17*(3), 569–579. https://doi.org/10.1039/C6RP00022C

Rose, D., & Martin, J. R. (2012). *Learning to Write, Reading to Learn: Genre, Knowledge and Pedagogy in the Sydney School.* Equinox.

Thummathong, R., & Thathong, K. (2018). Chemical Literacy Levels of Engineering Students in Northeastern Thailand. *Kasetsart Journal of Social Sciences, 39*(3), 478–487. https://doi.org/10.1016/j.kjss.2018.06.009

Vollmer, G. (1980). *Sprache und Begriffsbildung im Chemieunterricht.* Diesterweg.

Physics: Exploring Pluriliteracies through a Deeper Learning Episode on Rainbows

KLAUS WENDT, ANDREAS PYSIK & JOHANNES LHOTZKY

6.1 Synergies between Scientific Literacy and Deeper Learning

In our highly scientific and technology-dominated world, great importance is placed on learners' ability to navigate such an environment. Therefore, physics education is of the utmost relevance as it is a dedicated tool in the formation of scientific and technological competences. The goal of our educational efforts should be to provide learners not only with topical facts, knowledge and background but also with particular skills in approaching, handling, and specifically communicating 'science' in such a way as to successfully participate in any kind of purposeful exchange in the field's discourse. 'Scientific literacy' describes exactly this intersection between using scientific knowledge and skills to language addressee- and context-appropriate discourse in the field. A further characteristic of scientific literacy is the activity-related and application-oriented knowledge of essential underlying scientific cognition processes, such as ideation, formulation of hypotheses, planning of experiments, interpretation of results and deviations, and, finally, the deduction of general concepts and laws (Fischer, 1998). In physics education, 'scientific literacy' essentially comprises the three domains of

1. Explaining scientific phenomena
2. Developing, executing, and evaluating scientific research
3. Interpreting scientific evidence (Gebhard, Höttecke & Rehm, 2017; Prenzel et al., 2013).

Thus, the scientific use of knowledge can be defined as identifying objects for investigation, describing observation and phenomena and drawing conclusions based on evidence. In addition, scientific literacy involves understanding the relevance and importance of science and technology for our future existence and the future of our environment. Physicists must also be prepared to confront and reflect on topics and ideas related to other fields of science (Prenzel et al., 2013).

The appropriate and correct use of language and communication skills facilitates the acquisition and teaching of relevant, basic science skills (Gebhard, Höttecke & Rehm, 2017). Included here are the fundamental skills of analytical reasoning, complex problem solving and teamwork. Scientific literacy is, therefore, the competent and appropriate usage of instructional, educational, and technical language as well as the ability to transition from such academic registers to common everyday speech. To truly appreciate scientific observations, methodologies and theories, physicists must have a command of multi-modal discourse, for example, writing lab reports, solving equations and using digital tools.

The general goal of a literacy-based approach is the initiation of a deeper learning process, which entails the teaching of subject culture, methods, and content (Prenzel et al., 2013).

6.2 Deeper Learning in Physics Lessons

Language is the basic building block of classroom communication and paves the way to make knowledge transferable, understandable and usable. As pointed out above, its well-reflected application is thus of the utmost importance even in teaching physics and must adequately accompany the formation of essential subject-specific knowledge. According to the 2006 and 2012 PISA studies, the three aspects of scientific literacy (i.e. (1) explaining scientific phenomena; (2) developing, executing and evaluating scientific research; and (3) interpreting scientific evidence) are also identified by the terms (1) knowing, (2) doing, and (3) assessing. These aspects are further divided into a broad range of competences, such as linguistic and epistemological competence; learning, communicative, social, and procedural competence; and surely neither last nor least, ethical–moral and aesthetic competence (Prenzel et al., 2013).

In deeper learning, the concept of literacy refers not only to a deep understanding of subject-specific knowledge but also a command of discipline discourse (Meyer & Imhof, 2017). That is, deeper learning is based on the teaching–learning model of competence-oriented and cognitively activating education (Leisen, 2014) and is complemented by aspects of language formation. Here, language is an essential element in processes of so-called higher-order cognition, such as creativity, systematic decision-making, evaluative thinking, and brainstorming (Helmke et. al, 2011; Meyer & Imhof, 2017). In order to successfully navigate such cognitive processes, learners must gradually acquire ever-more sophisticated language within their discipline of study, and this language must be continuously refined.

However, languaging appropriately is one of the most fundamental challenges in educational contexts, especially in the natural sciences. One glance in a physics textbook quickly reveals the sheer quantity of specialised terms learners are confronted with: in a science textbook at secondary level, about 1,500–2,500 technical terms or phrases are introduced, which are often even characterised by a subject-specific syntax. On average, up to ten new technical terms appear in one lesson (Merzyn, 1998). Success in the classroom can only be achieved when such terms and syntax are mastered.

Cognitive Discourse Function

Vollmer and Thürmann describe basic cognitive and linguistic actions using the term cognitive discourse functions (CDFs), which are essentially linguistic patterns that show up time and time again during specific cognitive processes, for example, explaining, describing, or evaluating (Vollmer & Thürmann, 2010, p. 116). In terms of deeper learning, CDFs refer to both thematic and interdisciplinary language acts. Many CDFs can be used across disciplines, which helps learners make meaning regardless of school subjects. However, there are also subject-specific CDFs that focus on science education in particular. They are closely related to the linguistic term 'operator.' Though they can sometimes be shared with other disciplines, common operators in physics are usually very specific (Vollmer, 2011, pp. 1f). Fortunately, though, a number of science-oriented CDFs exist that can aid learners in effectively communicating in the natural science field (Table 6.1).

In order to simplify the CDFs even more, we have created 'illustrated discourse functions' specifically for our example. That means we have established a transparent system of pictograms that visually underline the work assignments within the learning unit discussed in this chapter. The symbols chosen provide learners with the specific information about the task's primary focus and the way it should be addressed and solved. From a collection of items, we have limited ourselves to a set of six icons: observing as a layperson, observing through a physics lens, performing, noting, verbalising and purposeful verbalising (see Figure 6.1). The symbols serve as anchor points and help learners quickly find their way around the teaching materials.

6.3   Deeper Learning Strategies in Physics

The successful achievement of deeper learning in physics teaching implies the ability to act and express oneself confidently and in depth within a specific context. Learners must be able to *do* physics (i.e. observe and conduct experiments), *organise* physics (e.g. describe physical phenomena), *explain* physics (i.e. provide an explanation for observations), and *argue* physics (e.g. evaluate the appropriateness of certain methods). Acquisition of such skills is guided by deeper learning strategies.

- The **deepening of the understanding of text and experimentation** is necessary to initiate research actions. In this process, the learners already draw on prior knowledge and established patterns in order to understand and process new knowledge and content.

Table 6.1 Physics-specific discourse functions

Discourse Function	Description	Activity Domains
Deduce	Draw appropriate conclusions based on findings	Explaining
Estimate	Indicate orders of magnitude through reasoned considerations	Arguing
Hypothesise	Formulate an educated guess	Arguing
Prove	Prove or disprove an assertion/statement with the help of factual arguments by logical deduction	Arguing
Document	Provide all necessary explanations, derivations, and sketches for a subject/procedure	Doing
Plan	Find an experimental setup for a given problem and create experimental instructions	Doing
Report	Report the course of events, observations, and results as well as evaluation (results protocol, progress report) in a discipline-appropriate manner	Explaining
Investigate	Search for objects; work out characteristics and connections	Doing
Derive	Solve equations using mathematical operations to determine physical quantity; comment on essential steps of the solution	Organising/ Explaining
Check	Measure facts or statements against facts or internal logic and, if necessary, uncover contradictions	Arguing
Summarise	Reproduce essential information in a concentrated form	Organising/ Explaining

Figure 6.1 Illustrated discourse functions

- **Commitment and accountability** can be increased by assigning learners partial responsibility for the layout and accuracy in planning, conducting and evaluating an experiment and in independently contributing interpretations, evidence and references.
- To **highlight** the **content relevance** for a given topic, it is essential to achieve an adequate mindset for the specific research task. Authentic contexts and relevance to everyday life can facilitate the learners' entry into and excitement for

the learning unit. Therefore, everyday prominence for the learners' personal experiences plays a central role in the acceptance and transfer of knowledge.

- Another substantial point is the **development of a critical cultural conscious-ness**. This facet, which at first glance might seem somewhat irrelevant or inappropriate for physics education, is of much importance. A central aspect of work in the sciences includes the ability to participate in current discipline discourse. Examples include topics such as climate change, energy and mobility.
- For the sake of supporting the learners in the best possible way, we must also mention the **differentiation and individualisation of the learning pathways**. The focus here is on both the work materials and the learning environment as well as the self-regulation and feedback by the teacher.
- To enforce deeper learning, a proper appreciation of the application of what is being learnt and what has been learnt is required. It is fundamental that learners acquire and fully establish a solid basis for the treatment of tasks as well as for a competent application of experimental instructions. This is a necessary condition for further action and is known as **deep (or even deeper) practice**.

Individualised learning paths can be developed using appropriate and targeted support given by verbal as well as written assistance. Learners at varying stages in the learning process can be aided by well-developed language and method supports (i.e. **scaffolding**). Thus, individualisation processes can be assisted with the help of sophisticated and evidence-based **scaffolding approaches**.

6.4   A Model Deeper Learning Episode in Physics

The Physics of the Rainbow

The occurrence of a rainbow in the sky is a truly impressive natural spectacle and addresses attention not only as a phenomenon of physics but also in cultural, socio-political and ethico-religious senses. In these contexts, it is considered a symbol of harmony, wholeness or nature conservation, or as a sign of the connection between heaven and earth. The first drawings of the rainbow date back to more than 5,000 years ago (Taçon, Wilson, & Chippindale., 1996) and therefore already testify its prominent relevance for ancient mankind and early cultures.

Similarly, rainbows are a worthwhile candidate for in-depth research in the context of science. An analysis of the phenomenon itself, as well as the underlying causes for its appearance, can be an insightful one. The study of rainbows sheds light on a variety of physical phenomena, such as ray optics, light refraction and light dispersion.

In the following pages, the learning unit will be introduced and explained in detail. In the learning episode, the learners research the natural phenomenon of rainbows based on clearly stated research hypotheses, which ultimately results in the creation of the final learning product: a technical article for publication on Wikipedia. The presentation and implementation of the presented teaching unit was deliberately created without external constraints. Additionally, it should be seen as an island of understanding showcased in a special learning unit, completely independent from prior learning units. Here, the topic is to be intentionally dealt with in a targeted and multi-faceted manner. The chapter shows the preliminary ideas and central planning steps and emphasises the importance and concrete influences of deeper learning aspects. Table 6.2 compiles a variety of the aspects and ideas covered in the preparation and implementation of the following teaching unit on the physics of the rainbow. The information in the table will be expanded on in the following pages as well as in the attached learning materials.

6.5   Alignment of the Deeper Learning Episode

Learner Strengths, Needs and Interests

In the eyes of learners, physics is often believed to be demanding in mathematics, rather boring and irrelevant. Therefore, it is extremely necessary to consider the individual preferences, interests and needs of the learners. It is essential to create an appealing, exciting and, nevertheless, challenging learning environment in which the learners can safely develop, experience, and test their skills regardless of their significantly varying ability levels and/or varying interests. To address the abilities of individual learners, the presented material is accompanied by a comprehensive collection of tools and resources. To cognitively activate different types of learners, a variety of task types, problems and display formats were chosen. The subject matter – rainbows – is highly relevant to learners as it is a phenomenon with which they are regularly confronted in their everyday lives. This should further strengthen their participation and develop personal interest. Based on clearly stated research hypotheses, the learners work on the specific topic – here, the rainbow – which ultimately results in the creation of the final learning product, a technical article for publication on Wikipedia.

Scientific Literacy

As already described, scientific literacy includes written, verbal, numerical and digital competence. In addition, observation, methodology and underlying scientific theories of scientific contexts play a central role. This holds true in the proposed learning unit as well. The observable characteristics of the rainbow, as collected in the initial experiment, provide the context and object of investigation for the learning unit. This is consolidated by a (first) hypothesis through guided

Table 6.2 Planning grid for a deeper learning episode in physics: 'The physics of the rainbow'

Designing Deeper Learning Episodes

Planning Grid for a Deeper Learning Episode in Physics

What do I want my learners to know or be able to do?	How will my learners demonstrate increasingly deeper understanding at the surface, consolidation and transfer levels?	How can I support active knowledge co-construction for my learners?	How can I support my learners every step of the way?	How can I generate and sustain learner commitment and achievement?
Basic Understanding: • Role of raindrops in rainbow creation • Weather conditions, positional relationships, appearance **Fundamental Skills:** • Describing a natural phenomenon and the required underlying causes • Describing experimental observations **Deeper Understanding and Practice:** • Experimental confirmation of the role of raindrops with a raindrop model • Application of prior knowledge to theoretical considerations of the path of light in the droplet	**Preliminary Learning Outcomes:** Diagnosis of the results of the worksheets • Worksheets 1 and 2 • Worksheets 3, 4 and 5 Process-accompanying diagnosis of learning status and learning difficulties Diagnosis of the Results of the Worksheets: • Worksheets 6–10 Process-accompanying diagnosis of learning status and learning difficulties **Main Learning Outcomes:** • Understanding and explaining the Rainbow • Wikipedia article • Review of progress by classmates	**Social Interaction:** Learner group work on experimenting, describing, explaining, etc. **Construction of Knowledge:** • Description of phenomena and their traceability to known physical relationships • Use of model concepts to gain knowledge • Use of idealisation (circular glass globe as a raindrop) • Formulation of hypotheses • Planning and documenting experiments • Carrying out experiments according to instructions • Opportunities and limitations of the physical point of view **Use of Media:** • Illustrations (change of presentation)	**Structure and Orientation:** • Use of clearly defined CDF • Clearly structured material User manual: symbols on worksheets, **Use of Scaffolding:** • Expressions for positional relationships and the structure of conditional sentences • Physical information with assignment tasks • Support for written explanations **Feedback:** • Individual teacher feedback on . . . • Worksheets 3, 4 and 5 • Final version Wikipedia article • Peer feedback on . . . • Wikipedia article about the primary rainbow **Feed-up:** • Research questions	**Engagement:** Context-oriented topics **Personal Meaningfulness/Relevance:** A well-known natural phenomenon **Opportunities for Autonomous Learning:** • Student experiments • Independent research on the secondary rainbow and Alexander's dark zone • Creating a Wikipedia article • Peer feedback

Table 6.2 (*cont.*)

Designing Deeper Learning Episodes

Planning Grid for a Deeper Learning Episode in Physics

- Explanation of the primary rainbow through synthesis of previous findings
- Reflecting the role of models and experiments in physics

Transfer:
- Media: Wikipedia article
- Content: Genesis of a secondary rainbow
- Alexander's dark zone and more

- Films, if necessary (to support teachers and learners)
- Scaffsheets
- Haptic and hands-on experiments
- (Optional Wikipedia on school server)

- Outlook: Wikipedia article

Feed-forward:
- Experiment planning
- Information about Wikipedia articles
- A pool of images and drawings for the production of the Wikipedia article

Assessment:
Quality of scientific explanations

observation. The learners formulate ideas and guesses about how the relative geometrical position of the sun, the observer, and the rain area affect the appearance of a rainbow (or lack thereof). Based on this information, they analyse the object of investigation independently or in teams and develop individual research questions about the cause of this optical phenomenon.

Activity Domains

In general, learners in the physics classroom are asked to actively observe phenomena, formulate hypotheses, plan, set up and perform experiments, interpret and evaluate findings, and, finally, transfer the knowledge obtained through experimentation to other contexts. Within the presented series of lessons of this model teaching unit, we focus on active observation, hypothesis formation, evaluation and knowledge transfer (i.e. writing a Wikipedia article).

Growth Mindset, Deep Practice and Deep Understanding

The learning unit provides learners with the opportunity to look at rainbows from a new, more scientific perspective. Rainbows are an everyday phenomenon but are not easily explained in a scientifically appropriate way. To create a real-world working environment, authentic material in the form of photographs and experimental equipment are made available to learners. By means of differentiated and individualised aids, the provided material enables and supports independent learning by accounting for varying levels of prior knowledge. Furthermore, learners are able to self-regulate their learning experience by deciding whether to complete tasks individually or in small groups. Throughout the classroom, learners have access to visual aids detailing common procedures in research (e.g. observation, experimentation or evaluation).

6.6 How Do Learners Move from Surface Learning through Consolidation to the Transfer Stage?

Description of the Learning Unit in Chronological Order

Activation of the Learners

To activate the learners' concepts of dispersion and optics in physics, the optimal position of the sun, rainfall and observer is discussed. This starts discourse on the topic of the appearance and visibility of the rainbow. Here, learners are asked to recall their prior real-life experiences (e.g. *When did I last see a rainbow? What were the conditions then?*) while also contributing their previous knowledge on the topic (e.g. *Which conditions must possibly be met to see a splitting of colours in the pattern?*).

Starting-Point

The deeper learning episode starts with some preparations in the first lesson. The learners form groups (e.g. groups of three) and receive the first and second work-sheet. The class then moves to the open school grounds to explore an artificial rainbow, which serves as the first experiment. This will allow the learners to directly observe the natural phenomenon and to formulate first hypotheses as starting-points for joint discussions and further investigations. They should independently figure out that the raindrops somehow act as the source of the colour effects. Propelled downward by gravity, the individual raindrops separate the different colours of which white sunlight is composed and each individual drop makes visible to the observer one specific colour. The succession of millions of raindrops, each 'revealing' another colour, makes it possible to observe all the colours of the rainbow, which serves as an important first insight (see 1st Experiment on Worksheets 1–4 and Table 6.2).

Promote/Acquire Basic Understanding and Acquisition of Foundational Skills

The artificial rainbow is also a good starting-point to achieve a basic knowledge. Specifically, learners can collect data on the appearance of the rainbow, the under-lying conditions for the formation thereof, the necessary conditions for its visual observation, the weather conditions, the shape and opening angle of the rainbow, the occurrence of individual colours, and the relationship between the positions of the light source, rain drops, and observer (i.e. the positional relationship). Additionally, they can consider other phenomena, like double rainbows, dark space and more, which can then be discussed. Worksheets 3–5 guide learners in develop-ing this basic knowledge (2nd Lesson, see Lesson Plan Table 6.3).

Studies have shown that these basics are not directly evident for schoolchildren or learners of higher grades:

> Thus, many do not realise that the observer must have the sun at his back. Very many learners are of the opinion before the lesson that one must look through the rain at the sun [5]. Others do not arrange the sun, the rain wall and the observer in one line, but see the rain wall like a mirror on which the sun shines obliquely (angle of incidence = angle of reflection). The correct arrangement must therefore be discussed in class and preferably demonstrated (Wilhelm, Horz & Schlichting, 2014, p. 6).

Supporting the Learners

As already described in Part I of this volume, differentiation of the learners' learning processes. In order to customise the learning material in an optimal way, special scaffolding materials called 'scaffsheets' have been developed. There are two types

Table 6.3 Lesson Plan

Lessons	Tasks for Learners (S) and Teachers (T)	Activity Domains	Time
1st	Organisation (T) Experiment 1 (S & T) Worksheets 1 & 2 (S)	Organising, Doing	45 minutes
2nd	Outlook: Your Wikipedia Contribution (T) Worksheets 3, 4 & 5 (S)	Doing, Explaining	45 minutes
Teacher Feedback (T)			
3rd	Experiment 2 (S & T)	Doing, Explaining	45 minutes
4th	Experiment 3 (S & T)	Doing, Explaining	45 minutes
Homework: Learning Task 1 (Tasks 8.1, 8.2, 8.3)			
5th	Learning Task 1 (Worksheet 8) (S) Experiment 4 (T)	Doing, Explaining	45 minutes
6th	Learning Task 2 (S) Creating a Wikipedia article (S)		
7th	Creating a Wikipedia article (S) (also as homework)	Explaining, Arguing	45 minutes
8th	Presentation and reflection (S & T)	Arguing	45 minutes
9th	More about rainbows	Doing, Explaining	45 minutes
Teacher Feedback (T)			

Figure 6.2 Initiate scaffolding

of scaffsheets (Figure 6.2), which are indicated in this learning episode by a specific colour and pictogram. Those providing language support are identified with a corresponding yellow pictogram (e.g. Scaffsheet 1). Scaffsheets primarily providing learners with subject information are identified with orange pictograms (e.g. Scaffsheet 5).

Scaffolding regarding the formulation of positional relationships and the necessary conditions for rainbow observation is provided by Scaffsheets 1–3, specifically addressing learners who do not yet have a firm comprehension of the corresponding linguistic basics (Table 6.2). Furthermore, information about the rainbow angles is scaffolded in a task to prevent problems with the comprehension of a corresponding text (see Worksheet 5). With respect to the final written learning product, learners also receive help in giving written explanations, provided by Scaffsheet 5, as well as in citing links correctly, organising their work, and addressing specific claims required in their explanations (see Scaffsheets 6–8).

Supplementary to this written scaffolding, learners are supported through personal feedback, feed-up, and feed-forward (Hattie, 2012). At the beginning of the learning unit, learners are presented with well-defined research questions as well as an in-depth look at the expected learning product (i.e. a Wikipedia article), which ensures clarity of purpose via feed-up. Later on, the student groups receive teacher-given feedback on their results from Worksheets 3–5 and then peer feedback on their Wikipedia article. Regarding feed-forward, learners are given the ability to monitor and assess their learning and thereby gain confidence to be able to complete a future task on their own.

These essential steps are supported by the following:

- lesson planning that is transparent to learners and allows them to successfully address the research questions
- well-structured information about the expected learning outcome, (here, e.g. the design of the Wikipedia article), leading to clarity in the evaluation criteria
- guidance on what is expected of written statements
- a pool of images, which allows learners to adequately design the article and their texts.

Learning Path: Experimental Setup and Construction – In the Rainbow Lab

After the introductory experiment and the acquisition of basic knowledge, the learners move on to the second experiment, which is preceded by a short thematic transition. Specifically, learners discuss ways to investigate specific colour observation in more detail. This discussion should initially lead to the suggestion to use a water-filled and illuminated round-bottom flask as a model of a water drop and lastly to the development of the following research questions: *Does the round flask 'show' the colours of a primary rainbow when it is illuminated and lowered? Does it 'show' the colours of a secondary rainbow? Does this lighting take place in the respective rainbow angles that we have discussed in class?* (Second Experiment on Worksheet 6).

A corresponding experimental setup is shown in Figure 6.3, with a clinometer (Figure 6.4, self-printed in a 3D printer) to measure the angle. The clinometer consists of a holder for a smartphone and a scope to aim the phone at the glass bulb. Instructions for 3D printing are included in Section 6.8 Learning Materials.

At the beginning the clinometer is used to set a starting angle of about 55°. A student observes the round-bottom flask with one eye right next to the clinometer while another student slowly lowers the flask, changing the angle. First, at the lower edge of the flask, light changing its colour from red to violet should be observed, followed by another reflex at the lower edge with colour change from violet to red.

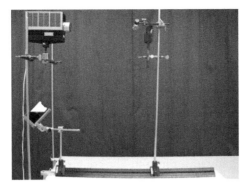

Figure 6.3 Experimental setup

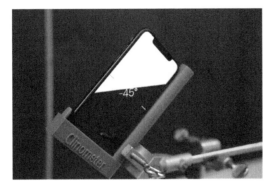

Figure 6.4 Clinometer in action

These findings with respect to the first research question should confirm the raindrop model.

However, the angles of 51° and 42°, as obtained from the artificial or real rainbow, cannot be confirmed in the angle measurements. Here, values around 46° to 48° are found. These findings give the opportunity to criticise the model and to make assumptions about possible reasons for the observed deviations (e.g. the influence of the glass envelope). The independent discovery and development of an explanation corresponds to an important aspect of scientific literacy i.e. the process of gaining knowledge. An experiment that can be used to properly reproduce the rainbow angles is described in the appendix (see Section 6.8 Learning Materials).

One question remains: *How do the raindrops create a curved arc?* This research question can be tested again with a water-filled round-bottom flask – ideally outdoors since the direction of the light source must be kept constant even under major changes in the flask positions. This experiment represents a student-centred extension to the second experiment in the rainbow lab with the clinometer (3rd Experiment on Worksheet 7).

The two rainbows can be simulated using flasks in the lab. Learners are asked to observe the colour glow that appears at the highest point (i.e. the pinnacle of an arc) when focusing their eyeline in the centre of the line that connects the sun, the observer and the flask. Moving away from that centre point, the colour glow is observed at an increasingly lower height. The colour always seems further away on the side of the flask rim – always oriented to the centre (i.e. to the observer) (Worksheet 7, task 7.4). If, finally, the glass bulbs are observed all around for colour impressions, it becomes clear that the spectral glow takes place around the direction of incidence. This shows that even raindrops near the edge of an arc can contribute to the observed colour of the whole arc.

Moreover, further questions are prompted by the second experiment: *How is it that round flasks or water drops emit light in spectral colours? What happens, scientifically speaking, in the flask or in the drop?* In Learning Task 1, learners outline and verbalise their ideas about appropriate processes (Worksheet 8). To test their hypotheses, an experiment is planned and carried out (4th Experiment on Worksheet 9). The processes which become evident in this experiment are secured as results. This fourth experiment can also be viewed via video, for example, on a website of the Ludwig Maximilian University of Munich:

http://www2.didaktik.physik.uni-muenchen.de/expvid/Optik/hd/brechung_
    regenbogen.m4v

Facilitate Transfer

Learners are asked to transfer the knowledge they have gained throughout the learning episode by writing a Wikipedia article on the topic. The task asks the learners not only to create a technical text explaining the phenomenon of a rainbow but also to prepare the appropriate illustrations using pictograms, photos or sketches and provide links to related information. By adopting this familiar format for Wikipedia articles (i.e. curating images and related information), learners gain a new and possibly different or more comprehensive grasp of the concept and the subject-specific content.

Additionally, the opportunity to transfer their gained understanding is offered once again in the form of presentations and discussions of their Wikipedia article. Learners transform prior knowledge into a new linguistic context, deepening their skills with the genre of the specialised text. When presenting, learners must be aware of the differences between spoken and written discourse and choose their wording accordingly.

In order not to overburden the learners, content transfers regarding additional questions and ideas are made no earlier than after the presentation and the reflection on their individual Wikipedia articles. Further investigation into the following phenomena could be added to the end of the learning unit:

- How exactly is a secondary rainbow formed?
- What is the cause of Alexander's dark zone between the two arcs?
- Under what circumstances could circular rainbows form?
- Are rainbows also possible in moonlight?

The observations and generalisations carried out during the experiments support the transfer of knowledge. For example, learners use their gained knowledge about the appearance of an initial primary rainbow to explain the double rainbow effect. They are aided in their efforts by the linguistic tools they have attained throughout the learning unit as well as by images of ray trajectories (Worksheet 13). Here, the learned strategies and skills are applied and thus further adopted.

In Table 6.3, we give a detailed lesson plan for the presented learning unit on the physics of the rainbow. It divides the material into nine lessons of forty-five minutes each. However, it should be considered more of a guideline in the creation of a personalised plan that takes into consideration individual concepts and preferences rather than a strict programme.

6.7   Conclusion and Outlook

This chapter presents a model deeper learning episode in physics on the rainbow. As shown in Table 6.4, each step on the learning journey moves learners along the pathway of deeper learning through deep understanding, deep practice and transfer activities. In this context, both the subject-specific content and language are essential elements for which aids (i.e. scaffsheets) have been provided. These scaffsheets, as well as other aids and a variety of detailed examples, can be found both above and in the appendix to the chapter (see Table 6.5). These were designed with the purpose of fostering learner growth within the classroom. The use of these engaging, supportive materials in combination with valuable feedback promotes learner involvement, participation and cognitive activation, which allow learners to demonstrate their understanding through the production of a discipline-appropriate text.

Table 6.4 Outline of the learning episode and its relations to deeper learning

Topics	Learning Steps and Objectives	Deeper Learning
Natural Phenomenon: Rainbow	**Experiment 1 (Outdoor): Artificial Rainbow** **Observation:** The falling drops emit an arc-shaped spectrum of colours from red to violet. **Focus on Main Research Question:** How can we study this emission of spectral colour in the lab? **Basic Knowledge:** Appearance, weather conditions, positional relationships, rainbow angles	Activate Learners' Basic Understanding and Foundational Skills
In the Rainbow Lab: Models and Experiments	**Experiment 2: A Water-Filled Round-Bottom Flask as a Drop Model** Successful reproduction of shining in spectral colours and colour sequences Different rainbow angles lead to model criticism: restricted suitability of the drop model **Research Question:** Why do the luminous drops form an arc? **Experiment 3 (Outdoor): Re-Enactment of a Bow with a Round Flask** Reproduction of the circular arc shape, annular emission of spectral colours Composition of the rainbow from many (secondary) light sources in the form of the drops **Research Questions:** What happens with the sunlight in a drop? How is it redirected to the observer? How are the spectral colours created? **Learning Task 1: Light Path in the Centre Plane of a Droplet** Assumption and construction **Experiment 4: Confirmation of the Light Path in the Centre Plane of a Droplet** Conformation: emergence angle of approx. 42°, larger for red than for violet **Learning Task 2: Explanation of Colour Sequences**	Deeper Understanding and Deep Practice
Understanding and Explaining the Primary Rainbow	**Media Transfer:** Wikipedia page about the primary rainbow Presentations and reflections on the Wikipedia pages	Transfer Knowledge, Present and Reflect
More about Rainbows	**Content Transfer:** Secondary rainbows, Alexander's dark zone, rainbows at night, circular rainbows, etc. **Media Transfer:** Content addition to the Wikipedia page	Transfer Knowledge, Present and Reflect

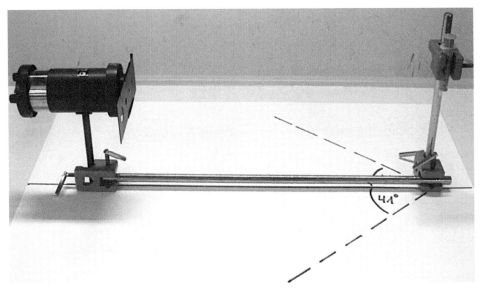

Figure 6.5 Water drop experiment

6.8 Learning Materials

Reproduction of Rainbow Angles with a Water Drop Experiment.

A drop of water hangs from a syringe (on the right in Figure 6.5) and is illuminated from the left. If the learners look along the two 41° sight lines and then move their heads back and forth, they discover colour reflexes in the spectral colours.

Instructions for the 3D Printing of the Clinometer

To determine the angle between the incident light and the light reflected by the raindrop (model) in the experiment (Figure 6.5), an angle-measuring instrument is required. In order not to have to make a special purchase for this, or to have to calculate via measuring, we developed a clinometer holder, through which any smartphone can be converted into a clinometer with a scope. A 3D printer is needed as well as a suitable app (pre-installed by default on iOS). As an alternative to the 3D-printed object, a smartphone can also be used as a scope with the help of a straw. In each case, however, it is important to ensure that the incident light in the model also hits the water drop model horizontally so that the angles can be determined correctly. The.stl file can be downloaded from https://www.larissa.physik.uni-mainz .de/rainbow/

WORKSHEET 6.1 Rainbows

Worksheet 1: Rainbows

1st Experiment: Inspecting an Artificial Rainbow

Task 1.1

Make a guess about the place where you can see a rainbow.

☐ A
☐ B
☐ C

Task 1.2

Now walk around the fountain. Check your assumption from Task 1.1

Result: ………………

Task 1.3: Observations

Watch the rainbow very closely!
Where do its colours come from?

....

....

....

....

....

WORKSHEET 6.2 Rainbows

Worksheet 2: Rainbows

Task 2.1

On the right you see <u>the same</u> falling raindrop in several images of a fast sequence.

Color this drop in the observed order of colors.

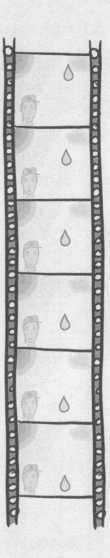

Task 2.2

Write down your research question(s).

....

....

....

....

....

....

WORKSHEET 6.3: Rainbows

Worksheet 3: Rainbows

 Using the photo below, describe what a rainbow looks like.

Note the order in which the spectrum of colours appear from top to bottom.

Distinguish between the (weak) upper and the (strong) lower arc.

Scaffsheet 1 provides words and phrases you can use for your description.

Scaffsheet 1

SCAFFSHEET 1: Rainbows

Scaffsheet 1: Rainbows

Here you can find words and phrases that you may use to describe the rainbow …

green   yellow

Between the arcs …

violet   red   orange   blue   indigo

For the first … the order of colours is:

secondary rainbow   primary rainbow

is darker than   is brighter than

WORKSHEET 6.4 Rainbows

Worksheet 4: Rainbows

At the fountain in the schoolyard, you have recognised that observers see the rainbow only if the sun, the rain area and the observers are arranged correctly.

Task 4.1

Use the following pictures to depict this arrangement. Choose pictures appropriately and put them in the right order. (*Several solutions are possible*)

Appropriate arrangement(s): ....

Task 4.2

Describe this arrangement in words!

....
....
....
....
....
....
....

Scaffsheets 2 & 3 might help you to write correctly!

Scaffsheets 2 & 3

SCAFFSHEET 2: Rainbows

Scaffsheet 2: Rainbows

Here you practise how to describe an arrangement of items. Build a suitable sentence for each speech bubble. Use the parts of the sentence given in the grey box.

Picture 2

Picture 4

		behind me.
		on my right side.
The sun	is	to my right.
The rain area	is located	in front of me.
		to my left.
		on my left.

1:...

2:...

3:...

4:...

SCAFFSHEET 3: Rainbows

Scaffsheet 3: Rainbows

Formulating conditions

Conditions are expressed with if-then sentences (conditional sentences).

Example:

If the rain stops, I go to the playground.

Sometimes there are also two conditions for something to happen:

Example:

If you feed the dog and do your homework, you can go to the tennis court.

WORKSHEET 6.5.1 Rainbow Angles

Worksheet 5a: Rainbow Angles

Assign a matching speech bubble to each of the seven pictures A to G.

There is no picture for four speech bubbles.

1 Attention: The rainbow angles are not angles between the horizontal and the light rays from the arc to the observer!

2 Accurate measurements show: In the secondary rainbow, the angle for violet is 52.7° and for red 49.7°.

3 Accurate measurements show: In the primary rainbow, the angle for red is 42.7° and for violet 41.1°.

4 Between the light beams is an angle of about 42°.

5 The angles 42° and 51° are characteristic for all rainbows. They are called 'rainbow angles'.

6 Between the light beams is an angle of about 51°.

7 Sunlight hits the primary rainbow. Coloured light reaches the observer from this point.

8 The centre C of the rainbow lies on the dashed line. The dashed line is the central perpendicular of the rainbow circle.

9 Sunlight hits the secondary rainbow. From there, coloured light reaches the observer.

10 An observer sees a primary rainbow P and a secondary rainbow S.

11 The image shows a beam of light from the sun to the observer. The beam is extended to the ground with a dashed line.

WORKSHEET 6.5.2 Rainbow Angles

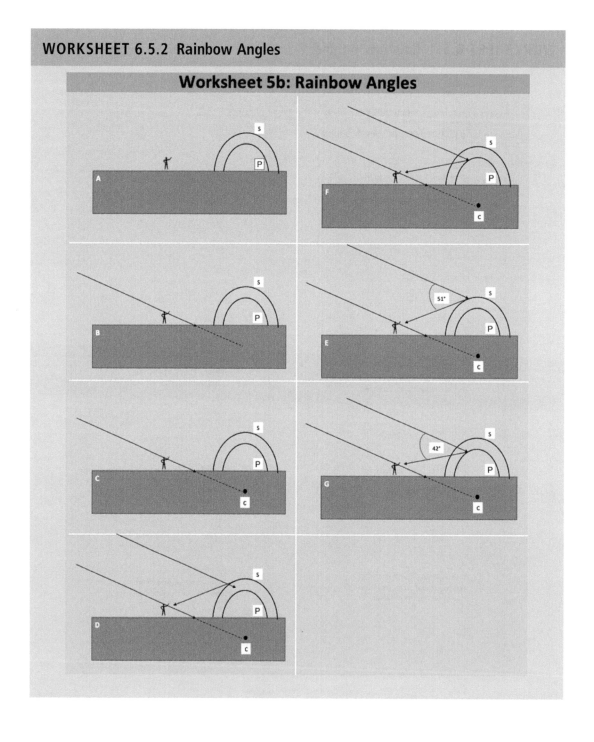

WORKSHEET 6.6 In the Rainbow Laboratory

Worksheet 6: In the Rainbow Laboratory

2nd Experiment: Investigations with a Waterdrop Model

Task 6.1

Write down our set of research questions.

....

....

....

Task 6.2

Describe the experiments we will use to answer our research questions.

....

....

....

....

....

....

....

....

....

....

....

....

Task 6.3

Conduct the experiment. Note your observations.

Colour sequence of the secondary rainbow observed?   YES / NO

Colour sequence of the primary rainbow observed?   YES / NO

	Rainbow Angles	Angles Measured in the Experiment
Secondary Rainbow		
Primary Rainbow		

Task 6.4

Make a reasoned judgement as to whether the round-bottom flask is a suitable model for a water droplet.

....

....

....

....

....

....

....

....

WORKSHEET 6.7 In the Rainbow Laboratory

Worksheet 7: In the Rainbow Laboratory

3rd Experiment: Waterdrop Model Rainbow

Task 7.1

Write down our research question.

....

....

So far we only have considered a flask (respectively a raindrop) in front of the observer, but we also have to take raindrops to the right and to the left into account. How do the raindrops create a curved arc?

Anyone from your group can try this outdoors! You can find out how in Task 7.1.

Task 7.2

Hold the water-filled flask in front of you, with the sun behind you.

Raise and lower the flask until you see the two lights again.

Now hold your position and turn the flask only by moving your arm to the right (about 40 cm). Raise and lower again ...

Repeat this once or twice more, each time further from the centre.

Do not look directly into the sun. If it is too bright for you, do not look into the water-filled flask.

Task 7.3

Describe your observations.

....

....

....

....

Task 7.4

Let us now focus on the lower luminous phenomenon, which belongs to the primary rainbow.

Examine where exactly the glow occurs in the round-bottom flask.

Enter the positions into the sketch.

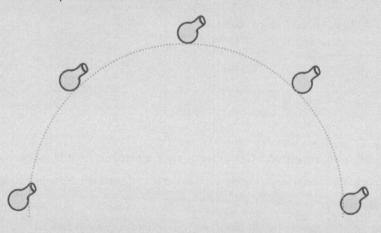

Task 7.5

How is it possible that the flask lights up from different positions in different directions?

One of you holds the flask in a fixed position in the sunlight and the others look at it from all sides

....

....

Task 7.6

Explain what this experiment tells you about the formation of the rainbow.

....

....

WORKSHEET 6.8.1 In the Rainbow Laboratory

Worksheet 8a: In the Rainbow Laboratory

Learning task 1: What Happens in a Raindrop?

Task 8.1

Write down the questions we now want to clarify.

....

....

Task 8.2

We first look at the sunlight moving towards the centre of a drop.

a) Make a guess as to what happens to this light. Draw the course of the light that you

suspect. (The grey arrow represents the sunlight).

....

....

....

....

b) Evaluate whether this light can contribute to the formation of the rainbow.

....

....

....

....

Task 8.3

We now look at sunlight entering a droplet in the upper half.

a) Make a guess as to what happens to this light. Draw the course of the light that you have guessed.

....

....

....

....

b) Evaluate whether this light can contribute to the formation of the rainbow.

....

....

....

....

WORKSHEET 6.8.2 In the Rainbow Laboratory

Worksheet 8b: In the Rainbow Laboratory

Task 8.4 Construction Task

Now we have a guess what happens to the light in the drop.
In optics, we can even predict by construction!

1. Take a sheet of graph paper and draw a circle with a radius of 5 cm in the right half. Mark

    the centre and draw a straight line (called an axis) across the centre.

Your drawing should look like this:

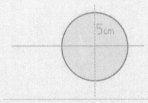

2. Draw a horizontal beam of light 4 cm above the axis and coming from the
    left onto the drop.

3. Now construct the path of the light beam into the drop and how it leaves it.

    Use this law of refraction to calculate the angles of refraction:

    $$\frac{\sin \alpha}{\sin \beta} = \frac{n_\beta}{n_\alpha}$$

    a: angle of incidence n_a: Refractive index for the medium in which the light is incident
    b: angle of refraction n_b: Refractive index for the medium into which the light is refracted

    $n_{Air} = 1.00$
    $n_{Water} = 1.33$

4. Describe also what happens with the light.

    Check your results, comparing them with the proposed solution on Scaffsheet 4.

    Scaffsheet 4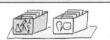

SCAFFSHEET 4: Proposed Solution for the Optical Construction

Scaffsheet 4: Proposed Solution for the Optical Construction

Angle of incidence into the drop: 53°
Total deflection angle: 42°

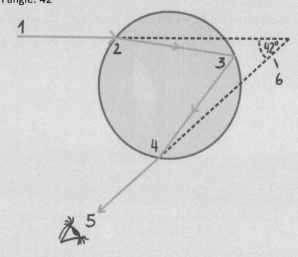

Description:

1. Sunlight enters in the raindrop.
2. This light is refracted for the first time.
3. The light is reflected (angle of incidence equals angle of refraction).
4. The light is refracted for the second time.
5. The light moves towards the earth at an angle of 42° to the direction of incidence (eventually towards an observer).

WORKSHEET 6.9 In the Rainbow Laboratory

Worksheet 9: In the Rainbow Laboratory

4th Experiment: Experimental Test

So far, we have used theoretical considerations to investigate what might happen to the light in a raindrop. You have applied your knowledge of refraction and reflection.

In physics, however, you are only convinced when your theoretical considerations pass an experimental test.

A suitable experiment will now be demonstrated to you: It shows a beam of light entering a circular bowl filled with water. This water bowl represents a raindrop.

Task 9.1: Experimental Demonstration
Write down our expectations.

....

....

....

....

....

....

Task 9.2: Conclusions
Evaluate whether our theoretical considerations (see Worksheet 8) pass the experimental test!

....

....

....

....

....

....

WORKSHEET 6.10: In the Rainbow Laboratory

Worksheet 10: In the Rainbow Laboratory

Task 10.1: Close to an Explanation ...

Think back to Task 2.1: You have coloured a raindrop in the order in which it shines in the primary rainbow. With our results from Experiment 2, we are close to an explanation!

The following picture should help you explain. Here you see the same drop three times as it falls. You also see the eye of the observer. Of course, it is much farther away from the drop than it is shown in the picture. This is illustrated by the dashed line.

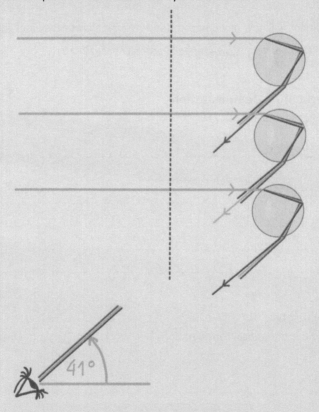

Write an explanation of why the raindrop appears first red, later green, then blue to the observer.

Scaffsheet 5 supports you in formulating!

Scaffsheet 5

SCAFFSHEET 5: How to Write a Good Explanation

Scaffsheet 5: How to Write a Good Explanation

An explanation is an answer to a scientific question based on facts, concepts or rules. It explains why things happen, what they are made up of or how they work.

In general, a causal explanation has the following structure:

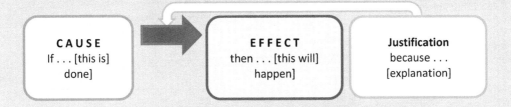

| **CAUSE** | **EFFECT** | **Justification** |
| If . . . [this is] done] | then . . . [this will] happen] | because . . . [explanation] |

Example: **If** I eat too much chocolate, **then** I will get fat **because** chocolate contains lots of unhealthy ingredients responsible for weight gain.

Now it´s your turn:
1. Select which box contains cause, effect and justification.
2. Then arrange them accordingly.
3. Add If, then and because. Write down the complete sentence.

... the raindrop is in it´s highest position ...

... it appears to be a red colour ...

... red light reaches the eye of the observer ...

4. You have formed the first sentence of your explanation. Continue your explanation!

A GOOD CAUSAL EXPLANATION HAS:

A GOOD CAUSAL EXPLANATION HAS:

❶ ideas connected with causal links

Incorrect	Correct
If I get in the pool, <u>then</u> I will get wet and <u>then</u> I will get cold. ☹ This is just a chronological order of steps.	If I get in the pool, I will get cold **because** water has a higher thermal conductivity than air. **As a result,** I lose heat much quicker and **consequently** feel cold.

❷ ideas ordered chronologically and linked by sequential connectives

Incorrect	Correct
<u>At the end,</u> I got in the pool <u>before</u> I got cold.	**First,** I got in the pool, **then** I got wet, **after that** I got cooler, **in the end** I was freezing.

❸ reasons based on relevant rules, concepts and definitions

Incorrect	Correct
If water is heated up to 100°C, it boils <u>because I say so.</u>	If water is heated up to 100°C, it boils **because** it has reached its boiling point.

❹ experimental data like observations and measurements as back up

Incorrect	Correct
… because <u>my father once told me so</u>	**The experiment showed that** water boils at exactly 100°C.

❺ present tense

Incorrect	Correct
Heat <u>caused</u> the water to boil.	Heat <u>causes</u> water to boil.

❻ scientific terms

Incorrect	Correct
bubbling point, burning, glass mug	boiling point, combustion, beaker

WORKSHEET 6.11.1 Your Wikipedia Article about the Primary Rainbow

Worksheet 11: Your Wikipedia Article about the Primary Rainbow

11.1 Create a draft for a Wikipedia article about the primary rainbow.

The article should be addressed to people of the same age as you, understandable for them and with everything you have learned about the rainbow so far.

Follow the usual Wikipedia structure!

As you can see below, a Wikipedia article usually consists of the following four parts, which are always arranged in the same way:

Abstract
In a few sentences you give an overview of what follows.

Table of Contents
Shows the headings of the main section.

Hard Facts
Key facts at a glance, mostly numbers.

Main Section
Contains all information you want to provide. Should be divided into sections, and these should have headings.

Use the following blank Wikipedia page

Print it in a large format and complete your article on it.

Blank Wikipedia page

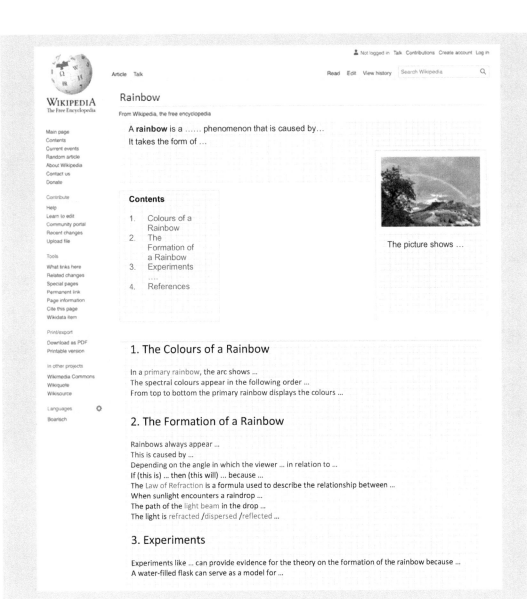

Article Talk

Read Edit View history Search Wikipedia

WIKIPEDIA
The Free Encyclopedia

Main page
Contents
Current events
Random article
About Wikipedia
Contact us
Donate

Contribute

Help
Learn to edit
Community portal
Recent changes
Upload file

Tools

What links here
Related changes
Special pages
Permanent link
Page information
Cite this page
Wikidata item

Print/export

Download as PDF
Printable version

In other projects

Wikimedia Commons
Wikiquote
Wikisource

Languages

Boarisch

Rainbow

From Wikipedia, the free encyclopedia

A **rainbow** is a …… phenomenon that is caused by…
It takes the form of …

The picture shows …

Contents

1. Colours of a Rainbow
2. The Formation of a Rainbow
3. Experiments ….
4. References

1. The Colours of a Rainbow

In a primary rainbow, the arc shows …
The spectral colours appear in the following order …
From top to bottom the primary rainbow displays the colours …

2. The Formation of a Rainbow

Rainbows always appear …
This is caused by …
Depending on the angle in which the viewer … in relation to …
If (this is) … then (this will) … because …
The Law of Refraction is a formula used to describe the relationship between …
When sunlight encounters a raindrop …
The path of the light beam in the drop …
The light is refracted /dispersed /reflected …

3. Experiments

Experiments like … can provide evidence for the theory on the formation of the rainbow because …
A water-filled flask can serve as a model for …

Your text should also contain blue links!

A useful feature of Wikipedia is the so-called 'hyperlink structure': terms that may be unfamiliar to readers are shown with a blue link. Below you can see an example of the term 'physics'. If a reader clicks on this link, they will get an explanation of this term.

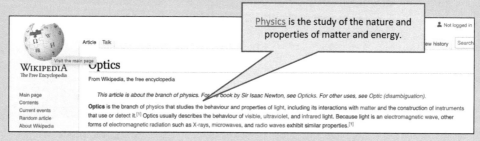

Create a table of links and drawings and add them to your Wikipedia article.

Hyper links
ScaffSheet 6

You're unsure about the claims that your explanations in the article should meet? **Scaffsheet 5 gives you clues.**

Organisation:
Scaffsheet 5

SCAFFSHEET 6: Hyperlinks

Scaffsheet 6: Hyper links

Here are some terms that might appear in your text and are explained with blue links.

Look for more terms when your main section is ready and complete the table with it.

Formulate definitions of these terms last. List these definitions in your document in an appendix.

Link-Term	Explanation
reflection	...
dispersion	...
refraction	...

WORKSHEET 6.11.2 Drawings Say More Than a Thousand Words

Drawings say more than a thousand words!

A good main section consists of an understandable text und matching drawings. Select some of the following drawings or make your own drawing if you like.

WORKSHEET 6.12: Feedback for Your Classmates!

Worksheet 12: Feedback for Your Classmates!

  WANTED: Your feedback!

Wikipedia's strength is its users, who keep the articles up to date with illustrations and topics and continually improve them.

Therefore, correct the article of another group!

Pay attention to ...

completeness

correctness of content

suitable for the addressees

other factors

Give your feedback in a comprehensive way!

WORKSHEET 6.13: There is More about Rainbows!

You have now explored and explained the primary rainbow. But more phenomena are still missing, for example, the secondary rainbow and the dark band between the arcs. The following tasks will guide you to explain these phenomena as well.

Task 10.1: The Secondary Bow

The following drawing shows you the path of light that enters a drop of water below the centre of the drop.

a) Describe the course of the light.

b) Explain the secondary rainbow with the help of this course.

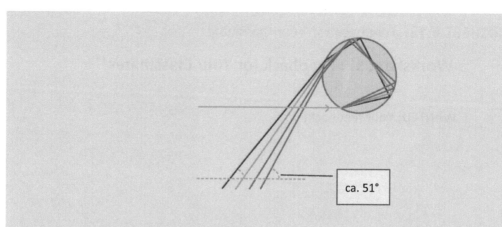

Task 10.2: Alexander's Dark Zone

Between the main and the secondary rainbow is a zone darker than the arcs and the rest of the sky. This is Alexander's Dark Zone, named after Alexander of Aphrodisias, a Greek philosopher.

Make a guess as to why this zone between the arches is so dark.

(Hint: Think beyond the visible spectrum!)

Task 10.3: Add to Your Wikipedia Article!

The extra content must <u>cover the secondary rainbow</u> and, if you like, something additional.

APPENDIX

Information on the Influence of the Glass Envelope on the Exit Angle

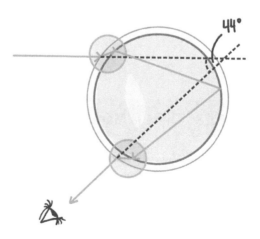

Table 6.5 Assessment grid: 'Wikipedia article on rainbows'

Assessment Grid 'Wikipedia Article on Rainbows'

	Wonderful!	Well done :)	OK, but …	Not quite OK …
Introduction	The rainbow is precisely introduced as a physical phenomenon using appropriate language and/or content.	The rainbow is introduced as a physical phenomenon using appropriate language and/or content.	The rainbow is introduced as a physical phenomenon, but not appropriately in terms of language and/or content.	The rainbow is not or not comprehensibly introduced as a physical phenomenon.
Description of the Colours of a Rainbow	The description of rainbow colours precisely presents the visible spectrum of the main arc in the correct order.	The description of rainbow colours presents the visible spectrum of the main arc.	The description of rainbow colours presents part of the visible spectrum of the main arc.	The description of rainbow colours does not present the visible spectrum of the main arc.
Explanation of the Formation of a Rainbow	The explanation of the formation of a rainbow includes accurate and comprehensive reasoning about the relation between the viewer, the light beam and the raindrop. Precise subject-specific language, including mathematical formula, is used, and technical terms are provided with well-defined hyperlinks.	The explanation of the formation of a rainbow includes correct reasoning about the relation between the viewer, the light beam and the raindrop. Subject-specific language, including mathematical formula, is used, and technical terms are provided with hyperlinks.	The explanation of the formation of a rainbow includes some or only partly correct reasoning about the relation between the viewer, the light beam and the raindrop. Some subject-specific language is used, and some technical terms are provided with hyperlinks.	The explanation of the formation of a rainbow includes some or only partly correct reasoning about the relation between the viewer, the light beam and the raindrop. Hardly any or no subject-specific language is used, and few or none of the technical terms are provided with hyperlinks.
Using Experiments to Provide Evidence	Experiments are stringently used to give evidence for the described physical phenomena and the theory explaining them.	Experiments are used to give evidence for the described physical phenomena and/ or the theory explaining them.	Experiments are mentioned but not related to the described physical phenomena or the theory explaining them.	Experiments are not mentioned.

REFERENCES

Fischer, H. E. (1998). Scientific Literacy und Physiklernen. *Zeitschrift für Didaktik der Naturwissenschaften*, *4*(2), 41–52.

Gebhard, U., Höttecke, D., & Rehm, M. (2017). *Pädagogik der Naturwissenschaften*, Springer.

Hattie, J. (2012). *Visible Learning for Teachers*. Routledge. https://doi.org/10.4324/9780203181522

Helmke, A., Helmke, T., Lenske, G., Pham, G. Praetorius, A.-K., Schrader, F.-W., & Ade-Thurow, M. (2011). Unterrichtsdiagnostik – Voraussetzung für die Verbesserung der Unterrichtsqualität. In S. G. Huber (Ed.), *Jahrbuch Schulleitung 2012: Befunde und Impulse zu den Handlungsfeldern des Schulmanagements*. Carl Link Verlag, pp. 133–144.

Leisen, J. (2014). Wie soll ich meinen Unterricht planen? – Lehr-Lern-Prozesse planen am Beispiel Elektrizitätslehre in Physik. In U. Maier (Ed.), *Lehr-Lernprozesse in der Schule: Referendariat: Praxiswissen für den Vorbereitungsdienst*. Klinkhardt, pp. 102–117.

Merzyn, G. (1998). Fachbestimmte Lernwege zur Förderung der Sprachkompetenz. *Praxis der Naturwissenschaften – Physik in der Schule*, *36*, 284–287.

Meyer, O., & Imhof, M. (2017). Pluriliterales Lernen. Vertiefte Lernprozesse anbahnen und gestalten. *Lernende Schule*, *20*(80), 20–24.

Prenzel, M., Sälzer, C., Klieme, E., & Köller, O. (2013). *PISA 2012. Fortschritte und Herausforderungen in Deutschland*. Waxmann. https://nbn-resolving.org/urn:nbn:de:0111-pedocs-188384

Taçon, P. S. C., Wilson, M., & Chippindale, C. (1996). Birth of the Rainbow Serpent in Arnhem Land Rock Art and Oral History. *Archaeology in Oceania*, *31*(3), 103–124. https://doi.org/10.1002/j.1834-4453.1996.tb00355.x

Vollmer, H. J. (2011). *Schulsprachliche Kompetenzen: Zentrale Diskursfunktionen*. https://www.home.uni-osnabrueck.de/hvollmer/VollmerDF-Kurzdefinitionen.pdf

Vollmer, H. J., & Thürmann, E. (2010). Zur Sprachlichkeit des Fachlernens: Modellierung eines Referenzrahmens für deutsch als Zweitsprache. In B. Ahrenholz (Ed.), *Fachunterricht und Deutsch als Zweitsprache*, 2nd ed. Narr, pp. 107–132.

Wilhelm, T., Horz, M., & Schlichting, H. J. (2014). Ein Regenbogen mit Glaskügelchen. *Praxis der Naturwissenschaften – Physik in der Schule*, *63*(6), 5–10.

7 Geography: Exploring Pluriliteracies through a Deeper Learning Episode on Global Warming

NICOLE BERG

7.1 Subject-Specific Literacy in Geography

Geography looks at Earth in a holistic way. The International Charter on Geographical Education defines geography as 'the study of Earth and its natural, physical, and human environment' (2016). Geographical knowledge is based on evidence-based investigations as well as theoretical, yet real-world-oriented, frameworks and concepts, and it is guided by a multitude of inquiry approaches. At the centre of geographical inquiry is always the following sequence of questions: *What is where? And how, when and why did it come to be there?* (Egli, Hasler, & Probst, 2016). However, these geographical inquiry practices require more than isolated competences related to discipline-relevant expertise and methodological skills. In geography, models and concepts are used to describe the causality and multi-dimensionality of specific local, regional or global phenomena and their corresponding problems, and students must be able to make meaning when confronted with or asked to produce such texts. So, what exactly are the competences needed to be literate in geography and deal with this interdependent study of Earth?

Geographic literacy (geo-literacy) is a concept combining different subject-specific skills and practices resulting in the mastery of a broad variety of media, databases, forms of representation and instruments relevant to geography. National Geographic (2012) defines geographic literacy as 'the ability to reason about Earth systems and interconnections to make far-reaching decisions' since humans are members of a global society and 'face decisions on where to live, what to build, where to travel, how to conserve energy, how to wisely manage scarce resources, and how to cooperate or compete with others' (Utami, Zain, & Sumarmi, 2018, p. 1). Thus, geographic literacy includes problem-solving skills, critical and creative thinking skills and the multi-causal reasoning skills needed to make those far-reaching decisions.

According to Edelson (2011b), learners are prepared to make far-reaching decisions when teachers take three crucial components of geographical literacy into account: how our world works (interactions), how our world is connected (interconnections) and how to make well-reasoned decisions (implications). This means that the geographically literate are able to consider the complex nature of both human and environmental factors and use those considerations to make decisions in the field (Edelson, 2011a). To achieve this, students need to acquire visual, spatial and linguistic literacy skills in the field. First, visual literacy skills are of the utmost importance to geography since the foundation of geographical knowledge is based on the analysis of data in maps, podcasts, pictures, videos and statistics. Students need to be able to make meaning out of the data communicated through these different (visual) modes.

Second, geographers analyse and observe spatial relationships between local, regional and global geographical areas to answer questions and solve problems (e.g. *Is fracking in the North Sea environmentally reasonable? How should we prepare for natural disasters in endangered areas?*). For decision-making like this in the real world, individuals need to think and act geographically to trace causes and effects across space and time (Edelson, 2009). However, students need to *do* geography – that is, do geographic inquiry, conduct fieldwork and communicate their results – in order to develop this form of geographic literacy, and this *doing* must be at the centre of deep learning (Harte & Reitano, 2016).

Specifically regarding communication in the field and its required linguistic skills, progress in geographic literacy entails an increase in the ability to make meaning across the four activity domains of deeper learning: *doing, organising, explaining* and *arguing* geography. To master meaning-making across activity domains, teachers need to include both general academic language structures as well as subject-specific geographical language functions, genre conventions and text types in their classroom. A repertoire of geography-specific cognitive discourse functions (CDFs) is essential because it not only guides learners in their geographical thinking but also leads them to precise meaning-making. For example, if students are to work with discourse functions displaying cause and effect, conjunctions in the form of linking words and causal connectors are of the utmost importance since these seemingly small bits and pieces contribute to a successful and targeted task fulfilment (Berg, 2020). Thus, learners need to use and understand not only a rich vocabulary with various technical terms but also sophisticated grammatical forms and patterns expressing a factual or neutral recollection of information to demonstrate an understanding of the multi-causal relationships of geographical issues.

Table 7.1 exemplifies the way in which activity domains and activities in geography can be related to CDFs and student output typical in geography.

7.2   Deeper Learning in Geography

As previously explained, at the centre of deeper understanding in geography are the abilities to successfully confront and understand its facts, concepts, inquiry methods and media (i.e. texts) and to effectively operate within the activity domains through the mastery of geographical output or text productions.

Table 7.1 Activity domains, language functions and student products in geography

Activity Domain in Geography	Sample Activities in Geography	Possible Learner Progression within These CDFs	Complex Student Products in Geography
Doing Geography CDFs • Report	Hypothesising and experimenting to study patterns/processes of the natural environment	Novice: 'I think that eating bread is not good for our environment.' Expert: 'Human diet has a **negative impact on our** climate.'	• Experiment and lab reports • (Mental) Maps • Maps • Concept maps/mind maps • Field trip protocols • Videos, podcasts • Portfolios • Spatial analysis of a (specific) geographical area • Analysis of climate graphs/climate maps, population charts, aerial views, satellite pictures, etc. • Flowcharts, cause–effect schemes • SWOT analysis • Role plays, podium discussions, debates • Cartoon analysis • Written comment • Geographical argumentation and discussion • •
	Collecting and examining real-world data to understand principles, compositions and different modes of action in geo-ecosystems		
	Drafting, creating and producing varieties of maps/cartographies or other discontinuous texts, such as video/audio		
Organising Geography CDFs • Describe • Classify	Describing geographical data orally or in written form	Novice: 'The speaker talks about our diet, what we eat and our climate.' Expert: 'In his radio interview, a local farmer speaks about the impact climate change has on his production of fruit and vegetables and relates that to our eating habits.'	
	Structuring or categorising geographical information systematically or thematically		
	Deciding upon the relevance of a variety of geographical materials at hand		
Explaining Geography CDFs	Explaining causes and effects of geographical processes to shed light on interdependencies	Novice: 'Meat production creates greenhouse gases which cause climate change. The cows produce methane, and that is not good for the environment.'	

Table 7.1 (*cont.*)

Activity Domain in Geography	Sample Activities in Geography	Possible Learner Progression within These CDFs	Complex Student Products in Geography
• Explain • Define	Explaining solution strategies, horizons or alternative actions to geographical problems and questions Explaining value, significance, perspectives, roles, etc. regarding geographical matters, problems, situations and facts Characterising the natural geographic conditions of a certain geographic area	Expert: 'There are **different causes** for global climate change. For example, with the rising population, **more food** is needed, so industry and agriculture expand, which leads to higher production. Production results in greenhouse gas emissions because there is a need for land, for example for cattle farming. The feed for cattle, like wheat, **must be grown. For this, space is needed, which leads to deforestation** (. . .).'	• • • • • • • • • •
Arguing Geography CDFs • Explore • Evaluate	Evaluating geographical problems, positions or roles critically while referring back to overarching concepts or principles Predicting possible outcomes by interpreting materials concerning geographical issues, e.g. caricatures or maps Discussing/arguing different perspectives on geographical issues in hindsight to overarching concepts or principles	Novice: 'I think our diet is not good for the environment because of the many greenhouse gases that are produced.' Expert: 'Human diet and nutrition can be highly problematic concerning climate change and sustainability. The main problem lies in our meat consumption because its production needs a lot of space, so rainforests are deforested. However, if we stick to a plant-based diet, less space is needed and less greenhouse gas emissions are produced.'	

To expand **textual understanding**, students need to be able to decode geographical genre conventions, which mainly build on disciplinary terminology as well as different media and forms of presentation (e.g. maps, tables and charts). Teachers need to provide task- and text-specific forms of scaffolding to help learners decipher academic and disciplinary lexis, linguistic elements and text structures. When teaching text production and genre conventions across the activity domains, **deep practice** should be a guiding principle. This includes teaching common features and structures found in geographical genres, such as map interpretations, map analyses and oral and written problem explanations. For instance, when producing an oral explanation, students need to practise sentence frames and conjunctions of cause and effect to successfully make meaning.

Content relevance is the foundation of student involvement and learner autonomy and applies particularly to geography: Most thematic fields dealt with in the geography classroom, such as global warming and climate change, the COVID-19 pandemic and its socio-economic impact or global deforestation, are of current relevance to society and science as they are twenty-first-century challenges. This relevance needs to be made transparent to learners to spur their motivation and interest. **Agency and accountability** can be increased by focusing on content relevance. Learners feel more obliged and responsible for their own learning pathway if they confront problems that are relevant to them.

Furthermore, **learning pathways** also need to be differentiated with joint **scaffolding development**. In our heterogeneous classrooms, different students need to be offered different input and output scaffolding, as well as different ways of reaching a common goal in a shared overall learning task. To achieve this, it is necessary to provide scaffolding mechanisms, such as structural and language/ phrase frames for output production on different levels. We can further enable personalised learning by using a variety of real-world forms of representation. By truly **differentiating and individualising learning pathways** in geography (e.g. through offering a choice of materials for a specific learning task or a variety of different assignments within an overall learning task), students are held accountable for their own learning process again.

Additionally, the understanding of multi-perspectivity in all sorts of texts also needs to be considered at all levels. **Critical cultural awareness** is developed in geography by considering the multi-perspectivity and interconnectedness of geographical problems. As students engage in a specific geographic subject area focusing on a precise and authentic problem, teachers need to lead them through a process of critically questioning and arguing different perspectives. This, in turn, is what **increases content relevance** for students again and **fosters agency and accountability**.

7.3   A Model Deeper Learning Episode in Geography: 'Human Diet, Food Consumption and the Environment – Are We Eating Up Our Planet?'

The main objective of this deeper learning episode (DLE) is to foster oral explanations by listening to authentic radio interviews with subject experts. It is designed for eighth-grade (lower secondary) students in geography, focusing on the thematic area of global climate change and its correlation with human diet and nutrition. The CDF *explaining* is at the centre of this geographical investigation since the students are asked to produce their own oral explanations on the aforementioned topic. Explanations are an essential feature of science as well as a 'fundamental classroom activity that engages students in epistemic practices of the discipline' (Kang, Thompson, & Windschitl, 2014, p. 677).

As a key competence of critical thinking, explanations serve different functions from different perspectives. First, students build understanding and factual knowledge about a certain problem through explaining. Second, student explanations mirror understanding and therefore disclose thinking structures to the subject teacher. Furthermore, students need to act faster and more spontaneously in oral explanations when compared to text production in the written mode. This spontaneity allows teachers to detect deficiencies and learning obstacles effectively and target these problem areas through scaffolding and deep practice.

Many considerations must be taken into account when designing task sequences aimed at explanation production (see Table 7.2). One key element in increasing competence in explaining builds on the foundation of explanations itself: *What accounts for a good explanation in geography? What differentiates a sound explanation from a less profound one?* Learners need to be able to verbalise their thinking structures and their reasoning for a specific conclusion. Moreover, learners need patterns and structures to **imitate, follow and adapt** to successfully master and communicate the causality represented in geographical problems. Therefore, students need deep practice in monological speaking in different ways and settings and concerning different aspects of a topic in order to become confident in explaining and to establish a routine in oral communication situations.

7.4   Alignment of the Deeper Learning Episode

High task fidelity is ensured by combining scientific information with real-world knowledge and hands-on practical skill training in oral explanations based on decoding, adaptation and transfer of patterns found in the audio materials.

Table 7.2 Planning grid for a deeper learning episode in geography

Designing Deeper Learning Episodes

Planning Grid for a Deeper Learning Episode in Geography

What do I want my learners to know or be able to do?	How will my learners demonstrate increasingly deeper understanding at the surface, consolidation and transfer levels?	How can I support active knowledge co-construction for my learners?	How can I support my learners every step of the way?	How can I generate and sustain learner commitment and achievement?
Basic Understanding: • Causes of greenhouse gas emissions from food production and its effects **Foundational skills:** • Organising basic information for oral explanations with PREP-Sheet • Decoding information from podcasts through listening for prosody and listening for structure in the audios • Organising information from the audio materials in a visualisation • Practising monological speaking • Criteria-based evaluation of other explanations (i.e. content, structure and prosody)	**Preliminary Learning Products:** • Hypotheses about the connection between a loaf of bread and greenhouse gas emissions • Prosodic analysis of expert explanation • Calculation of greenhouse gas emissions for an exemplary consumer good • Flowchart of gas emissions in grain production • Flowchart about the causes and effects of meat production in the Amazon • Oral explanation about meat production **Main Learning Product:** Podcast containing an oral explanation about the guiding question Purpose: educating the broad public	**Construction of Knowledge:** (X) Inquiry-based learning (X) Problem-based learning () Experimenting () Project-based learning **Social Interaction:** • Thorough comparison of preliminary results in groups • Group work practising and evaluating oral explanations **Use of (Digital) Media:** • NPR podcasts with written transcripts • Flowcharts/cause–effect schemes • Main learning product is recorded with smartphones	**Scaffolding:** • Organisation of explanation with key elements (introductory sentence, terminology, adjectives, cause and effect, linking words, specifying verbs) is scaffolded by providing PREP-Sheet • Verbalisation of oral explanations is scaffolded by language frames • Causality of explanation is scaffolded by cause–effect schemes (structural scaffolding) • Understanding of podcast is scaffolded by tasks focusing on speech prosody and vocabulary help **Feedback:** • Individual teacher feedback on task completion • Peer feedback with evaluation grid for improvement	**Engagement:** Personal meaningfulness/ relevance: • Personal dietary choices are the foundation for engagement with the topic and personal/ individual influence on the problem • Listening to podcast is a real-world experience for students • All learners enhance monological, subject-specific speaking ability Opportunities for autonomous learning: • Independent, (faster) work on worksheets and topics is possible • Production of own cause–effect schemes (e.g. for classroom use) • Research for further

Table 7.2 (cont.)

Designing Deeper Learning Episodes

Planning Grid for a Deeper Learning Episode in Geography

Deeper Understanding:
- Awareness of prosodic strategies and their use to detect meaning
- Applying prosodic strategies in oral explanations to support presentation of information
- Using linguistically versatile structures for expressing cause and effect

Deep Practice:
- Recurring tasks on prosody in other material
- Organising information in more complex cause–effect schemes
- Verbalising causality orally

Transfer:
- Complete, criteria-based oral explanation

Genre: podcast
Mode: oral explanation
Style: academic style with subject-specific terminology and aspects of colloquial spoken language

Transfer Task:
- Evaluating the effects of greenhouse gas emissions on specific areas/countries
- Evaluating strategies to reduce greenhouse gas emissions by changing dietary habits

possible podcasts about (sub)topic
- Creation of a podcast

Reflection and Revision:
- Reflection on oral explanations with assessment grid
- Discussion on the value of the DLE (metacognition)

Feed-Up:
- PREP-Sheet as model for oral explanations
- Language frames for verbalisation
- Vocabulary help for listening comprehension
- Written transcripts
- Assessment grid for oral explanations as improvement strategy

Feed-Forward:
- teacher feedback on cause–effect schemes for verbalisation of explanation
- Peer feedback with evaluation grid for improvement

Assessment:
- Assessment grid for oral explanations in geography

Learner Strengths, Needs and Interests

Learners are generally interested in digital modes of representation, such as radio shows, podcasts and listening materials. Moreover, speaking and communicating in a foreign language motivates and interests them (Vandergrift, 2003). For students who are afraid of orally explaining in a foreign language, specific skill training with step-by-step increases in complexity and scaffolding on different levels caters to their needs through deep practice. To decode authentic scientific discourse as well as encode it through their own oral explanations, students need not only explicit structural scaffolding and subject-specific language structures but also knowledge about prosodic features or patterns in spoken discourse (Berg, 2020). Examples of prosodic features are the use of breaks, tempo, intonation or time-management strategies. Knowledge of these enables learners to decode information in spoken discourse more effortlessly, as well as to encode it in their own communication.

Geographic Literacy

The interdependence between the human diet and global warming can only be articulated if students work with the given materials, which require them to be geographically literate. To decode the audio materials, students need instruments and skills to gain understanding and verbalise the connection themselves in the form of oral explanations. Therefore, students acquire their understanding gradually by focusing on the different structural and content aspects given in the audio materials, with the help of prosodic scaffolding, and finally apply this understanding by producing their own oral explanations to answer the guiding question about the relationship between human diet and global warming.

As stated before, geographically literate students must be familiar with the overarching principles in in the field. One of these principles is sustainability. Specifically, '[g]eography helps people to think critically about sustainable living locally and globally and how to act accordingly' (International Charter on Geographical Education, 2016, p. 6). Since the anthropogenic influence on the environment is the main focus of this DLE, sustainability serves as its guiding principle. The objective of this learning episode is for students to reflect on the foods they buy and consume and how these habits relate to the bigger issue of greenhouse gas emissions. Developing in students the ability to critically think about and reflect on such an essential and decisive lifestyle choice and its effect on the global environment lies at the heart of (school) geography.

To produce profound oral explanations about this relationship, students need to be directly exposed to example explanations. However, the simple reception of oral discourse will not lead to successful engagement and deep understanding. Therefore, students work with transcripts and structural scaffolding (e.g. in the form of structured visualisations) that will, in turn, guide them to producing their own oral explanations. This way, students attain the necessary skills and instruments to both decode as well as encode meaning in a subject-specific form of representation (i.e. an oral explanation). Within the DLE, students engage with both the formal academic and subject-specific discourse patterns and the instances of less academic and rather informal language patterns presented in the audio materials. Students observe key elements of explanations within the audio materials and transfer them to their own explanations.

Activity Domains

Learners are *doing* geography at various points within the learning episode, specifically when they hypothesise about the questions and/or the connection between human diet and the environment. Another instance of *doing* geography occurs when students read, analyse and produce flowcharts and cause–effect schemes, since the ability to create these forms of discontinuous texts is considered a methodological key competence in geography. Along with that goes the conversion of numerical data about consumerism-related greenhouse gas emissions into another form of representation, which requires students to *organise* the given information into a structured format. Through a concluding oral explanation of these more abstract and condensed representations of information, students verbalise cause-and-effect relations, which, as is implied, refers to *explaining* geography.

Growth Mindset, Deep Practice and Deep Understanding

Using authentic subject-specific spoken discourse in a classroom is a challenging task for learners of a foreign language because they can only attain full understanding of spoken subject-specific discourse when given a range of instruments, tasks and skills to scaffold their understanding. In this learning episode, successful listening comprehension is accomplished through a specific listening comprehension approach called 'Listening for Literacies' (Berg, 2020). This newly developed listening approach focuses on the decoding of different aspects of the audio material. Students need to decode structural aspects of a text in order to understand cause-and-effect structures and to deduce understanding and knowledge. Prosodic patterns (see Worksheet A1), especially, help to decode meaning in spoken discourse as there are many specificities in spoken language that make up meaning. Prosody-related activities support the learning of subject-specific discourse (functions) via a process called 'phonological chunking' (Lewis, 2012). Analysing prosodic features of subject-specific discourse raises learner awareness of both the prosodic and lexical/semantic features of chunks. Asking learners to emulate subject-specific discourse by role-playing, recording, providing feedback and re-recording their utterances will support the acquisition of chunks and their accompanying prosodic features while also facilitating memorisation and retention of subject-specific discourse functions as applied in real-world contexts. Transfer in the learning process is facilitated through the students' analysis of prosodic features (both in the given audio materials and their own explanations), the recording of their own explanations, the subsequent feedback of said recordings and the re-recordings of their explanations post feedback. Taken together, this constitutes deep practice. With the help of this prosodic knowledge, students can decode subject-specific meaning more easily and effectively. Deep practice in the form of repetition and increasing complexity in the audio materials is needed to not only raise awareness about discourse strategies but also to actively engage students in meaning-making. Through this deep practice, learners will master both decoding and encoding subject-specific discourse in the form of oral explanations over time.

7.5 How Do Learners Move from Surface Learning to Consolidation to the Transfer Stage?

The implementation of listening material according to the Listening for Literacies model serves as the vehicle to move students from surface learning to deeper learning. Specifically, it is the combination of focusing on subject-specific aspects as well as general structural aspects in oral explanations that helps learners to move along the learning pathway.

Engage the Learner

At the beginning of this DLE, the teacher presents two photos: one of a loaf of bread and another one displaying exhaust fumes or a deforested area. Looking at a typical food item, such as a loaf of bread, and a photo of a deforested area or an example of exhaust gases, students are asked to comment on the possible correlation between the photos. This activates the learners since they are presented photos that appear to have no connection to each other and asked to find one. Learners are likely to engage in the opening discussion by posing hypotheses. Prior knowledge they might have is activated, and they are prompted to participate by the cognitive dissonance that occurs. Moreover, using tangible consumer goods often consumed by the students in order to teach about a global geographical problem has a special relevance to them (content relevance, agency and accountability).

Promote/Acquire Basic Understanding and Acquisition of Foundational Skills

To create high transparency for learners and lead them towards the desired learning output, they are provided with a lesson plan giving an overview of the worksheets and materials with which they will work. The worksheets have been designed in such a way that scaffolding in different forms is already available in order to facilitate learning. Especially in phases where students need to organise given information into flowcharts or cause–effect schemes, they are free to choose from given visualisations or develop their own. However, it is advisable that rather inexperienced students, in particular, stick to the given templates, leaving the option to develop their own design for later when they have more experience.

In terms of foundational skills, students first organise basic information on how to give an oral explanation in the form of a PREP-Sheet. This is a crucial step in the learning pathway since students actively and consciously deal with the question of how an oral explanation is accomplished in terms of structure, language and subject-specific conventions. It is of the utmost importance that students are confronted with high-quality explanations that can serve as a model for their subsequent text production. However, students must also be given unfounded and poorly developed examples so that they can discover keys and characteristics of sound versus unsound explanations. The PREP-Sheet serves as scaffolding throughout the DLE in the form of a checklist for the production of oral explanations.

Regarding the promotion of understanding when dealing with the audio materials, the concept of Listening for Literacies prescribes that students listen to the audios on MP3 players/mobile phones individually. This will allow learners to slow down the audio material and to stop and replay difficult passages. This is particularly important for the first listening phase (listening for content) as this is where the course is set for the rest of the learning task. The transcript can be used by the teachers at any time as a support measure or scaffolding. The learners will always find the most important vocabulary of the audio text on the first worksheet.

Provide Feedback, Feed-Up and Feed-Forward/Demonstrate Basic Understanding and Reflect

There are different opportunities for feedback and reflection within this DLE. First and foremost, the teacher serves as a mentor and observer and gives individual feedback on the completion of the task sequence. Especially at the beginning, the teacher ensures that students have a clear understanding of the demands of an oral explanation (feed-up) with the help of the PREP-Sheet. Moreover, the teacher can give feedback on the cause-and-effect schemes since these are used as structural support for the verbalisation of the explanation (feedback and feed-forward), using the assessment grid in Table 7.3. Finally, students demonstrate their understanding about the content and their knowledge about prosody and structure in using the evaluation grid (Table 7.4) while listening to other explanations (feedback, feed-up, feed-forward). Particularly during the phases of repetition and practice, teachers are free to give feedback (e.g. with the assessment grid introduced later in this chapter).

Facilitate/Acquire Deeper Understanding and Deep Practice

With the materials of this DLE, deeper understanding of its topics is closely linked to raising awareness about the function of prosody in spoken communication. In Part A of the DLE, learners listen to a specified part of the audio, read the printed transcript excerpt and conjecture why the words are printed in different sizes. That way, they learn about content words (i.e. the words in an utterance that carry meaning), helping them to understand that knowledge about stress patterns can enable them to hear details of a given text better. Afterwards, information about the ecological footprint of consumer goods is further decoded by analysing the structural composition of the explanation(s) in the audio text. For this, students follow a sequence of tasks where they organise the causes of an ecological footprint as well as its effects in a graphic visualisation. This visualisation again scaffolds the oral explanation at the end of the task sequence. As deep understanding requires deep practice, students work on a task demonstrating strategies to gain time while speaking. This serves as further scaffolding for the final oral explanation concerning Part A because students are enabled to gain time while speaking. To support transfer into real-world situations, learners look for examples of these strategies in the listening text and eventually use these strategies playfully in the last task. This way, students transfer their newly acquired strategic knowledge and embed this independently in their knowledge construction.

In Part B of the DLE, students focus on the deforestation caused by meat production. They practise applying their knowledge about prosodic cues (here, content words) from Part A of the episode directly into Part B (deep practice). Here, they are to focus only on content words during the first hearing. This helps them both understand the text and realise their own potential to decode spoken discourse. In line with deep practice, students expand their prosodic knowledge with a focus on word stress by analysing speech pauses within the audio material. This knowledge can be applied while listening and, in turn, serves as a scaffold for the following task, where causes and effects for changes in the environment due to our diet are distinguished.

Facilitate Transfer/Transfer Knowledge

Following the task sequence, students acquire transferable knowledge through the process stated above. What is particularly striking about it is that with the help of the prosodic as well as the structural knowledge, they are enabled to transfer these skills to other geographical topics that they need to explain in future lessons. Helping students organise and explain the impact of our diet on the environment through visual and content input scaffolding (e.g. through cause–effect templates) as well as verbal output scaffolding (e.g. through phrase frames and sentence starters) ensures that the learner output can be individually optimised and transferred to other geographic topics.

Assessing Progress in Oral Explanations

In the context of this DLE, extensive formative assessment is paramount. It is through continuous feedback and ongoing formative assessment over an extensive period that learners will move from surface learning to transfer. The assessment grid (Table 7.3), adapted and revised from Berg (2020, pp. 83–84), shows how teachers can assess oral explanations recorded by students. It was developed alongside the aspects learners are dealing with in the DLE in the context of a good oral explanation (PREP-Sheet). With the assessment grid, teachers can detect and communicate possibilities for improvement with learners, freely deciding whether to focus on only one or several aspects of the assessment continuum. The nuances between the points are always in relation to text length. If teachers are transparent about the feedback they give and communicate with their students as mentors, the assessment grid can also be used as a summative assessment at the end of a DLE.

7.6   Conclusion and Outlook

Adapting the pluriliteracies teaching for deeper learning model to a geography context, teachers must rethink their way of lesson planning, their own understanding of subject-specific literacy and the implementation of methods that foster the development of such literacies. It demands great openness in terms of time structures as well as material development. By focusing on the language use in geography within different forms of representation, as shown here with audio materials, students can acquire a subject-specific literacy if they are exposed to a learning environment that puts emphasis on scaffolding the various obstacles to mastering subject-specific language. Knowledge about speech prosody is paramount for understanding spoken (academic) discourse, so the biggest challenge geography teachers face is to finally consider and apply this into their material design and lesson planning. Key to the acquisition of such linguistic knowledge are well-designed learning opportunities in which students detect, identify, practise, apply and transfer language structures in all modes, for all text types, and on all levels to different geographic topics.

7.7   Learning Materials

Geography for Everyone: Human diet, food consumption and the environment – are we eating up our planet?

Listening to the radio, checking social media, or watching TV, we notice something that is often discussed is the impact we as consumers have on the environment. But what exactly is that impact, and how can its causes and effects be explained? Are we

Table 7.3 Assessment grid for oral explanations in geography (adapted and revised from Berg [2020, pp. 83–84])

Score in Points

	3 Points: Excellent!	2 Points: Well done!	1 Point: Not there yet!	0 Points: Not OK.
Cause-and-Effect Relations	A clear framework of causes and effects is detectable in your explanation. There is a combination of multiple causes and effects that relate in different aspects to one another.	You used different causes and effects and related them to each other rather than just listing them. However, you did not put the causes and effects into a bigger topical framework.	You named different aspects in your explanation; however, you didn't distinguish clearly between causes and effects. At this point, your oral explanation sounds more like a description because there are no connections between your mentioned aspects.	Your explanation was rather incomplete or incorrect.
Linking	All your sentences are consistently linked with a broad variety of different linking words and phrases.	Most of your sentences are linked with different linking words and phrases. However, you used a few repetitions.	A few of your sentences are linked with one or two similar linking words or phrases, but most of your aspects are listed.	You forgot to use linking words or phrases.
Geographical Terminology	You used all necessary or even more subject-specific terms in your explanation. You used them thoroughly and correctly.	You used a lot of subject-specific terms; however, some were used incorrectly and/or some are missing in your explanation.	You used a few subject-specific terms. Some of them were used correctly. Some incorrectly. Some terminology was even missing.	You didn't use subject-specific terms correctly or didn't use any at all.
Specifying Verbs	Whenever possible, you used a specifying verb in the correct context.	You often used specifying verbs within the correct context.	In most sentences, you used general verbs; however, there were few instances of specifying verb use.	You did not use specifying verbs or used them inappropriately.

eating up our planet? Let's explore this question and record our own podcast, *Geography for Everyone*. Why? Because everyone needs to be able to answer this question, whether schoolteachers, students or parents – it's our planet. Sounds good? Let's start!

In the following, you will work with real podcasts that deal with the guiding question. With the help of these audio materials, you will be able to explain and answer this question to record a professional yet understandable answer for our *Geography for Everyone* podcast at our school. You will work with two different podcasts, A and B. Listen to the texts on your own and in your own tempo. Do not rush but take your time.

Follow the task sequence in the order of the worksheets. With each worksheet, you will have more information and knowledge. Also, you will feel well prepared for your podcast recording. For better orientation, see the lesson plan below.

Lesson plan		
Lesson	Associated Worksheets	Approximate Time Frame
1. Preparation	PREP-Sheet (obligatory)	45 minutes
Podcast A: *What's the environmental impact of a loaf of bread? Now we know. (Chatterjee, 2017)* 🎧 https://www.npr.org/sections/thesalt/2017/02/27/517531611/whats-the-environmental-footprint-of-a-loaf-of-bread-now-we-know?t=1614339378381		
2. Word stress (LfP[1])	Worksheet 1	140–180 minutes
3. The ecological footprint (LfS[2])	Worksheet 2	
4. Time to fill time (LfP)	Worksheet 3	
Podcast B: *Congress to Nutritionists: Don't talk about the environment. (Dan Charles, 2014)* 🎧 https://www.npr.org/sections/thesalt/2014/12/15/370427441/congress-to-nutritionists-dont-talk-about-the-environment		
5. Word stress (LfP)	Worksheet 1	180 minutes
6. Finding details in the podcast (LfC[3])	Worksheet 2	
7. Pausing and word stress (LfP)	Worksheet 3	
8. Human diet and the environment – causes and effects (LfS)	Worksheet 4 + Visualisation	
9. Finale – Recording of *Geography for Everyone*	Worksheet 5	60 minutes
10. Peer and teacher feedback on student podcasts	Evaluation Grid	90 minutes

---

[1] LfP: Listening for Prosody (Stage Two in *Listening for Literacies*)
[2] LfS: Listening for Structure (Stage Two in *Listening for Literacies*)
[3] LfC: Listening for Content (Stage One in *Listening for Literacies*)

WORKSHEET 7.1 PREP-Sheet: How Can I Give a Good Explanation?

PREP SHEET: How Can I give a Good Explanation?

WHAT?	HOW?	Bad example	Good Example	Own Example
Introduction	Introduce topic you're going to talk about in **one sentence**	In the water cycle, water evaporates and then condenses.	The water cycle is a climatological process that describes how water changes its aggregate shape over time.	
Terminology	Name **specific terms** and processes like an expert	rain	*precipitation*	
Adjectives	Use **adjectives** that **underline** and support your idea when talking about something extreme or very striking	precipitation	*extreme* precipitation	
Cause and Effect	Include **causes** (C) that **lead to one certain effect** (E) **or multiple effects** and say that reason A causes effect Y to happen	There was extreme precipitation, and the city was flooded.	Because of the extreme precipitation the city was flooded. The extreme precipitation led to the flooding and destruction of the city and left homeowners homeless.	
Linking Words	**Structure and connect** your ideas and **causes/ effects** like an expert without using only 'and .. and ... and'	The extreme precipitation led to the flooding of the city. And most of the houses were destroyed.	First of all, the extreme precipitation led to the flooding of the city. Moreover, most of the houses were destroyed because of that.	
Specify Verbs	Talk like an expert and use **specific verbs** rather than general verbs	The air gets warmer due to the sun.	The air heats up due to the sun.	

💬 Linking Words

In the ... there are several important steps.

Firstly/ First of all, ... , Secondly, ...

Next ...

Similarly, ...

The **most important effects**/aspects are ...

The ideas are related in the following way ...

This is related to ...

Moreover/Furthermore/Additionally ...

Another point is ...

Accordingly/Therefore/Because of that/Due to ...

In the end ...

Finally, ...

In fact, ...

🔊 Expressing Cause and Effect

The **reason** for this is ...

This **leads** to ...

There are **multiple causes for** ...

Several **causes lead** to ...

The **result** of X is ... . This, **in turn, causes** ... to ...

X **causes** Y to ...

The **effect is due** to ...

As a **result** ...

Therefore/Because of that/Due to ...

It **follows** that .../It **results** that ...

Consequently/As a consequence ...

The causes/effects are **related** because ...

WORKSHEET 7.2.1 Worksheet A I: The Carbon Footprint of a Loaf of Bread

Worksheet A I: The Carbon Footprint of a Loaf of Bread

1) While you **listen to** 1:06–1:46 (slow: 1:22–2:13) of the interview, **read** the short passage in the box below. **Concentrate on the stress and loudness of the speaker. Why** do you think the words are printed in different sizes? **Write down** your ideas and **compare** with a partner.

'So, they were looking at greenhouse gas emissions.

And what they found is if you look at a single loaf of bread,

they found the entire process that went into making it releases about 21 ounces of greenhouse gases into the atmosphere.

That's about the weight of this loaf of bread.

It doesn't seem much. But if you look at it at the country level,

the U.K., where the study was done, consumes over 4 billion loaves every year.

And using the researchers' calculations, that means about 2.6 million tons of greenhouse gases in the atmosphere

just from the bread consumed in the U.K. That's not insignificant.'

Source: Chatterjee, Rhitu (2017): What's the environmental footprint of a loaf of bread? Now we know from NPR, February 27, 2017,
https://www.npr.org/sections/thesalt/2017/02/27/517531611/whats-the-environmental-footprint-of-a-loaf-of-bread-now-we-know?t=1614339378381

The words are printed in different sizes because ...

_____

_____

_____

_____

_____

_____

VOC & PHRASE DOs:
greenhouse gas emissions – Treibhausgase
loaf of bread – Laib Brot
entire – gesamt(er)
(to) release – freisetzen
ounces – Unze (Masseinheit statt kg)
insignificant – unbedeutend

1) **Read the yellow info box about content words.**

2) **Listen to** the whole dialogue and **read** the transcript[5]. While listening, <u>**underline**</u> all content words you can hear in the text due to their pronunciation.

3) **Get together** with a partner and **practise** the dialogue aloud. Both of you should practise both roles, so **switch roles** after a while. With your annotated script and the underlined content words, **pay close attention to your pronunciation and** stress the content words when speaking.[6]

4) **Give feedback** to each other with the help of the sentence starters below the box.

Info box: Content Words in Speech

Most of the words that are printed in a bigger size are **content words**. Content words are the words in speech that have the *strongest stress*. This is the reason why the listener – in that case you– *understands these words best*. That means that they are pronounced **louder, clearer** and **often slower** than other words. This is because they carry the *highest meaning* and tell the listener what the sentence is about: they are the content of the message.

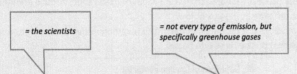

Example: So **they** were looking at **greenhouse** gas emissions.

Sentence starters for giving feedback about content words
You fully/partly concentrated on content words and paid special attention to word stress in both/only one of the roles.
You didn't pay any attention to your word stress.
Try varying with …
 … the loudness of your voice.
 … the tempo of your speech.

---

[4] Transcripts of the full podcast can be found online on NPR and are not published here due to copyright reasons.

[5] Here students can also record themselves, give feedback and re-record themselves again.

WORKSHEET 7.2.2 Worksheet A 2: The Carbon Footprint of a Loaf of Bread

Concentrate on the stress and loudness of the speaker

Worksheet A 2: Carbon Footprint of a Loaf of Bread

1) **Search** the passage in the transcript where the speaker explains the quantity of greenhouse gas emissions produced due to one loaf of bread. **Calculate** how many grams of greenhouse gases are produced per one loaf of bread. **Write** down your calculation below.

1 ounce = 28.34 g

2) **Read M1.**
3) **Listen** to the audio again. **While listening,**
   a) **list** all the steps of the process that lead to making a loaf of bread that produce greenhouse gas emissions on the left side in the box below
   b) **give** reasons **how** emissions are produced in each step (example: driving a car → burning of fuel → carbon emissions) on the right side below

M1: Definition of Carbon Footprint

The carbon footprint is the total amount of greenhouse gas emissions produced by human activities. Everything produced and done by humans creates carbon emissions and therefore has a carbon footprint. Therefore, the sources of emissions are industry (21%), agriculture & forestry (24%), electricity & heat production (25%), transportation (14%), housing/ buildings (6%) and other (10%).

a) Factors that lead to carbon footprint	b) How?
Example: A Loaf of Bread	

-
-
-
-

Phrase Bank: Linking Words

The starting point is ...	As a result (of) ...	The reason for this is ...
To begin with ...	As a consequence, ...	This affects ...
It shows the process of ...	This causes ...	One factor is ... another factor ...
Due to ...	... is caused by ...	When ... then ...
Because of ...	That leads to ...	
	Therefore ...	

4) **Draw** a pie chart about the different sources of greenhouse gas emissions listed in M1.

WORKSHEET 7.3 Worksheet A 3: Tiiiiime to Fill Tiiiime

Worksheet A 3: Tiiiime to fill tiiiime

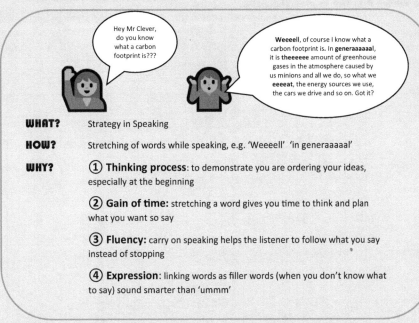

Hey Mr Clever, do you know what a carbon footprint is???

Weeeell, of course I know what a carbon footprint is. In **generaaaaal**, it is **theeeeee** amount of greenhouse gases in the atmosphere caused by us minions and all we do, so what we **eeeeat**, the energy sources we use, the cars we drive and so on. Got it?

WHAT?   Strategy in Speaking

HOW?   Stretching of words while speaking, e.g. 'Weeeell' 'in generaaaaal'

WHY?   ① **Thinking process**: to demonstrate you are ordering your ideas, especially at the beginning

② **Gain of time:** stretching a word gives you time to think and plan what you want so say

③ **Fluency:** carry on speaking helps the listener to follow what you say instead of stopping

④ **Expression**: linking words as filler words (when you don't know what to say) sound smarter than 'ummm'

Task: Listen to the examples below. **Underline** the plateau boundaries (the words that are looooonger). Decide the function(s) (①-④) of each example. Sometimes, there can be more functions than only one.

Time	Transcript	Example for ①–④
0:24–0:35	'So, you know, think about a loaf of bread, which I brought with me. It's an average – you know, you can find this loaf of wholewheat bread in a grocery store.' (Chatterjee, 2017)	
1:09–1:26	'And what they found is if you look at a single loaf of bread, they found the entire process that went into making it releases about 21 ounces of greenhouse gases into the atmosphere. That's about the weight of this loaf of bread.' (Chatterjee, 2017)	
2:24–2:36	'They did. One of their solutions was, you know, start with the nitrogen fertilisers that are applied on the farms because 40 per cent of the emissions are coming from the manufacture and the use of nitrogen fertilisers on farms.' (Chatterjee, 2017)	

Action Task: *NEVERSTOPSPEAKING*

Get together with a partner. Each of you has to **explain M1**. The important thing is that you are not allowed to stop speaking, soooooo **use plateau boundaries**, foooooooor example when you have to think about what to say next. **Repeat the task until both of you succeeded without pausing!** Have Fun!

*If there is no partner working at the same task, **take** your mobile phone and **record** a speech memo. Hand it in for feedback.*

WORKSHEET 7.4 Worksheet B I: The Louder, the Better

Worksheet B I: The Louder, the Better

1) **Listen** to Podcast B. While **listening, write down** the words you understand easiest and which you hear loud and clear.

Attention: It is not important to list as many words as possible, but only the content words. If the audio is too fast, simply stop after every sentence. However, **only listen once**.

WORKSHEET 7.5 Worksheet B 2: Finding Details in 'Nutrition and the Environment'

Worksheet B 2: Finding Details in 'Nutrition and the Environment'

1) **Listen** again. Afterwards, **match** the phrases (1–7) with the endings (a–g) in the box below. **Listen** as often as you need. **Compare** with a partner.

1 Kate Clancy makes her case by saying that	**a** is a major source of greenhouse gas emissions.
2 The Dietary Advisory Committee	**b** is one of the biggest sources of greenhouse gases in the atmosphere.
3 Meat Production	**c** less forests would be cleared by deforestation.
4 If people eat less meat	**d** nutritionists should also think about the environment when they give advice.
5 To talk about sustainability in nutrition	**e** already claims half of all vegetated land.
6 Producing food	**f** is a big shift.
7 Farming in general	**g** is working on new guidelines that include sustainability.

(Dan Charles, 2014)

VOC & PHRASE DOs

nutrition – Ernährung
nutritionist – Ernärungsberater
diet – Ernährung(sweise)
to maintain a healthy diet – sich gesund ernähren
to back off – zurückweichen
environmentalism – Umweltschutz
soil – Boden
to advise sb. of sth. – jmd. zu etwas raten

to make a case – sich für etw. stark machen
sustainability – Nachhaltigkeit
deforestation - Entwaldung
to supply – liefern
demand – Nachfrage
cattle – Rinder
feed – Futter
to demand – verlangen

---

2) **Organise and make short notes**: What does the speaker mean when he talks about *'a marriage of nutrition and environmentalism'* (00:29)? What does 'marriage' normally stand for?

_____
_____
_____
_____
_____
_____

WORKSHEET 7.6 Worksheet B 3: Pausing & Word Stress in Speech

3) In the blue box (**M4**) below, the speaker makes many pauses while he speaks. The pauses are shown by slashes between the words (**|**). For each pause or group of pauses, **identify** the reason(s) behind it. Therefore, **listen** to the beginning (until 0:24) and **match** the reasons in the cloud (a–d) to the correct blank box above the pauses.

M4: 0:00–0:24

[ ]

There's that catchy phrase **|** 'you are what you eat'. Well, some nutrition experts say it's much more than

[ ]

that. What we eat **|** can affect the world around us. A group of those experts – the Dietary Guidelines

Advisory Committee – is meeting in Washington today. They're working on new guidelines for how to

[ ]   [ ]

maintain a healthy diet, **|** and for the first time, they are examining how **|** our diet **|** affects **|** the

[ ]

environment. We are about to hear why lawmakers are telling those nutritionists **|** to back off. Here's

NPR's Dan Charles. (Dan Charles, 2014)

Reasons for Pausing:

a) underlining/highlighting an important point

b) punctuating the speech (commas)

c) preparation to 'listen up' and introducing the topic

d) preparation to 'listen up'

WORKSHEET 7.7 Worksheet B 4: Human Diet and the Environment – Causes and Effects

Worksheet B 4: Human Diet and the Environment – Causes and Effects

1) **Check** M6 below and **decide** for each aspect whether it is

   a)   a **cause for** changes in the environment or

   b)   a resulting **effect** observable in the environment.

   M6:

	cause for changes in environment	effect that results as a consequence
cattle farming		
higher meat production		
rising population		
methane		
deforestation		
greenhouse gases		
meat production		
less trees to absorb CO2		
growing/supply of feed		

VOC & PHRASE DO's

diet – Ernährungsweise
methane – Methan (Treibhausgas)
deforestation – Entwaldung
to absorb – absorbieren, aufnehmen
supply – Versorgung/Bereitstellung
feed – Futter

Remember that there can be many causes for one effect. Causes are often connected to each other. Sometimes, one aspect can be an effect of something and be the cause for another effect at the same time. In speech, causes (mainly the content words) are characterised by a **strong stress**.

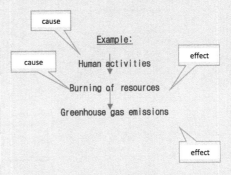

Example:

cause → Human activities ← effect

cause → Burning of resources ← effect

Greenhouse gas emissions

2) **Organise and explain** the information:
   a) **Turn** to the next page and **complete** the flow chart with the aspects/terms of the table from M6.

   b) **Skim** the phrase bank. **Find** fitting phrases or short linking words to **add** them on the arrows of your flowchart.

3) **Get together in groups of two or three** and **explain** your flowchart to each other. Group member 1 starts and the others listen. While listening, they **fill out the evaluation grid** for feedback. **Start your explanation** with the sentence in the speech bubble!

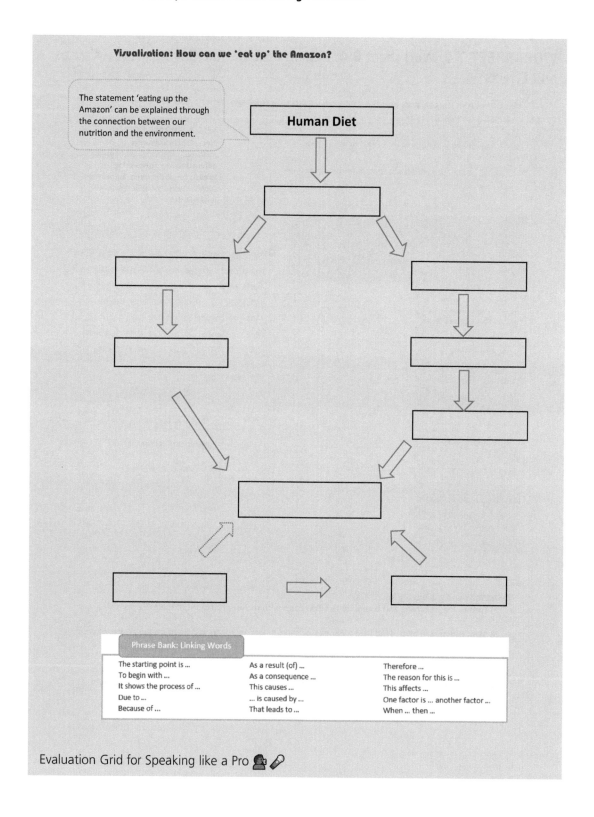

Visualisation: How can we 'eat up' the Amazon?

The statement 'eating up the Amazon' can be explained through the connection between our nutrition and the environment.

Human Diet

Phrase Bank: Linking Words

The starting point is ...	As a result (of) ...	Therefore ...
To begin with ...	As a consequence ...	The reason for this is ...
It shows the process of ...	This causes ...	This affects ...
Due to ...	... is caused by ...	One factor is ... another factor ...
Because of ...	That leads to ...	When ... then ...

Evaluation Grid for Speaking like a Pro

Table 7.4 Evaluation grid for speaking like a pro

The speaker ...			
Content			
... produced a well-structured speech/explanation/... that helped the listener to notice and remember significant points.			
... named causes and effects.			
... explained how causes relate to effects.			
... used linking words to connect ideas.			
Intonation and Rhythm			
... used word stress effectively to sound clear and comprehensible.			
... focused on speech rhythm, meaning that the voice was louder and clearer when signalling content words and weaker and faster when words were less important.			
... did not sound abrupt and spoke with a flow that made it easy for the listener to follow.			
Pausing			
... made appropriate pauses to put emphasis on specific aspects (e.g. after giving an example).			
... used pausing successfully instead of abruptly stopping to give the listener time to follow or think.			

WORKSHEET 7.8 Worksheet 5: Record your Podcast *Geography for Everyone*

Worksheet 5: Record your podcast *Geography for Everyone*

1. **Take the flowcharts** from worksheets A2 and B1 and **put** them **next to each other**. **Organise** the information in a structured way. For this, **create** a final flowchart/visualisation that helps you answer the guiding question. It **needs to include** but is not limited to the following:
   - *terminology*: ecological footprint, deforestation, greenhouse gas emissions, rising population, consumers, resources
   - *causes* of a rising ecological footprint
   - *effects* on the environment.
2. On all arrows of your flowchart, **add** fitting phrases (*this leads to, this causes ...*). Think of specifying verbs to use in your explanation – **write** them next to the subject-specific terms for orientation.
3. Before recording, **check** the PREP-Sheet again. **Stick** to the characteristics of a good explanation and **practise** your explanation as often as you need to in order to achieve a recording with as few disruptions as possible. To sound as fluent and professional as you can, **use** the phrase boxes on the PREP-Sheet!
4. **Record** your podcast. Remember: Nobody sees you – it's only your voice.

REFERENCES

Berg, N. (2020). *Listening for Literacies – Effekt von fachspezifischem Hör-Verstehenstraining auf die Entwicklung der mündlichen Sachfachliteralität im bilingualen Geographieunterricht* Unpublished doctoral dissertation, Johannes Gutenberg University Mainz. http://doi.org/10.25358/openscience-3591

Charles, D. (2014, December 15). Congress to Nutritionists: Don't Talk about the Environment. *NPR: The Salt.* https://www.npr.org/sections/thesalt/2014/12/15/370427441/congress-to-nutritionists-dont-talk-about-the-environment

Chatterjee, R. (2017, February 27). What's the Environmental Footprint of a Loaf of Bread? Now We Know. *NPR: The Salt.* https://www.npr.org/sections/thesalt/2017/02/27/517531611/whats-the-environmental-footprint-of-a-loaf-of-bread-now-we-know?t=1614339378381&t=1642421329281

Edelson, D. C. (2009). Geographic Literacy in U.S. by 2025. *ESRI: Geo Learning.* https://www.esri.com/news/arcnews/spring09articles/geographic-literacy.html

Edelson, D. C. (2011a). The Challenge of Defining Geo-Literacy. *ESRI: Geo Learning.* https://www.esri.com/news/arcnews/summer11articles/the-challenge-of-defining-geo-literacy.html

Edelson, D. C. (2011b, March 25). Geo-Literacy: Learn about Geo-Literacy – What It Is, Why It's Important, and What We Can Do to Advance Geo-Literacy in the U.S. *National Geographic Society.* https://www.nationalgeographic.org/article/geo-literacy-preparation-far-reaching-decisions/

Egli, H.-R., Hasler, M., & Probst, M. (Eds.). (2016). Geografie: Wissen und verstehen: Ein Handbuch für die Sekundarstufe II, 4th ed. hep der Bildungsverlag.

Harte, W., & Reitano, P. (2016). 'Doing Geography': Evaluating an Independent Geographic Inquiry Assessment Task in an Initial Teacher Education Program. *Journal of Geography, 115*(6), 233–243. https://doi.org/10.1080/00221341.2016.1175496

International Charter on Geographical Education (Ed.). (2016). *2016 International Charter on Geographical Education.* http://www.cnfg.fr/wp-content/uploads/2017/12/Charter_2016-IGU-CGE_May_9.pdf

Kang, H., Thompson, J., & Windschitl, M. (2014). Creating Opportunities for Students to Show What They Know: The Role of Scaffolding in Assessment Tasks. *Science Education, 98*(4), 674–704. https://doi.org/10.1002/sce.21123

Lewis, M. (2012). *The Lexical Approach: The State of ELT and a Way Forward.* Cengage Learning EMEA.

What is Geo-Literacy? (2012, May 24). *National Geographic Society.* https://www.nationalgeographic.org/media/what-is-geo-literacy/

Utami, W. S., Zain, I. M., & Sumarmi. (2018). Geography Literacy Can Develop Geography Skills for High School Students: *Is It True? IOP Conference Series: Materials Science and Engineering, 296,* 012032. https://doi.org/10.1088/1757-899X/296/1/012032

Vandergrift, L. (2003). Orchestrating Strategy Use: Toward a Model of the Skilled Second Language Listener. *Language Learning, 53*(3), 463–496. https://doi.org/10.1111/1467-9922.00232

8 History: Exploring Pluriliteracies through a Deeper Learning Episode on the German Empire

SUSANNE STASCHEN–DIELMANN

8.1 Inquiry and Literacy in History

Historical knowledge evolves from evidence-based investigations of what happened and its significance for us and, therefore, history is a problem-solving discipline that involves questioning, investigating, understanding and interpreting past developments and events. Historical inquiry starts with open-ended, guiding questions that are 'answered with selected facts arranged in the form of an explanatory paradigm' (Fischer, 1970, pp. xv, 4). The process can be deductive, which means a historian can prove or refute a hypothesis about a historical process (e.g. 'Bismarck managed to unify Germany as a nation'). Additionally, a historian can approach problems inductively, meaning he or she investigates sources in order to find a pattern or concept and then develops a theory from those findings (e.g. 'What evidence do the sources provide about diversity and uniformity in the German Empire?'). Either way, a historian must have both *narrative* and *historical literacy* to understand and contribute to the discipline's knowledge base and research efforts.

For the subject of history, terms such as *narrative literacy* or *historical literacy* have been developed to characterise the ability to participate in historically oriented discourses. Maria José Rodrigo (1994) described *narrative literacy* as the ability to arrange information around protagonists while preserving the temporal–causal structure and *historical literacy* as the ability to master key historical concepts and be scientifically active like a historian. To accomplish this, key historical concepts, such as 'nation', have to be recognised by the learners and used as time- and location-bound. Since historical reconstruction and presentation of results are closely linked to the competence of storytelling, as well as the abilities to criticise, argue, form judgements and present information on the basis of the professional handling of sources and representations, the terms *narrative* and *historical literacy* have been used synonymously in more recent curricula and publications, especially in the German context (Ministerium für Kultus, Jugend und Sport Baden-Württemberg, 2004).

The main task of the historian is to deal with primary and secondary sources and the historical evidence they contain. Students have to learn to evaluate a source's reliability in both written and spoken modes, recognise the author's subjectivity and resolve contradicting findings (Rodrigo, 1994). This requires sophisticated grammar skills that allow the learners to differentiate between perspectives, time levels and degrees of probability as well as an elevated vocabulary rich in technical terms that make it possible to speak about the time period they wish to refer to. In order to promote historical literacy in history lessons, it makes sense to work with the linguistic and cognitive pattern of the text types students are supposed to produce (e.g. primary or secondary source analysis, historical evaluation or argumentation).

As far as register is concerned, the subject of history uses so-called *colligations* or *colligatory concepts*. These are terms for larger contexts or connections between individual events or phenomena that also have an explanatory function (e.g. 'Renaissance', 'Industrial Revolution') (Walsh, 1960). In addition to that, there are technical terms in the narrower sense of the word, like 'Berlin Blockade' or 'Iron Curtain', which are more specific to a single historical process. The historical–political register also contains subject-relevant collocations, which include expressions such as 'to pass an Act' or 'to negotiate an armistice'. In comparison to the technical terms, these subject-specific phrases can help the learners to language historical narrations on a more general level and in an authentic and appropriate way. By enhancing their knowledge of historical jargon and collocations, students can make progress in discipline-specific meaning-making.

Progress in meaning-making in history entails an increase in competence in the activity domains of *doing, organising, explaining* and *arguing* history, which can be observed in the students' presentation of historical information and the quality of their production of historical text types. Historical meaning-making can be enhanced by enlarging the students' repertoire of general academic language structures as well as specific historical language functions and their command of genre conventions of historical text types, which show them a pathway to history-specific ways of meaning-making. The more precisely the students can follow history-specific genre conventions and the wider repertoire of history-specific discourse functions they have, the greater the opportunity for precise meaning-making to take place in the course of a historical investigation.

Table 8.1 shows the way in which activity domains and activities in history can be related to cognitive discourse functions (CDFs) and student products that are typical in history.

8.2   Deeper Learning in History

Deeper understanding in history means that historical events, structures and processes can be described, analysed and assessed in order to create a narration in accordance

Table 8.1 Activity domains, language functions and student products in history

Activity Domains in History	Sample Activities in History	Cognitive Discourse Functions and Learner Progression in History (How these CDFs might be languaged by learners at different stages)	Complex Student Products in History
Doing Historical Research Investigate, research, find, select CDFs • **Report** (inform, recount, present, summarise, relate)	Collecting historical data from a variety of primary and secondary sources Selecting relevant historical data with respect to the guiding question Presenting research results	Novice: 'I have been collecting information on the tools people used in prehistoric times.' Expert: 'In order to answer my guiding question, I have been investigating evidence for and against the legality of Hitler's takeover of power.'	**Preliminary:** • Chronology • Statistics • Maps • Lists • Bibliography • Structured notes • Mind maps, • Concept maps • Document archives **Oral:** • Presentations • Discussions • Historical debates • Talk shows • Role plays • Simulations **Written:** • Historical analysis and/or comparison of primary source/comparison of primary sources (texts, cartoons, pictures, posters, maps, charts, statistics, tables) • Historical analysis of secondary sources/comparison of secondary sources • Historical evaluation • Historical argumentation • Historical expert opinion • Newspaper article or comment on historical phenomenon • Comics
Organising Historical Data CDFs • **Describe** (describe, label, identify, name) • **Classify** (classify, compare, contrast, match, structure, categorise, subsume)	Organising the historical data chronologically or thematically Describing or summarising a historical event, structure or process orally or in writing	Novice: 'The Stone Age started 2.5 million years ago. Then the Bronze Age began around 3300 B.C. and the Iron Age started between 1200 B.C. and 600 B.C.' Expert: 'After his appointment as Reich Chancellor on 31 January 1933, Hitler established the National Socialist dictatorship, starting with the Decree for the Protection of the People and the State on 28 February 1933, one day after Reichstag Fire, and followed by the Enabling Act on 23 March 1933.'	
Explaining History: CDFs • **Explain** (explain, reason, express, draw conclusions, deduce) • **Define** (define, identify, characterise, compare, contrast)	Explaining change or continuity in historical events, structures or processes	Novice: 'When the people in the Iron Age could use more stable tools, they could build better houses, develop more dangerous weapons and improve farming.' Expert: 'With Hitler's accession to power, basic rights were abolished, the federal states were synchronised with the Reich, the separation of powers was eliminated, and thus the Führer state was established."	

Table 8.1 (*cont.*)

Activity Domains in History	Sample Activities in History	Cognitive Discourse Functions and Learner Progression in History (How these CDFs might be languaged by learners at different stages)	Complex Student Products in History
	• Explaining the significance of historical events, structures or processes • Explaining causation and the agency of people involved in historical events, structures or processes • Explaining by using time and chronology • Explaining and comparing different contemporary or retrospective perspectives on historical events, structures or processes • Explaining by providing accounts and evidence of historical events, structures and processes Assessing contemporary and retrospective perspectives on historical events, structures or processes		Digital: • Documentary • Animation • Radio show or feature • Instructional video • Blog/vlog
Arguing History: CDFs • Explore (explore, hypothesise, speculate, predict, guess, estimate, simulate, take other perspectives) • Evaluate (evaluate, judge, argue, justify, take a stance, state, critique, recommend, comment, reflect, appreciate)	Supporting or refuting historical hypotheses by giving accounts and evidence of historical events, structures or processes Assessing and evaluating historical hypothesis on change and continuity, significance, causation, chronology, perspectives and evidence (Downey & Long, 2016)	Novice: 'I think that the material people had for making tools was important for their development, because the tools …' Expert: 'The legality of Hitler's power grab can be disputed: although he might have followed the letter of the law, he certainly violated the spirit of the democratic Weimar Constitution because it is evident that …'	

with the scientific standards of the subject. Therefore, the learners need patterns of inquiry and representation that can scaffold historical thinking and narration:

To **deepen textual understanding**, the students need to be able to decipher technical terms and abstract concepts, which can be done by defining advanced words or by annotating difficult passages, especially if the text is written in the learners' second language. **Content relevance can be increased** by relating the historical matter into a present-day context or by using a mode they are interested in (e.g. digital modes). **Critical cultural consciousness can be developed** by presenting and critically questioning different contemporary and/or retrospective perspectives. **Agency and accountability can be increased** by giving students responsibility for the accuracy of the historical investigation and asking for evidence and referencing. **Learning pathways can be differentiated** by offering optional input and output scaffolding for learners with different language backgrounds as well as providing different assignments within the overall learning task. **Deep practice can be fostered** by practising recurring genre conventions (e.g. source analysis and historical evaluation) with different types of sources and in different historical contexts. **Scaffolding can be offered on different levels** by using language and method frames for text production on varying language levels.

8.3 A Model Deeper Learning Episode in History: 'After Unifying the German Reich with "Blood and Iron" in 1871, Did Bismarck Manage to Unify German Society as a Nation?' (Year 11)

The main objective of the following deeper learning episode (DLE) in history for upper secondary learners is the narrativisation of the social tensions following the formation of the German Empire in 1871, which is guided by the following question: 'After unifying the German Reich with "blood and iron" in 1871, did Bismarck manage to unify German society as a nation?'

The topic has relevance to the learners as it deals with the concept of national identity and diversity, which is part of the current political discourse. Moreover, the learning product is chosen according to learners' interests: students will create an instructional video to answer the guiding question in an evidence-based yet creative way by portraying the varying views of the different groups within German society at the time.

During the project, the learners are supposed to acquire and analyse information on different social and political groups in the German Empire (e.g. their power status and their relation to Reich Chancellor von Bismarck) and evaluate Bismarck's domestic policy, with special attention paid to his approach to dealing with potential opposition.

On the following pages, a grid with an overview of the planning aspects is shown, which are meant to be aligned with each other based on the principles of the pluriliteracies approach to deeper learning (Table 8.2). A didactic commentary explains this process and how learners move from surface learning to consolidation and finally to the transfer stage.

8.4   Alignment of the Deeper Learning Episode

In alignment with deeper learning principles, the proposed learning episode takes into account students' strengths, needs and interests, provides opportunities to build their historical literacy and successfully implements tasks that cover all activity domains. High task fidelity in this DLE is achieved by combining academic research on a social and political history topic with the entertaining element of role play and a digital mode of representation.

Learner Strengths, Needs and Interests
Learners are often interested in digital modes of representation and highly capable of using them. Therefore, an instructional video has been chosen to make use of its motivational qualities and to emphasise learners' strengths. The students are also responsible for the historical quality of their contribution and are trusted to carry out proper research and provide evidence for their research results. However, they might need academic language scaffolding to formulate an answer to the research question on an appropriate level, using historical evaluation criteria as well as academic and subject-specific language structures.

Historical Literacy
By completing this DLE, students become more familiar with different key historical concepts and thus become more historically literate. The first key concepts used in this episode are continuity and change because the formation of the German nation state was a major change that had not been brought about by the people but by diplomacy and military success. Since the Napoleonic Wars, the German people had demanded national unity and liberty, but with the rather authoritarian German Empire, only national unity was accomplished, and liberal ideals, such as effective participation rights for the different social groups, were not fully realised. Furthermore, religious and social disparities, as well as the integration of other nationalities into the German Empire, caused social tensions to mount. Another important concept is that of perspective because the views of different social,

Table 8.2 Planning grid for a deeper learning episode in history: Making an instructional video: 'After unifying the German Reich with "blood and iron" in 1871, did Bismarck manage to unify German society as a nation?' (Year 11)

Designing Deeper Learning Episodes

Planning Grid for a Deeper Learning Episode in History

What do I want my learners to know or be able to do?	How will my learners demonstrate increasingly deeper understanding at the surface, consolidation and transfer levels?	How can I support active knowledge co-construction for my learners?	How can I support my learners every step of the way?	How can I generate and sustain learner commitment and achievement?
Basic Understanding: • Information on different social and political groups in the German Empire, including their power status and their relation to Reich Chancellor von Bismarck • Understanding of Bismarck's domestic policy, especially his approach to potential opposition **Foundational Skills:** • Doing research on a specific social or political group in the past • Organising the information on a fact sheet • Explaining the group's power status and relation to Reich Chancellor von Bismarck	**Preliminary Product Outcomes:** • Fact sheet on social or political group • Interview with fictional representatives of that group in writing • Interview with a fictional representative of that group in a video clip • Script for frame narration: introduction and historical evaluation **Main Learning Product:** Purpose: educating other students Genre: instructional video Mode: digital (i.e. video) Style: academic and contemporary colloquial style **Possible Transfer:** • Evaluating to what extent Bismarck's foreign policy was successful in creating lasting peace in Europe	**(Co-)Construction of Knowledge:** [X] Inquiry-based learning 0 Problem-based learning 0 Experimenting [X] Project-based learning **Social Interaction:** • Groups work on one social or political group • Instructional video integrates the result of group work and frames it with a joint narration	**Scaffolding:** • Fact sheet is scaffolded by providing aspects for the research (situation, interests, power status, relation to Bismarck) • 'Historical evaluation' is scaffolded by a language frame • Instructional video is scaffolded by language frame **Feedback:** • Individual teacher feedback on fact sheet and interview script • Peer feedback on interview video clips with comparison to fact sheets	**Engagement:** Personal Meaningfulness/ Relevance: • Use of the instructional video for the education of younger learners • All learners perform in the instructional video Opportunities for Autonomous Learning: • Independent research on a political or social group

Table 8.2 (*cont.*)

Designing Deeper Learning Episodes			
• Evaluating the extent to which Bismarck unified the German Empire domestically	• Making an instructional video or audio on political and social groups in the Weimar Republic	**Use of (Digital) Media:** • Fact sheets and interview scripts are typed and exchanged digitally	**Feed-Up:** • Language frame and assessment grid 'Historical Evaluation'	• Creative writing and recording of the interview, including costumes and scenery
Deeper Understanding: • Society and political participation in the German Empire	• transforming a text, making it more academic and concise	• Interviews are recorded on video with the help of smartphones or iPads	**Feed-Forward:** • Individual teacher feedback on fact sheet and interview script	**Reflection and Revision:** • Joint revision of the instructional video, including a reflection taking the possible audience into consideration
Deep practice: • Using nominalisations to make a text more academic and concise • Evaluating a historical process using criteria		• Instructional video is created in iMovie	• Peer feedback on interview video clips with comparison to fact sheets	
Transfer: • Colloquial *vs* academic language • Criteria-oriented historical evaluation			**Assessment:** • Assessment grid 'Historical Evaluation'	

religious and national groups in imperial Germany are articulated by the learners via a role play. Lastly, the topic also includes the concept of agency (i.e. an individual's influence on a historical process) because Bismarck's outstanding role in the unification of Germany, especially his suppressive domestic policy, is a matter of historical debate.

Students are steered to these key concepts by a guiding question. The guiding question can only be answered if the groups carry out historical research, analyse and assess primary and secondary sources and share their evidence and results with the other groups. The results of the different groups' analyses are synthesised in a final historical evaluation, which is presented at the end of the instructional video.

An instructional video offers the possibility of combining scientific research with the entertaining elements of role play and motivates learners by being addressed to a younger audience. The instructional video incorporates two different discourse structures. The narrator will follow the academic discourse patterns of the historical narration: describing, explaining and arguing the historical structures and processes that are presented. The different social, religious and national groups of society will be presented in a role play that explains the different perspectives on the German nation state, so the language level is less academic and might also include colloquial language or simulate the style found in the primary sources. While the role play leaves more room for creative freedom and could also integrate colloquial language, the narrator's comments need a strictly academic code. Learners can choose from conventions found in instructional history videos on the internet or in historical documentaries, and they can integrate different language levels. This way, the learners can learn how to modify the language level deliberately using academic and subject-specific language structures (e.g. when formulating a historical evaluation as an answer to the guiding question).

Activity Domains

Learners are *doing* history when they collect historical data on their group and their attitude towards the German nation state and Reich Chancellor von Bismarck. They *organise* the information in a fact sheet, which can be structured as a mind or concept map or a structured list of information. This fact sheet must be made available to the other groups, should be properly referenced and should *explain* the specific viewpoint of the respective social group concerned. Using the perspectives of the different groups as arguments in favour or against, learners then have to *argue* to what extent Bismarck was able to create national unity in German society in order to completely fulfil the task set out for them by the guiding question.

Growth Mindset, Deep Practice and Deep Understanding

The task drives learner commitment and achievement by being fun-oriented and allowing students to dress up and take on the role of historical groups but also by demanding academically responsible research. The learning process is mentored by providing scaffolding in the form of pre-writing activities and language frames for the text and video production. Additionally, feedback is given on the academic research as well as on the scripts for the fictional interviews and the historical evaluation. This way, the learners can build knowledge autonomously and demonstrate their understanding by creating fact sheets, scripts and then an instructional video while still keeping scientific standards and practising discipline conventions through the staggered revision process. The fact that the video is to be presented to other classes provokes reflection on the joint work and the individual contribution.

8.5   How Do Learners Move from Surface Learning to Consolidation to the Transfer Stage?

In this DLE, text production is the major vehicle for the movement from surface to deeper learning. Because the historical knowledge derived from the research first has to be written and arranged on a fact sheet (i.e. a mind map or structured notes), then presented orally in class, then transformed into a script for a fictional interview and finally recorded, there is a lot of practice in organising and communicating historical information in varying forms of representation, language styles and modes. The most difficult step in the process is the shift from more informal, less sophisticated language to a more academic language in the final historical evaluation, which is the most advanced text type and summarises the whole learning process. This progression along the mode continuum consolidates learning.

The following section will outline the different stages of the DLE, explaining each stage through both the perspective of the teacher and learner. The process can be seen in the depiction below.

Engage the Learner

In order to activate the learners' concepts of national identity, they are asked about their national identity and who they consider part of their nation. They are likely to engage in this discussion since the recent rise of right-wing populist parties with their demands for the exclusion of certain groups of people has triggered a debate about the diversity of modern societies. For German students, this question has a special relevance as the aggressive and then also racist interpretation of nationalism led the German people into two world wars and the Holocaust.

Promote/Acquire Basic Understanding and Acquisition of Foundational Skills

The learners are then introduced to the learning task for the whole episode with a worksheet, which includes a lesson plan (see Table 8.3), and scaffolding language frames (see Worksheet 8.2 and Tables 8.4, 8.5 and 8.6). They must first collect historical information on their social, political, religious or national groups as well as organise the data into a fact sheet (e.g. mind map, concept map or structured notes) according to the following aspects: the situation of the group, its interests, its position of power and its relation to Bismarck.

Provide Feedback, Feed-Up and Feed-Forward/Demonstrate Basic Understanding and Reflect

There are five opportunities for feedback and reflection in the learning episode: the first, second and fourth are teacher feedback on the fact sheets, the video scripts and the historical evaluation, which make sure that the learners have a clear understanding of what the task demands (feed-up) and that the historical information passed on to the other students and used for the instructional video is accurate (feedback and feed-forward). The students demonstrate their understanding by providing a revised fact sheet, video script and historical evaluation (see Table 8.7).

Facilitate/Acquire Deeper Understanding and Deep Practice

Deeper understanding and deep practice are provided by the movement along the mode continuum (i.e. researching, writing and presenting the fact sheet, transforming the information into a script for the instructional video and finally recording it). The meaning-making in this process is scaffolded by pre-writing tasks (e.g. on nominalisations), genre-specific language frames and learning conversations on the basis of feedback criteria. These criteria can be made transparent by creating competence grids for the task so that expectations concerning the use of methods and language become clear to learners. This enables them to language their learning process and deliberately modify their language level.

Provide Feedback, Feed-Up and Feed-Forward/Demonstrate Basic Understanding and Reflect

The third feedback opportunity is peer-driven: the fact sheet and the video interview is presented to the class with the task to check whether the information in the fact sheet has been appropriately used in the video interview. This requires each learner to formulate goals (feed-up), assess the product (feedback) and suggest modifications (feed-forward) as well as be receptive to feed-up, feedback and feed-forward on his or her own product.

This feedback exchange serves an additional purpose, specifically imparting the information collected by the individual groups on the other groups who worked on a different topic. The comparison of fact sheets and video interviews in the feedback process gives the entire class a more holistic picture of imperial German society. This is the basis on which the guiding question is to be answered.

Facilitate Transfer/Transfer Knowledge

This DLE facilitates transfer skills in a number of ways. First, by comparing the information about all other social, religious or national groups according to their situation, interests, power status and relation to Bismarck, the learners become aware of the diversity of the society in imperial Germany as well as critically assessing the unifying ideas of nationalism and militarism. Secondly, the learners also acquire transferable knowledge concerning the concepts of continuity and change as well as perspective and agency when they critically evaluate Bismarck's attempt to unify the German Empire with a suppressive approach to domestic policy. Thirdly, they can also transfer the concepts of diversity and authoritarianism to modern societies, which are just as diverse, and debate concepts like national identity and the move to a more authoritarian approach in order to make society more homogenous by suppressing or excluding minorities. Lastly, by answering the guiding question on an academic language level and according to the conventions of the historical discourse community, learners acquire transferable knowledge about the method of historical evaluation and its academic discourse structures (Kayser & Hagemann, 2010).

Mentor Reflection/Present and Reflect

The learning offers multiple opportunities for learners to reflect on the material and their learning process. The mentor gives individual feedback on the historical evaluations and chooses the best version before the recording of the final cut of the instructional video. The 'winning' student receives praise for his or her work, and the other students have a model from which to learn that reflects the standards of the genre. Moreover, presenting the whole instructional video in class triggers reflection not only on the accuracy of the historical facts, concepts and strategies but also on the style, tone and mode of the communication, which is specific for the instructional video as a genre. Knowing that they will have to present the instructional history video to other classes will make the learners self-reflective and open to self-assessment, especially with regard to the consistency of narration and the impression the instructional video might make on the audience. Lastly, this learning episode provides learners with the opportunity to reflect on the content of their own narration (i.e. in what way their presentation is biased because of their specific selection of historical data).

8.6 Conclusion and Outlook

Pluriliteracies teaching for deeper learning makes sense for history teachers who want to make full use of language as a driving force for learning history. By focusing on the language use in different modes and text types, students can acquire a subject-specific language repertoire along with the historical facts, concepts, procedures and strategies they need to produce an accurate historical narration. By giving and receiving criteria-oriented feedback on various historical text types, the learners are empowered to language their learning process as well as their historical narration and thus experience deep historical learning.

Digital learning environments, such as the one from this learning episode, can help mentors to provide learners with history learning tasks that are motivating and offer students a self-empowering, transparent path towards subject-specific progress via extensive scaffolding and efficient assessment tools.

8.7 Learning Materials

WORKSHEET 8.1 'After unifying the German Reich with "blood and iron" in 1871, did Bismarck manage to unify German society as a nation?'

Instructional History Video: 'After Unifying the German Reich with "Blood and Iron" in 1871, Did Bismarck Manage to Unify German Society as a Nation?'
The history teachers in your school need an entertaining instructional history video for their students on the topic of the foundation of the German nation state, explaining the domestic situation after the foundation of the German Empire in 1871 and focusing on the question of whether the unification of German society was successful.

In order to capture the perspectives of different political, social, religious and national groups in Germany at that time, you are tasked with enacting interviews with (alleged) contemporary witnesses on video, who will be asked about their social and political status in society, their interests and their relation to Reich Chancellor von Bismarck. We will then combine the different perspectives in an instructional history video, adding an introduction explaining the historical context and a conclusion arguing and evaluating the guiding question.

Work in Groups with up to Three Students

Imagine you belong to one of the following groups who are looking for their role in the newly founded German Empire:

- Women (bourgeois and working class)
- Nobility and military
- Liberal bourgeoisie (including national and social liberals)
- Socialist workers (focusing on the Social Democratic Party, SDP – later the SPD)
- Catholics (focusing on the Centre Party)
- Jews
- Danish minority in Schleswig

The representatives of these groups should be interviewed with the following question:

- Situation: How are you doing? (Don't elaborate too much!)
- Interests: What is it you want to achieve or keep for your social, religious or national group?
- Power position: How is your social and/or political position in the empire? Can you articulate your interests and achieve your goals? How are you represented in parliament?
- Relation to Bismarck: How does Reich Chancellor von Bismarck treat your group? What do you think about Bismarck?

Tasks

1. Collect historical information – texts and pictures – on your social, religious or national group using the following material and the internet and try to find precise answers to the interview questions:
   - Kursbuch Geschichte' (Cornelsen) 2017, pp. 81–85, 110–118
   - Das deutsche Kaiserreich 1971–1914' (Buchner) 1987, pp. 35–62, 8 –115
   - https://www.bpb.de/geschichte/deutsche-geschichte/kaiserreich/
2. Organise your information in a structured way in an A4-sized fact sheet (e.g. mind map, concept map or structured notes) for the other groups. Include the most important facts on the group's situation, interests, power position and relation to Bismarck. Hand this in for feedback. After a revision, be prepared to present your fact sheet to the class together with the video interview.
3. Formulate an interview script on the basis of your fact sheet and record the interview with a smartphone, answering the interview questions in a role play. Please use costumes and the linguistic style of the primary sources to make your language sound more authentic.
4. Present your video to the class. Give and receive feedback on the basis of the fact sheets:
   - Have all the important facts been included and presented in a historically precise way?
   - Is the role play authentic?

5. After seeing all the interviews and doing the pre-writing tasks, please answer the guiding question in writing, providing a reasoned historical evaluation for the concluding part of the video: 'After unifying the German Reich with "blood and iron" in 1871, did Bismarck manage to unify German society as a nation?' Use the language frame and hand in your historical evaluation for feedback. The best evaluation will be used for the instructional history video.

6. Write an introductory text and choose freely usable picture material for the general introduction, the introduction to your respective interview scene and the conclusion of the instructional history video.

Lesson Plan

Table 8.3 Lesson plan

Lessons and Feedback (90 minutes twice a week)	Tasks	Time
1st lesson	Tasks 1 & 2: Research and fact sheet	90 minutes
Teacher feedback on fact sheets	Task 2: Revise fact sheet	Homework
2nd lesson	Task 3: Interview script	90 minutes
Teacher feedback on video script	Task 3: Revise video script	Homework
3rd lesson	Task 3: Video recording	90 minutes
4th lesson Peer feedback on video interview	Tasks 2 & 4: Presentation of Fact sheets, video and interview with peer feedback	90 minutes
Teacher feedback on historical evaluation	Task 5: Pre-writing tasks and historical evaluation	Homework
5th lesson	Formulation of introduction and conclusion of the instructional history video	90 minutes
	Cutting and integrating voice-over in instructional history video	Homework (for two students and/or teacher)
6th lesson Peer and teacher feedback on the instructional history video	Watching instructional history video and reflection	90 minutes

WORKSHEET 8.2 Language Scaffolding Activities and Language Frames

Language Scaffolding Activities and Language Frames
(Expected student products in italics)

Pre-Writing Activities
1. Before writing your historical evaluation, please reflect on the term 'national unity'. Complete the sentence with at least three different endings.
   A nation is unified if the people . . .
   - *share common values.*
   - *accept economic disparities.*
   - *integrate minorities.*
   - *identify with the political system.*
2. Now rephrase these sentences expressing them in one complex noun each. Use these nominalisations as criteria to structure your historical evaluation of the 'national unity' of the German Empire:
   - *Community of values*
   - *Acceptance of economic disparities*
   - *Integration of minorities*
   - *Identification with the political system*
3. Please define the following historical or political terms that you could use in your historical evaluation of the national unity of the German Empire:
   Militarism – *strong appreciation of soldiers and the military as an institution*
   Nationalism – *strong appreciation of one's nation*
   Belief in Authorities – *attitude of obedience towards the government*
   Anti-Semitism – *attitude of prejudice against Jewish people*
   Social Question – *problem of social inequality and bad living conditions for the working class*
   Anti-Socialist Laws – *legislation which banned socialist political activity 1878–1890*
   Kulturkampf – *Reich Chancellor von Bismarck's fight against the influence of the Catholic Church on politics in the German Empire implementing restricting legislation 1872–1878*
   Protectionism – *raising import tariffs in order to protect national producers*
   Gender Equality – *desired outcome of women's fight for equal access to rights or opportunities*
4. Have a look at the fact sheets of all groups and find one or two historical arguments per **criterion** that either confirm or reject the existence of national unity. Make sure you use logically consistent *connectors* to structure your arguments and complex nouns or nominalisation to make your text concise. For example:

The people in the German Empire were a **community of values** since the ideas of nationalism and militarism put forward and represented by the aristocracy and the military were widely accepted throughout society. *Nevertheless*, there were national minorities, like the Danish people in Schleswig, who preferred to identify with Denmark as their nation state.

5. Now start writing following the language frame 'Historical Evaluation'.

Model Historical Evaluation

In 1871, the German Empire was founded in the Hall of Mirrors in the Palace of Versailles in the presence of the German nobility, but the German people were not invited. The German Empire was founded from the top, establishing a monarchy with a constitution, which included authoritarian and liberal elements. But was that enough to unite people in the German Empire?

The powers of the Reichstag, the parliament, were restricted by prerogatives of the Emperor and the Federal Council, but it nevertheless offered a platform for the different social, political and religious groups to articulate their interests: The nobility and the military were represented through the Conservative Party; the Catholics were represented by the Centre Party; the Liberals had a spectrum of parties, like the National Liberal Party or the Progress Party; and the working class were mainly represented by the Social Democratic Party. Women and national minorities were not represented in the Reichstag.

In the following text, the national unity of the German Empire will be examined, specifically to what extent the German people formed a community of values, accepted economic disparity, integrated minorities and identified with the political system.

The predominance of militarism and nationalism as shared values can be taken as evidence that German society was indeed a **community of values***. The strong* **identification with the emperor** *and monarchy, as well as the widespread belief in authorities, formed a strong foundation for this, enforced by the economic upswing in the early years of the German Empire.*

However, the empire seemed less unified concerning the **economy because huge disparities** *between the social classes seemed to persist despite the economic prosperity of the so-called 'Gründerzeit', and the social question remained unresolved: The poverty of the working class and their families caused them to turn to the revolutionary idea of communism and demand the nationalisation of the means of production owned by aristocratic or bourgeois elites. The political activities of the Social Democrats were suppressed by Bismarck's anti-socialist laws of 1878 so that an* **integration of this large political minority** *could not take place. Earlier, the Catholics, as a religious minority, had been excluded as Bismarck's Kulturkampf tried to reduce the influence of the Catholic Church and the Pope through repressive legislation. During the reign of the German Empire, large parts of the Jewish* population assimilated, but widespread anti-Semitism, tolerated by Bismarck, prevented the **integration of the Jewish minority as well**.

Because the Social Democrats as well as the Catholic Centre Party continued gaining more and more votes and seats in the Reichstag, Bismarck changed his strategy against his domestic enemies. He established the Centre Party as a political partner by including them in his protectionist policy and tried to take the ground from under the Social Democrats by implementing major social legislation and improving the situation of the working class considerably. With this, he managed to tame the revolutionary drive of the Social Democrats, who started to become reform-oriented rather than strive for a revolution.

Women had to wait until 1918 and the collapse of the German Empire before they finally gained gender equality concerning suffrage in the Weimar Constitution.

All in all, Bismarck's domestic policy can be judged as a sincere attempt to unite German society in a more homogeneous, Prussia-dominated and authoritarian German Empire. Focusing on the **integration of minorities**, especially his relation to religious or political opponents, it must be noted that Bismarck did not manage to unite German society. His suppressive approach clashed with the emancipatory ambitions of Socialists, Catholics and women. The anti-Semitism of the elites alienated the Jewish population, and the liberal economic elites were frustrated by protectionism. **Militarism** and nationalism were broadly effective in creating a **community of values**, but the economic, social and cultural problems were only suppressed, not resolved.

In hindsight, Bismarck's approach could be seen as an unsustainable attempt to contain the growing diversity of the industrialised society by imposing the dominant Prussian culture, values and politics on the whole of Germany.

Language Frame 'Instructional Video'

Table 8.4 Composing an instructional video

Genre Moves	Considerations	Language Help	Options
Introducing the Topic: • Outlining a problem • Showing its relevance • Developing a guiding question	What is interesting about the topic? In what way is it relevant today? Do scientists or political interest groups argue about the topic? What needs to be investigated? Is the topic open to judgement? What are the categories and criteria for the judgement?	Today we will talk about … because … For us today the topic is relevant because … Why should you learn about …? Here is why: … Leading scientists/historians/ politicians/interest groups have argued whether … We want to investigate … We will help you to make up your mind on the question of … focusing on the following criteria …	• Narrator in shot (natural background setting or greenscreen) • Voice-over (commentary heard by viewer without speaker being in shot) • Subtitles or captions • Background music • Introductory video clip presenting the subject matter with or without commentary
Explaining the Topic: • Organising information • Developing concepts and understanding • Analysing the topic with reference to the guiding question	Does the topic predetermine a certain structure (e.g. comparison or process)? Are there different perspectives that structure the topic (e.g. workers vs employers)? What have different scientists/ politicians/interest groups written or said about the topic? What facts and processes need to be presented and explained? How reliable are the sources? Is their use limited by copyright?	First, we are going to look at … Second, … Third, … We need to take the following perspectives into account … Let's have a look at the different factors/people/stakeholders involved … On the one hand … On the other hand … What were the causes for this development? Why did X happen? How can we explain X? Like a …	• Structuring in chapters • Demonstrating an experiment • Presenting primary sources (e.g. contemporary cartoons) • Narrating a process • Giving explanations: sequential, factorial … • Articulating perspectives (dialogue, interview, recorded speeches) • Analysing along categories (e.g. efficiency) and criteria (e.g. costs and benefits)

Table 8.4 (cont.)

Genre Moves	Considerations	Language Help	Options
		If we want to have a look at (the efficiency of . . .) we need to take the (costs and benefits) into account.	• Using rhetorical means (rhetorical questions, metaphors, antithesis, etc.)
		Judging in hindsight	• Using video effects (screenplay clips, flashback/flash forward, freeze-frame, fade in, fade out, split screen)
		From today's point of view . . .	
		The contemporary perspective . . .	
Concluding the Topic:	How can the answers to the guiding question be summarised?	Back to our guiding question: . . .	• Reference to guiding question
• Providing an overview	Which aspects are most relevant? Why?	What are our most important results?	• Visualisation of key points, hierarchy of key points, mind map
• Providing judgement or conclusions	Are the results in accordance with the earlier analysis?	The major reason for . . . was . . .	• Summarising conclusions
• Providing an outlook	If judgement is involved, what are the categories and criteria for the judgement?	The more/less . . ., the more/less	• Judging along categories (e.g. efficiency) and criteria (e.g. costs and benefits)
	What questions remain to be investigated at a later date?	In a nutshell, ...	• Outlook to further questions to be investigated
		Judging (the efficiency of . . .) one has to say that (the costs exceed the benefits of) . . .	
		It would be interesting to know more about	
		In our next tutorial we will . . .	

Table 8.5 Developing a storyboard

	Introducing the Topic	Explaining the Topic	Concluding the Topic
Image/Video	Lead in with title '...', name of the series and the authors Example: *History before Noon* by 11b	Introducing structure (e.g. via mind map, bullet points, collage of historic pictures representing elements of the topic)	Showing introductory structure again (mind map, bullet points, collage of historic pictures representing elements of the topic) and the guiding question
Length	5 seconds	15 seconds	60 seconds
Spoken Text/Music	Music playing, then fading out	'What aspects are relevant to ...?' 'What elements have to be considered to investigate ...?'	'How can we answer the question ...?' 'Let's summarise ...'
	Narrator greets the audience and introduces the topic (e.g. with the help of a historical picture in the background), giving basic information and formulating the guiding question.		
	60 seconds		
	'Hello and welcome to a new episode of our series *History before Noon*. Today we will introduce you to the time of ..., when .... Now, the question is ...'		

Language Frame 'Historical Evaluation'

Table 8.6 Language frame: 'Historical Evaluation'

Genre Moves	Considerations	Stylistic Advice	Useful Phrases
Contextualisation	• Introduce the guiding question by explaining the historical context	• Focus only on necessary general information, no details	• In 1871 … • In the process of … • … faced the problem of … • The question of … is important because …
Development of Evaluation Criteria	• Focus on key terms of the guiding question (e.g. 'national unity') • Subdivide categories, like 'national unity', into characteristics or criteria that you can examine (e.g. shared common values, acceptance of economic disparities, integration of minorities, identification with the political system) • Alternatively, distinguish between different aspects (e.g. social, political or economic unity)	• Write an introduction that explains the question with reference to the historical context	• In order to be able to answer the question of … (e.g. national unity), one has to examine the following characteristics of …/criteria … • Distinguishing … • In the following text, the question of … will be discussed • First of all, … has to be defined: … • In order to assess whether …, the following aspects need to be investigated: … • Evaluation criteria can be derived/ deducted from … • With regard to political, economic and social aspects, … can be examined
Criteria-Oriented Argumentation	• Find historical evidence that can be related to the criteria outlined in the introduction	• Name the criteria and then provide the historical evidence in favour or against	• Concerning the question of … (criterion), the following historical structures/ events/aspects are relevant … • One also has to take into account how … (historical evidence) • This … (historical evidence) can be taken as an indication that … (characteristic) indeed …

| Historical Judgement | • Weigh the arguments with reference to the criteria according to their significance for your judgement
• Make a reasoned judgement

• Refer back to the guiding question and the arguments and criteria you find most relevant
• Use careful language expressing degrees of factuality | • This … (criterion) can be substantiated by looking at … (historical evidence)
• A counter-argument could be the existence of … (historical evidence)
• The fact that … (historical evidence) speaks against/in favour of …(criterion)
• Regarding political/social/economic aspects, …
Assessing the question of …/the criterion of …
Focusing/putting special emphasis on … (criterion), one can come to the conclusion that …
In my opinion, … (criterion) has a special relevance because …
All in all, the question of … can be answered by …
• In hindsight, it seems that …
• In conclusion, one could say that … |

Assessment grid 'Historical Evaluation'

Table 8.7 Assessment grid: 'Historical Evaluation'

Assessment Grid 'Historical Evaluation'

	Wonderful!	Well done :)	OK, but …	Not quite there yet …
Contextualisation	The historical context of the guiding question is precisely explained.	The historical context of the guiding question is appropriately explained.	The historical context of the guiding question is explained comprehensibly with few factual mistakes.	There is little or no reference to the historical context and/or the reference to the historical context is incorrect.
Development of Evaluation Criteria	Evaluation criteria derived from the key term(s) of the guiding question are stringent and complete.	Evaluation criteria derived from the key term(s) of the guiding question are appropriate and nearly complete.	Evaluation criteria derived from the key term(s) of the guiding question are comprehensible but incomplete.	No or only incomprehensible evaluation criteria are derived from the key term(s) of the guiding question.
Criteria-Oriented Argumentation	The evaluation process includes accurate and comprehensive facts and subject-specific language. The evaluation is developed coherently by checking the criteria on the basis of historical arguments.	The evaluation process includes appropriate facts and subject-specific language. The evaluation is developed in a mostly coherent way by checking the criteria on the basis of historical arguments.	The evaluation process includes some appropriate facts and subject-specific language. The evaluation is developed in a partly coherent way by checking the criteria on the basis of historical arguments.	The evaluation process includes little or no appropriate facts and subject-specific language and/or the evaluation is developed incoherently and/or lacks criteria orientation.
Historical Judgement	The judgement is made by comprehensively weighing the significance of the historical arguments and the criteria. There is a precise distinction between factual judgements and value judgements.	The judgement is made by aptly weighing the significance of the historical arguments and/ or the criteria. There is a clear distinction between factual judgements and value judgements.	The judgement is made by weighing the significance of the historical arguments. There is some distinction between factual judgements and value judgements.	The judgement is made without weighing the significance of the historical arguments and/or there is little or no distinction between factual judgements and value judgements.

REFERENCES

Downey, M. T., & Long, K. A. (2016). *Teaching for Historical Literacy: Building Knowledge in the History Classroom*. Routledge/Taylor & Francis Group.

Fischer, D. H. (1970). *Historians' Fallacies: Toward a Logic of Historical Thought*. Harper Perennial.

Kayser, J., & Hagemann, U. (2010). *Urteilsbildung im Geschichts- und Politikunterricht (eine Publikation von Cultus e. V. - Bildung - Urteil - Kompetenz, Berlin)*. Schneider.

Ministerium für Kultus, Jugend und Sport Baden-Württemberg (Ed.). (2004). *Bildungsplan 2004 – Allgemein bildendes Gymnasium*.

Rodrigo, M. (1994). Promoting Narrative Literacy and Historical Literacy. In M. Carrettero & J. F. Voss (Eds.), *Cognitive and Instructional Processes in History and Social Sciences*. Lawrence Erlbaum Associates.

Walsh, W. H. (1960). *Philosophy of History: An Introduction*. Hutchinson.

Political Science: Exploring Pluriliteracies through a Deeper Learning Episode on Electronic Waste

SUSANNE STASCHEN–DIELMANN & SASKIA HELM

9.1 Inquiry and Literacy in Political Studies

Political knowledge evolves from evidence-based investigation of power structures, political interests and decision-making in societies. Therefore, political science is a problem-solving discipline that involves questioning, investigating, understanding and interpreting political developments and events. Inquiry into political science aims at revealing the relationships underlying political events and conditions while also constructing general principles about the way the world of politics works. In order to build and refine precise and persuasive theories about these relationships and general principles, it is important for the written work of political scientists to be conceptually precise and well substantiated by empirical evidence (The Writing Center, University of North Carolina at Chapel Hill, n.d.). Though this may be true, the term *political literacy* is often used to describe the goal of political education in schools, such as citizen competence or preparing citizens for democracy, with little reference to the importance of discipline-specific language (Westholm, Lindquist & Niemi, 1990). For example, Denver and Hands (1990) define political literacy as 'the knowledge and understanding of the political process and political issues which enables people to perform their roles as citizens effectively' (p. 263). That being said, for political participation to be successful, effective communication and appropriate languaging is undoubtedly essential.

One essential aspect of political literacy is understanding political vocabulary, which can be understood both in a broad and narrow sense. Looking at it more broadly, political vocabulary can be considered anything talked about in political discussions. Words such as climate, vaccination or taxation are politically relevant because the issues they refer to are the subject of controversial disputes in public communication. Thus, political vocabulary is littered with many words from our everyday life and various professional fields due to the all-encompassing nature of politics. Many words that are not 'political' in the strict sense of the word are, therefore, semantically charged in certain contexts and then receive an additional meaning in the political sphere (Grinth, 2010). This additional political use of language must be distinguished from political vocabulary in the narrower sense, which can be divided into four groups: vocabulary referring to political institutions (e.g. 'constitution'), vocabulary referring to particular policy areas (e.g. 'trade agreement'), vocabulary for political interaction (e.g. 'declaration of solidarity') and vocabulary referring to ideology (e.g. 'conservatism') (Grinth, 2010). Additionally, within this vocabulary are subject-relevant collocations, which include expressions such as 'to amend a resolution' or 'to draft a proposal'. More general than the technical terms, these subject-specific phrases can help the learners to language political texts in an authentic and appropriate way.

In addition to the importance of language, it is also important that political scientists understand the key concepts on which the discipline is built. This includes basic concepts like power (*Who can exercise it?*), laws (*How do they come about and do they provide justice?*), common good (*What is good for the community?*), system (*What characterises coexistence in modern societies?*), public life/policy (*What is the difference between human activity in public and private life?*) and scarcity (*How should the handling of scarce goods be politically regulated?*) (Sander, 2009). These concepts and their sub-concepts provide a basis for the construction of knowledge in politics and are the main instruments of meaning-making – that is, understanding and being understood in political discourse.

Progress in meaning-making in political science entails an increase in competence in the activity domains of *doing, organising, explaining* and *arguing* politics, which can be observed in students' presentation of political information and the quality of their production of political text types. Therefore, meaning-making in political science can be enhanced by enlarging the students' repertoire of general academic language structures as well as specific political language functions and their command of the genre conventions of political text types. Essentially, the more precisely the students can follow the specific genre conventions of political text types and make use of specific cognitive discourse functions, the more precise the meaning-making that can take place in the course of a political investigation.

Table 9.1 shows the way in which tasks in political science and the activity domains are related to cognitive discourse functions (CDFs) and student products that are typical in political communication.

9.2   Deeper Learning in Political Science

Deeper understanding in political science means that political measures, events, structures and processes can be described, analysed and assessed in accordance with the scientific standards of the subject. Therefore, the learners need patterns of inquiry and representation that can scaffold political thinking and communication.

Table 9.1 Activity domains, language functions and student products in political science

Activity Domains in Political Science	Sample Activities in Political Science	Cognitive Discourse Functions and Learner Progression in Political Science (How these CDFs might be languaged by learners at different stages)	Complex Student Products in Political Science
Doing Political Research: CDFs • **Investigate, research, find, select** • **Report** (inform, recount, present, summarise, relate)	Collecting political data from a variety of primary and secondary sources Selecting relevant political data with respect to the guiding question Presenting research results	Novice: 'We asked people in the street to say what they think about a longer school day. 70% thought that this was a good idea.' Expert: 'We used a sample size of 100 people and found that 70% of our respondents were in favour of a longer school day.'	**Preliminary:** • Chronology • Statistics • Maps • Lists • Bibliography • Structured notes • Mind maps • Concept maps • Document archives **Oral:** • Presentations • Discussions • Political debates • Talk shows • Role plays • Simulations **Written:** • Political analysis and/or comparison of texts, cartoons, pictures, posters, maps, charts, statistics, tables • Policy cycle analysis • Conflict analysis • Political scenario • Political evaluation • Political argumentation • Political expert opinion
Organising Political Data: CDFs • **Describe** (describe, label, identify, name) • **Classify** (classify, compare, contrast, match, structure, categorise, subsume)	Organising the political data chronologically or thematically Describing or summarising a political event, structure or process orally or in writing	Novice: 'In the 1970s and 1980s, people were unsure about making the school day longer. It caused many people to ask themselves questions about the role of the government and the role of parents, especially the role of mothers.' Expert: 'In the 1970s and 1980s, the political decision of establishing longer school days also raised questions about the proper role of the state, parenting and the value of paid employment for women.'	
Explaining Politics: CDFs • **Explain** (explain, reason, express, draw conclusions, deduce) • **Define** (define, identify, characterise, compare, contrast)	Explaining aspects of power in political measures, events, structures or processes Explaining the legal framework of political measures, events, structures and processes Explaining the **common good** of people, groups or societies involved in political measures, events, structures or processes	Novice: 'Some people still think that women should stay at home and do household work but men can have a job and earn money.' Expert: 'Female employment is still strongly determined by socio-economic constraints and pressure to conform to traditional gender roles.'	

- Newspaper article or comment on political phenomenon
  - Comic

Digital:
- Documentary
- Animation
- Radio show or feature
- Instructional video
- Blog/vlog

Explaining the political system that shapes political measures, events, structures or processes

Explaining the role of public life/policy in political measures, events, structures or processes

Explaining aspects of distribution and scarcity in political measures, events, structures or processes

Exploring the validity of a theory about a political measure, event, structure or process

Evaluating the legitimacy of political measures, events, structures or processes

Evaluating the efficiency of political measures, events, structures or processes

Novice:
'Longer school days should (shouldn't) be established because a lot of people (don't) want this.'

Expert:
'Longer school days would/would not be a legitimate solution to the persistent gender gap in the labour force because a majority/only a minority of mothers would be more able and willing to enter the labour force knowing that they had reliable and educational childcare while they were working.'

Arguing Politics:
CDFs
- Explore (explore, hypothesise, speculate, predict, guess, estimate, simulate, take other perspectives)
- Evaluate (evaluate, judge, argue, justify, take a stance, state, critique, recommend, comment, reflect, appreciate)

As educators, there are many things we can do to help students foster these deeper learning strategies. For example, by defining difficult words or annotating hard-to-understand passages, especially when a text is written in a learners' second language, we help learners decipher technical terms and abstract concepts and thus **deepen** their **textual understanding**. When we relate political matters to their lives and challenge them to take a stance, **content relevance can be increased**. Moreover, when we present and critically question different ideological perspectives or interests, our students' **critical cultural consciousness can be developed**. **Agency and accountability can be increased** by giving students responsibility for the accuracy of the political investigation and asking for evidence and referencing. Furthermore, we can **differentiate learning pathways** by offering optional input and output scaffolding for learners with different language backgrounds, as well as providing different assignments within the overall learning task. **Deep practice can be offered** by practising recurring genre conventions (e.g. policy cycle or conflict analysis based on a variety of sources and with reference to different political contexts). By providing language and method frames for text production on different levels, we can **scaffold students' learning** and provide level-appropriate guidance.

9.3   A Model Deeper Learning Episode in Political Science: Online Model United Nations Debating the Question of 'Reducing the Harmful Impact of Informal E-Waste Recycling' (Year 10)

The main objective of the following deeper learning episode (DLE) in political science is developing a deep understanding of the way in which political problems can be solved multilaterally by simulating the formal and informal problem-solving procedures of the United Nations. This includes learning about the social and linguistic conventions of the diplomatic process, with a special focus on diplomatic language in oral formats, such as opening speeches, negotiations during the lobbying process and debates in committee sessions, as well as written genres, such as amendments and resolutions.

The concept of a *Model United Nations* (MUN) is not new, seeing as simulations of the United Nations have been practised since the 1950s, and prior to that, simulations of the League of Nations took place from the 1920s. Usually, a MUN is practised in a club at school or university, preparing the learners for a large-scale official conference event, such as The Hague International Model United Nations. Typically, only a few ambitious students from each club can take part in the conferences as participation is limited to a small number per school or university. Being a part of the club means travelling, having international encounters and dressing appropriately for the various MUN events.

This DLE makes use of the enormous learning opportunities that this format offers with respect to plurilateral learning. However, it brings the concept of a MUN conference to the school level and uses normal school lessons for the preparation of the conference. The conference itself then only needs one school day, in which the learners attend the conference online or live at school, dressed appropriately for the occasion. Teachers can choose to limit the participation to one grade level (e.g. all of Year 10) or even just a single class, which reduces the number of participating member states. Nevertheless, all participants are still able to benefit from the great plurilateral learning opportunities provided by such a format.

The conference will be built around making a resolution to the political problem of 'reducing the harmful impact of informal e-waste recycling'. The topic is relevant to the learners as it deals with a pressing environmental problem caused by the unsustainable way in which electronic products are used in the Western world – that is, their world. Specifically, informal e-waste recycling refers to when electronic devices are sold to scrap dealers, who improperly handle and dispose of the equipment and its parts, which leads to the release of the toxins contained within the devices.

The learning episode begins with an introduction to the concepts of MUN and informal e-waste recycling. Students then work in teams to research the different aspects of informal e-waste recycling (e.g. economic, environmental, and social). This research will serve them in the next step, where they choose a country and analyse the problem from that country's perspective. Once each student knows his/her country's stance on the matter, they individually draft a resolution on how to manage informal e-waste recycling, in which the problem and its possible solutions are laid out. In the following step, students prepare an opening speech for the General Assembly, in which they once again explain the problem and suggest possible solutions. The culmination of their research and text production (i.e. the resolution and opening speech) is the conference on the last day, in which students represent their countries as delegates, propose their solutions to the problem, and come to a final co-constructed resolution on how to handle the matter via lobbying, negotiating and debating.

The learning product (i.e. the co-constructed UN resolution) promotes creativity and problem-solving skills while also providing authenticity by giving students a realistic insight into the way multilateral political decision-making works. The DLE is structured in such a way that it leads the learners through different modes of political communication, culminating in a public debate at a MUN Conference. The public nature of the event motivates learners to properly prepare themselves for the debate, which includes the acquisition of profound knowledge on the topic and the languaging of their respective political positions. In order to be able to play their role as a UN member state authentically, the learners must acquire information on the member state they represent, its power status and its political position concerning the issue of electronic waste, analysing the environmental, economic, social and political dimensions of the problem from that state's perspective.

In Table 9.2, a grid is shown with an overview of the planning aspects guided by the principles of the pluriliteracies approach to deeper learning. Afterwards, a didactic commentary explains how this DLE is aligned with the aforementioned principles and how learners move from surface learning to consolidation and finally to the transfer stage.

9.4   Alignment of the Deeper Learning Episode

In alignment with deeper learning principles (Table 9.2), the proposed learning episode (see Table 9.3) takes into account learners' strengths, needs and interests, provides opportunities to build their political literacy and successfully implements tasks that cover all activity domains. High task fidelity in this DLE is predominately achieved by the authentic UN simulation – that is, by researching, presenting, speaking and writing like a diplomat with the task of finding and negotiating political solutions to a global problem.

Learner Strengths, Needs and Interests

To ensure the success of the learning episode, it is important to keep in mind learner strengths, needs and interests. Setting up a MUN highlights students' strengths because it lets them draw on the cultural knowledge they already have about relevant topics. This is even more the case for multicultural classrooms in which students come from different backgrounds. Such a learning episode can provide the opportunity for learners with an L1 different from the school language to research their L1 country's position on the problem and lobby for its political interest.

Though students will come to the learning episode with many strengths, there will also be knowledge gaps that need to be filled. A MUN is very structured and guided by many rules. Some students might need advance organisers, like an explanatory video to understand the concept of MUN and its rules. In a similar vein, many of the formats of MUN, such as policy cycle analyses, the opening speeches for the General Assembly, a MUN resolution, and committee debates, are highly conventionalised regarding purpose, mode, genre and style. Therefore, it would be necessary to provide learners with method and language scaffolding so they can successfully navigate these formats (see Table 9.4). Another need that may arise regards the research phase. The students are responsible for the depth of their research but might

Table 9.2 Planning grid for a deeper learning episode in political science: Model United Nations debating the question of 'Reducing the harmful impact of informal e-waste recycling' (Year 10)

Designing Deeper Learning Episodes

Planning Grid for a Deeper Learning Episode in Political Science

What do I want my learners to know or be able to do?	How will my learners demonstrate increasingly deeper understanding at the surface, consolidation and transfer levels?	How can I support active knowledge co-construction for my learners?	How will I support my learners every step of the way?	How can I generate and sustain learner commitment and achievement?
Basic Understanding: • Multilateralism: political decision-making in international organisations • Understanding of the impact of generating increasing amounts of e-waste **Foundational Skills:** • Doing international (and multilingual) research on the environmental, social, economic and political dimensions • Translating and organising the information for a policy cycle analysis in English • Explaining the impact of increasing e-waste generation while using different subject lenses • Formally arguing solutions to the problem of informal e-waste recycling	**Preliminary Product Outcomes:** • Country profile and political position • Policy cycle analysis, taking political, environmental, social and economic aspects into consideration • MUN opening speeches reflecting the member states' positions **Main Product Outcome:** Purpose: Presenting a solution to the problem of informal e-waste recycling Genre: UN resolution Mode: (Digital) text document Style: Diplomatic language **Possible Transfer:** • Translating subject-specific texts into English	**Construction of Knowledge:** (X) Inquiry-based learning (X) Problem-based learning ( ) Experimenting (X) Project-based learning **Social Interaction:** • Individual research in respective L1 • Collaborative work on the policy cycle analysis (Part I) • Individual completion of policy cycle (Part II) • Individual preparation as ambassador to the Model UN General Assembly and Economic and Social Council • Collaborative lobbying process • Plenary work in the MUN General Assembly and the Economic and Social	**Scaffolding:** • Research is scaffolded by providing starting websites • Policy cycle analysis, country profile and position paper are scaffolded by structuring worksheets • Opening speech is scaffolded by a writing frame • UN resolution is scaffolded by a writing frame **Feedback:** • Individual teacher feedback on policy cycle analysis (Part I) and draft resolution • Peer feedback on policy cycle analysis (Part II), opening speech	**Engagement:** **Personal Relevance:** • Use of the MUN conference as an engaging setting demanding contributions from all delegations • Relevance of the topic for students as owners of electronic goods (e.g. smartphones) **Opportunities for Autonomous Learning:** • Independent research on one of the dimensions of the global impact of e-waste • Individual development of solutions to the problem and evaluation of these • Formulation of a well-founded position on the problem

Table 9.2 (cont.)

Designing Deeper Learning Episodes

Deeper Understanding:
- Global dimension of consumption and waste

Deep Practice:
- Translation or mediation of L1 information into English
- Using subject-specific language
- Using formal debate code for argumentation
- Writing formal texts

Transfer:
- Subject-specific translation
- Debate code and conventions
- Global learning dimensions

- Giving a public speech
- Debating procedures
- Writing formal texts
- Analysing a political problem according to the principles of global learning or the policy cycle

Council

Use of (Digital) Media:
- Policy cycle analysis as a collaborative document, opening speeches and resolutions are presented and exchanged digitally (e.g. via Padlet)
- MUN Conference can be held onsite or digitally via Teams or Zoom.

Feed-Up:
- Structured worksheets, writing frames and assessment grids 'Opening Speech' and 'MUN Resolution'

Feed-Forward:
- Individual teacher feedback
- Peer feedback

Assessment:
- Assessment grids 'Opening Speech' and 'MUN Resolution'

- Creative writing of the opening speech and the draft resolution
- Interpretation of the member state's delegate in a formal debate

Reflection and Revision:
- Commenting and debating draft resolutions, negotiating the wording of amendments and subject-specific terminology
- Closing ceremony presenting the final resolutions and awarding the best delegation award

need help finding the right resources and mediating information from their L1 into the conference language.

In addition to addressing students' needs and strengths, this learning episode also takes into account learners' interests. Based on professional experience, learners tend to enjoy the challenge of taking on an identity that is different from their own. Diplomats have a high prestige and represent an academic and political elite that is stereotyped as being very well mannered, eloquent and well informed. Motivated by their desire to successfully and authentically portray their selected diplomat, students undergo intensive preparation of appropriate, eloquent and well-informed written and spoken communication.

Political Literacy

The language the learners use in this DLE is pluriliteral in many different ways: As mentioned in Section 9.1, political science is an all-encompassing discipline, dealing with topics from both everyday life as well as other professional disciplines. Thus, in order to prepare themselves fully for the conference, the learners need to analyse the political problem of e-waste from the perspective of a variety of different disciplines. This multi-disciplinary problem analysis confronts students with subject-specific language. For example, when researching the biological impact of the chemicals and materials involved in e-waste recycling as well as the geographical distribution and economic and social structure of e-waste trafficking, students are confronted with specialised biological terms, from which they have to pull meaning. The written explanation of the information they gather from their research will require subject-specific language, which they then have to transform into language for a political context for use at the conference. All the while, students must keep in mind the many different facets of conference language, which means making their discourse understandable enough for a lay person but still precise enough to address the details of the problem.

With regards to political language in the narrower sense, formal, legal and institutional language has to be mastered by the learners in order to successfully complete the task. This includes the language used in the resolutions and amendments and that of certain persuasive political genres, such as speeches, negotiations and debates, all of which require rhetorical skills and creativity.

In addition to language, students must be literate in the key concepts of politics. The predominating key concepts used in this episode are law and common good because the MUN conference simulates the quest for a global solution to e-waste recycling via the formulation of a legal text. However, other concepts, like power, public life/policy and scarcity, also play a key role since the international arena is marked by significant imbalances concerning power, public life/policy and/or economic strength, all of which determine how member states deal with scarcity of resources, especially those hidden in recyclable waste.

Activity Domains

This learning episode touches on each of the four activity domains. Learners are *doing* political science when they collect subject-specific data on the political, environmental, economic and social dimensions of informal e-waste recycling and research their member state's political position on the problem using a variety of resources. Then they *organise* the gathered information in the policy cycle analysis for each dimension and *explain* one of the dimensions of the informal e-waste recycling to their peers. Those dimensions reflect the political complexity of the problem with its political framework, the economic, environmental and social impact and the resulting interests involved, as per the policy cycle analysis. The formulation of a political position of the member state, the opening speech, the draft resolution and the contributions to the committee debate also integrate the activity domains of *organising* and *explaining* but predominantly represent the activity domain of *arguing*.

Growth Mindset, Deep Practice and Deep Understanding

The task drives learner commitment and achievement by demanding a research-based role play whose successful completion requires problem solving, negotiating and debating in front of an audience of peers. Throughout this challenging learning process, a growth mindset is fostered through mentorship, feedback and reflection. Students are mentored and encouraged by the teacher, who consistently models the diplomatic code and provides method and language scaffolding in the form of structured worksheets and language frames for both the text production and the debate. Additionally, feedback given at regular intervals provides students the opportunities to improve their work. Peer feedback is given on the policy cycle analysis (Part II) and the opening speech, and teacher feedback is given on the policy cycle analysis (Part I) as well as the drafts of the resolution. Lastly, student growth is fostered by reflection on the success (or lack thereof) that they achieved in their lobbying, debating and voting processes.

In addition to a growth mindset, students are able to develop a deep understanding of both political practices and the effects of informal e-waste recycling through their self-driven research on the different dimensions of consumption and waste and the multilateral approaches to the solution of such problems. They then demonstrate their understanding through the presentation of their policy cycle analyses, their opening speeches and, finally, their draft resolution.

All the while, learners are engaged in deep practice by maintaining scientific standards and diplomatic conventions. The social interaction in the informal lobbying process, the formal public debating and the voting procedure on amendments and resolutions provides a high degree of reflection on the success of the work and the individual contribution.

This way, deeper understanding can be achieved concerning the global dimension of consumption and waste and multilateral approaches to the solution of such problems.

Deep practice is offered concerning translation and mediation skills, the use of subject-specific language and the practice of formal written and oral argumentation as a form of political articulation.

9.5 Movement from Surface Learning to Consolidation to the Transfer Stage

In this DLE in-depth research, organisation of information and text production are the major vehicles for the movement from surface to deeper learning. Specifically, the political knowledge derived from the research is first rearranged in a collaborative policy cycle analysis, then used to formulate a political position in accordance with the country profile, transformed into a draft resolution and, finally, reduced to be presented in an opening speech. This process provides ample opportunity to practise organising and explaining political information in different forms of representation, in different language styles and in different modes. Approaching political knowledge from these different angles propels students from surface learning to consolidation to knowledge transfer. The most difficult move is the switch to a diplomatic language level in the draft resolution, which requires intensive teacher feedback concerning content and language. The formal language and adherence to the UN rules of procedure is even more challenging in their spontaneous use during debate and, therefore, also needs intensive scaffolding (see Worksheet 9.7 – Conference Outline) and exemplary behaviour by the mentor or student chairing the committee sessions and the General Assembly. So, learning is consolidated by moving along the mode continuum.

Engage the Learner
In order to activate the learners, the setting of a United Nations conference is introduced along with a documentary on informal e-waste recycling that impressively shows the impact on the people involved (The Documentary Channel, 2019). For secondary school students, this question has a special relevance because they are digital natives, used to smartphones and computers that they frequently exchange for newer versions.

Promote/Acquire Basic Understanding and Acquisition of Foundational Skills
The learners are then acquainted with the learning task for the whole episode via a detailed handout in which the learning unit is laid out and scaffolding language

frames are given (see Section 9.7). They first collect political information on one of the dimensions of the problem, such as environmental, social or economic impacts, in order to co-construct the first part of a policy cycle analysis. Afterwards, they choose a member state of the UN they want to represent, research the profile of that country and, with the help of the second part of the policy cycle analysis, develop a well-founded political position.

Provide Feedback, Feed-Up and Feed-Forward/Demonstrate Basic Understanding and Reflect

Teacher feedback via assessment grids and comments on the language use is necessary in the early stages of the project in order to ensure the correctness and depth of the information that is passed on to peers during the first part of the policy cycle analysis. It is also necessary to ensure the political position the students have developed is authentic and coherent.

Facilitate/Acquire Deeper Understanding and Deep Practice

Deeper understanding and deep practice are provided by movement along the mode continuum (i.e. researching and organising information, writing and debating about the problem of informal e-waste recycling). The meaning-making in this process is scaffolded by genre-specific language frames and learning conversations on the basis of feedback criteria. In addition to feedback, expectations concerning the use of methods and language are made transparent via assessment grids and a detailed task prompt (see Tables 9.5, 9.6 and 9.7). This enables the learners to language their learning process and deliberately modify their language level.

Provide Feedback, Feed-Up and Feed-Forward/Demonstrate Basic Understanding and Reflect

The third opportunity for teacher feedback concerns the draft resolution and is important to ensure its authenticity as well as correctness in form and content. One of the most difficult movements in this learning episode is the switch to a diplomatic language level in the draft resolution, which requires intensive teacher feedback concerning content and language. If language problems are confronted in these feedback sessions, the delegates do not have to argue about mistakes in resolutions or amendments during the debate but can rather work on the formulation of a consensus while co-constructing a joint resolution.

Additionally, students receive peer feedback on their opening speeches. This feedback is backed by an assessment grid that gives clear quality criteria and, therefore, also offers opportunities for self-reflection and serves as a feed-forward.

Facilitate Transfer/Transfer Knowledge

By collecting information about the political, economic, environmental and social dimension of the problem, learners become aware of the global dimension of their consumption habits, which is transferable to other global environmental issues. They also acquire transferable tools for working on global problems: translation and mediation skills, political analysis tools and the linguistic means to articulate a political position publicly and in a formal context. Moreover, the learners acquire transferable knowledge concerning the procedures of the multilateral process in international organisations and might be able to develop an understanding of the complexity of democratic decision-making on an international level.

Mentor Reflection/Present and Reflect

Apart from the individual feedback that is given by the mentor, refection is mainly triggered by the obligation to perform in front of an audience in the committee sessions. Such a challenge creates an opportunity for self-awareness and can make students more open to direct feedback they might receive during the debate and voting procedures. Additionally, they will be assessed by their peers, especially with regard to the consistency of the political position and their conduct as delegates, which provides another opportunity for reflection. An option would also be to set up a press team that comments on the debate in a conference newsletter. Such journalistic feedback could enhance the reflection process.

9.6   Conclusion and Outlook

Pluriliteracies teaching for deeper learning makes sense for political science teachers who want to make full use of language as a driving force for learning political science. By focusing on the language use in different modes and text types, the students can cultivate a subject-specific language repertoire while also acquiring the political facts, concepts, procedures and strategies they need to produce appropriate political communication. By giving and receiving criteria-oriented feedback on various political text types, the learners are empowered to language their learning process as well as their political communication and thus experience deep political learning.

Digital learning environments can facilitate the setting up of complex learning task, such as a MUN conference, and help to save time, paper and organisational work, which might put off teachers from entertaining such formats. To make use of them can prove very rewarding in terms of achieving the main goal of political education, which is for the learners to become politically literate and empower themselves as citizens.

9.7   Learning Materials

WORKSHEET 9.1 Online Model United Nations Debating the Question of 'Reducing the Harmful Impact of Informal E-Waste Recycling'

Imagine you are a diplomat working at United Nations in New York. With your delegation, you represent a member state or a non-governmental organisation (NGO) and have been assigned to the Economic and Social Council, a sub-committee to the UN General Assembly that deals with environmental problems that need to be solved on a global level.

One of those problems is the question of reducing the harmful impact of informal recycling of electronic waste, which has economic, environmental (i.e. geographical, biological and chemical) and political dimensions.

In order to integrate all those dimensions and develop a well-founded political position based on thorough research, you will divide up the research of those three dimensions in your delegation and then inform your colleagues about your findings.

Tasks

1. Please work in **groups of four** and do research for the first part of a policy cycle analysis, dividing up the work so that **each member of the group does research on one of the following dimensions** of the problem of informal e-waste recycling. Add your research results to the respective section of the collaborative worksheet 'Policy Cycle', then explain your research results to your group and answer questions.

   - **Political Framework (legal and institutional aspects):** In what way does informal e-waste recycling reflect global and domestic imbalances of power? What measures has the international community, especially the United Nations, taken to tackle the problem?
   - **Economic interests:** What is the economic value of e-waste, and what impact does that have on the distribution of wealth? What economic

interest groups are involved, what are their interests, and in what way do they articulate those interests?

- **Environmental interests:** In what countries does informal e-waste recycling take place, and which countries benefit? What chemicals can be recycled, and what dangers do they pose to the environment if they are not recycled appropriately? What are the effects of informal e-waste recycling on humans involved in the process, especially children?
- **Social Interests:** What is the situation of families who earn their living with informal e-waste recycling? What kind of social policy could the countries with a large informal e-waste recycling sector implement to improve this situation?

You can start with the following websites. Please also include information from non-English websites if possible.

- https://ourworld.unu.edu/en/informal-recycling-of-e-waste-a-serious-problem-expert-says (10.7.2021)
- https://www.unep.org/news-and-stories/press-release/un-report-time-seize-opportunity-tackle-challenge-e-waste (10.7.2021)
- http://www3.weforum.org/docs/WEF_A_New_Circular_Vision_for_Electronics.pdf (11.7.2021)
- https://www.researchgate.net/publication/223018238_Key_drivers_of_the_e-waste_recycling_system_Assessing_and_modelling_e-waste_processing_in_the_informal_sector_in_Delhi/link/5bfd02d3458515b41d108848/download (10.7.2021)
- https://www.sciencedirect.com/science/article/pii/S2214999614003208 (10.7.2021)
- https://www.itu.int/en/ITU-D/Environment/Pages/Spotlight/Global-Ewaste-Monitor-2020.aspx (10.7.2021)

As homework, read through your teacher's feedback and improve your group's collaborative document.

2. As an individual, **choose one of the following UN member states**, which you will represent as national ambassador in the MUN General Assembly and in the Economic and Social Council, by adding your name and member state to the collaborative document 'Delegations'. **You may also represent a country of your choice and do research in the language of your choice**, but each member state can only be represented by one ambassador.

3. Use the worksheet 'Country Profile and Position' and the following link https://imuna.org/resources/country-profiles/ to do research on the member state you represent and the political position it might have on the question of informal e-waste recycling.

Countries Sending E-Waste	Countries Receiving E-Waste	Countries with Little or No E-Waste Export or Import	NGOs
USA	Nigeria	Russian Federation	UNEP (United
Canada	Mexico	North Korea	Nations
Federal Republic	Brazil	Iran	Environment
of Germany	Senegal	Chile	Programme)
France	Ivory Coast	South Africa	Greenpeace
UK	Benin	Nepal	CTA (Consumer
Norway	Ghana	Uganda	Electronics
Italy	Egypt	Ethiopia	Association)
Denmark	India	Afghanistan	
Japan	People's Republic of	Niger	
South Korea	China		
Australia	Thailand		
	Vietnam		

Based on: World Economic Forum (2019)

Please download a copy of the revised collaborative document 'Policy Cycle Analysis' and complete it from the perspective of the member state you represent. Answer the following questions.

- **Possible solutions**: What political measures appear feasible for the future? How could formal e-waste recycling be economically stimulated in your member state? What is your member state prepared to do concerning the prevention of the negative environmental and social impact of informal e-waste recycling?
- **Efficiency of the solution:** What are the costs of the solution? What are its benefits? Do the benefits outweigh the costs?
- **Legitimacy:** Is the solution in accordance with the Charter of the United Nations and previous UN resolutions? Is the solution likely to be approved by a majority of the Economic and Social Council or the General Assembly?

4. With the help of the respective writing frame, draft a UN resolution from the perspective of the Economic and Social Council that is in accordance with your member state's political position.

5. With the help of the respective writing frame, write a one-minute opening speech for the General Assembly that introduces your political position on the question of informal e-waste recycling as persuasively as possible. Exchange your opening speech with a partner and give feedback with the help of the 'Assessment Grid: MUN Opening Speech'. Revise your own opening speech according to your partner's feedback.

Lesson Plan

Table 9.3 Lesson plan

Lessons and Feedback (90 minutes twice a week)	Tasks	Time
1st lesson	Introduction of MUN and the problem of informal e-waste recycling	90 minutes
2nd lesson	Task 1:Individual research and entry in collaborative document	90 minutes
Teacher feedback on collaborative document 'Policy Cycle'	Task 1: Revision of the collaborative document	Homework
3rd lesson	Task 2: Research on country profile and political position	90 minutes
Teacher feedback on country profile and political position	Task 2: Revision of country profile and political position	Homework
4th lesson	Task 2: Completing the policy cycle analysis from country's perspective, including peer feedback and revision	90 minutes
5th lesson	Task 3: Drafting of MUN resolution	90 minutes
6th lesson	Task 3: Drafting of MUN resolution	30 minutes
	Task 4: Writing opening speeches, including peer feedback and revision	60 minutes
Teacher feedback on UN resolution	Task 4: Revision and publication of MUN resolution via Padlet Informal lobbying via Padlet	Homework
Full school day (9 am to 4 pm)	MUN conference with opening ceremony, committee sessions and closing ceremony	420 minutes (including breaks)

WORKSHEET 9.2 Country Profile

Country Profile:

Your country's official name:

The region your country is located in:

Physical features and climate:

Ethnic composition:

Official language and other languages:

Country's capital and other major cities:

(*cont.*)

Quality of life for an average person:

Date of foundation of the country:

Type of government:

Natural resources:

Major imports and exports:

Biggest trading partners:

WORKSHEET 9.3 Political Position on the Question of Informal E-Waste Recycling

Political Position on the Question of Informal E-Waste Recycling:

_____
_____
_____
_____
_____
_____
_____
_____
_____
_____
_____
_____
_____
_____
_____
_____
_____
_____
_____
_____
_____
_____
_____
_____
_____
_____
_____
_____

WORKSHEET 9.4 Policy Cycle Analysis

Policy Cycle Analysis

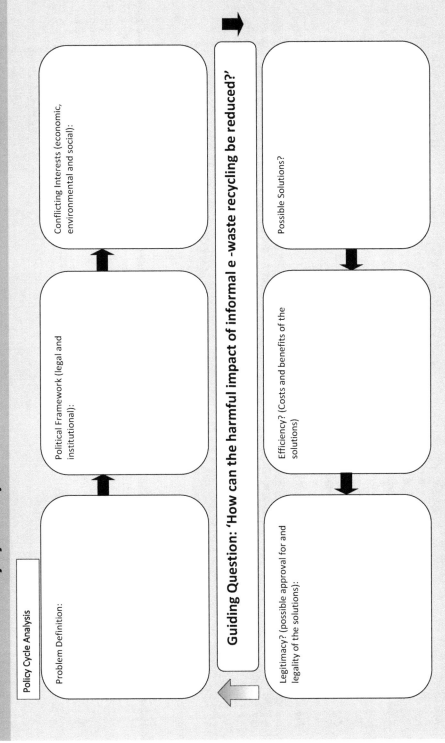

Problem Definition:

Political Framework (legal and institutional):

Conflicting Interests (economic, environmental and social):

Guiding Question: 'How can the harmful impact of informal e-waste recycling be reduced?'

Legitimacy? (possible approval for and legality of the solutions):

Efficiency? (Costs and benefits of the solutions)

Possible Solutions?

Writing Frame: Opening Speech (max. 1 minute)

Table 9.4 Writing frame: Opening speech (max. 1 minute)

Parts	How to Proceed	Useful Phrases	Example Opening Speech
Address	First, you address the chairperson of the committee and the delegations of the other member states. In formal debate you speak of yourself and others only in the third person. The tradition is also to refer to others exclusively as 'the Distinguished Representative of (member state)'. To omit the word 'Distinguished' would be a significant faux pas and possibly a deliberate slight.	Honourable Mr/Madam Chairman, Honourable/Distinguished Delegates of the . . . (committee)	Honourable Madam Chairman, Distinguished Delegates of the Social Council, . . .
Hook	The opening speech should go straight to the point. The hook tells the listener what clash, problem or conflict you want to focus on. This part shouldn't take more than ten seconds.	. . . once said: ' . . . ' Following this quotation . . . . . . million people in . . . are . . . It is a fact that . . .; however, ... (member state) is here today, in another United Nations conference, to discuss . . . The latest statistics issued by . . . on . . . say that . . . Do we really want . . .? Is it inevitable that . . .?	Do we really want to deny Syrian refugees who have spent over three years in refugee camps the right to work?
Point	Then you should explain your main point and why your approach to the problem is the correct one.	The delegation of . . . (member state) would like to . . ./thinks that . . . It is essential to . . . . . . (member state) suggests that/wants to contribute to . . . It is not acceptable that . . . This is an outrage!	Germany thinks that work visas could be an essential tool to mitigate the most severe effects of the refugee crisis brought about by ongoing war in Syria. It is not acceptable that those who had to flee from war and destruction are not allowed to use their skills and talents to feed their families and to contribute to the welfare of their host countries.

Action	You should describe your policy/solution halfway through your speech at the latest. This is because you need time to elaborate on your solution. No idea is clear in one sentence. You will need time to explain why it is important and why it is going to work.	The UN should … This is why the UN is called upon to … Nonetheless, a resolution is necessary to do nothing more and nothing less than to … … (member state) is in favour of/supports a resolution that will, finally, request …	The UN should support this by asking the member states hosting Syrian refugees to issue work permits to those who have spent more than one year in a refugee camp. Germany is aware of the fact that large numbers of refugees can be difficult to integrate into the labour market, but the state is optimistic that it is possible by providing accompanying measures.
Final Words	You could end with an appeal to the committee expressing your hopes for a successful outcome of the following negotiations. Don't forget to thank the audience for listening to you.	… (member state) hopes that … will make this conference fruitful and productive Thank you for your attention!	Germany hopes that the Economic and Social Council will be able to have a fruitful debate on this issue and come to solutions that can really improve the lives of the Syrian refugees. Thank you for your attention!

Table 9.5 Assessment grid: Opening speech

Assessment Grid: Opening Speech

	Excellent!	Well Done!	Improvement Possible	Improvement Necessary
Address	You welcome the chairman of General Assembly and the delegates of other member states in perfect form and in accordance with diplomatic conventions. You always speak of yourself and others in the third person.	You welcome the chairman of General Assembly and the delegates of other member states appropriately and in accordance with diplomatic conventions. Most of the time you speak of yourself and others in the third person.	You welcome the chairman of General Assembly and the delegates of other member states. Occasionally you speak of yourself and others in the third person.	You forget to welcome the chairman of General Assembly and the delegates of other member states. You never speak of yourself and others in the third person.
Thematic Anchor	Your opening speech gets to the point very quickly but precisely. The thematic anchor focuses the listener clearly on the problem or conflict.	Your opening speech gets to the point quickly. The thematic anchor focuses the listener on the problem or conflict.	Your opening speech takes a comprehensible direction. The thematic anchor does not necessarily focus the listener on the problem or conflict.	Your opening speech appears long-winded. The thematic anchor hardly focuses the listener on the problem or conflict.
Explanation of the Problem	You accurately address the main aspect of the problem concerned and explain clearly why the proposed approach is the right one.	You address the main aspect of the problem concerned and explain why there is a problem.	You address the problem concerned and explain roughly why there is a problem.	You don't address the problem concerned and/or there is no comprehensible explanation of the problem.
Demand for Action	After about half of the speaking time, you present the policy or the solution to the problem and convincingly explain why the solution could be promising.	After about half of the speaking time, you present the policy or the solution to the problem and comprehensibly explain why the solution could be promising.	After about half of the speaking time, you present a rough sketch of a solution to the problem and roughly explain why the solution could be promising.	You don't present a comprehensible solution to the problem and/or explain why the solution could be promising.
Closing Remarks	You end the speech confidently with a clear conclusion and politely thank the audience.	You end the speech with a conclusion and thank the audience.	You end the speech with a conclusion or by thanking the audience.	You end the speech without a conclusion or thanking the audience.

WORKSHEET 9.5 How to Write a UN Resolution

How to Write a UN Resolution (Created Using: **https://bestdelegate.com**)

A resolution has three main parts: the **heading**, the **pre-ambulatory clauses** and the **operative clauses**.

Table 9.6 How to write a UN resolution

Parts	What is the Purpose of the Part and What Needs to be Included?	Examples and Useful Phrases
1. Heading	There are four main pieces of information in the header of the resolution. **Committee:** The name of the committee you're representing **Topic:** The name of the topic you're debating **Sponsors:** The main authors that wrote the clauses of the resolution **Signatories:** The delegates that would like to see this resolution introduced in the committee. They don't necessarily support the resolution but want it to have the requisite number of signatories so it can be accepted by the Chair (usually about 20% of the committee is required)	Committee: Security Council Topic: The Use of Unmanned Aerial Vehicles (UAVs) Sponsors: Argentina, Ethiopia, Germany, Kazakhstan Signatories: Poland, Somalia, South Africa, Sudan, etc.
2. Pre-Ambulatory Clauses	The pre-ambulatory clauses state all the issues that the committee wants to resolve on this issue. It may state reasons why the committee is working on this issue and highlight previous international actions on the issue. Pre-ambulatory clauses can include: • Past UN resolutions, treaties, or conventions related to the topic • Past regional, non-governmental, or national efforts in resolving this topic • References to the UN Charter or other international frameworks and laws • Statements made by the Secretary-General or a relevant UN body or agency	The Security Council, recalling its resolution A/ RES/68/178, which sought to limit the use of UAVs in combatting terrorism without the express permission of Member States, ... Concerned by the recent high rate of civilian casualties in the rate of armed UAV strikes, ... Pre-Ambulatory Phrases: Acknowledging Affirming Alarmed by Guided by Having considered Mindful of Noting Reaffirming

Table 9.6 *(cont.)*

Parts	What is the Purpose of the Part and What Needs to be Included?	Examples and Useful Phrases	

	• General background information or facts about the topic, its significance and its impact
	
	First, take a statement that you want to write about (perhaps an issue you want to solve or a specific fact from one of the five bullet points above). You then take that statement, combine it with an <u>underlined pre-ambulatory phrase</u>, and end it with a comma.
		Bearing in mind
		Deploring
		Emphasising
		Expressing concern
		Expressing its
		  appreciation
		Fully aware
			Recalling
			Recognising
			Regretting
			Taking into
			  consideration

3. Operative Clauses	Operative paragraphs determine what action the UN will take on the issue. This can mean funding solutions, directing members of the UN Secretariat what to do, or requesting actions by UN Member States. Each paragraph takes action, so it is important to be careful with each of the operative paragraphs in a resolution!
	
	First, take a solution that you want to include in the draft resolution. You then take that solution, combine it with an underlined *operative phrase in italics*, and end it with a semicolon (the last operative clause ends with a period). Operative clauses are also numbered. This differentiates them from pre-ambulatory clauses, helps show logical progression in the resolution, and makes the operative clauses easy to refer to in speeches and comments.
		1. *Encourages* countries to adopt a UN High Commissioner for Refugees (UNHCR) and UN Office for Disarmament Affairs (UNODA)-orchestrated 2014 Covenant on Extrajudicial Drone Strikes that:
		  a. Treats extrajudicial targeted assassination outside declared conflict zones as violations of the 1966 Covenant on Civil and Political Rights,
		  b. Reaffirms the rights of nations to develop drones, especially for nonviolent purposes,
		  c. Acknowledges that drone use in self-defence and inside declared war zones is acceptable in accordance with existing international law;
		
		2. *Strongly encourages* the use of drones in peaceful and primarily civilian affairs within each nation for instances of agricultural progress, surveillance, monitoring natural disasters and the environment; (…)
		
		Operative Phrases: Insists that
		Acknowledges Instructs
		Adopts Invites	

Affirms

Approves

Authorises

Believes that

Calls attention to

Calls upon member states

Condemns

Confirms

Decides

Demands

Determines that

Emphasises

Endorses the Declaration

Establishes

Expresses its appreciation

Expresses its concern

Notes that

Demands

Determines that

Realises

Recalls

Recognises

Recommends

Reminds

Requests

Resolves

Suggests that

Supports

Takes note

Urges

Welcomes

Table 9.7 Assessment grid: UN resolution

Assessment Grid: UN Resolution

	Excellent!	Well done!	Improvement Possible	Improvement Necessary
Resolution Head	In the resolution head you can find the committee, the topic, the authors and the signatories in the correct order.	In the resolution head you can find the committee, the topic, the authors and the signatories, but not in the correct order.	In the resolution head some information is missing.	There is no resolution head, or a considerable part of the information is missing.
Pre-Ambulatory Clauses	The pre-ambulatory clauses provide a precise and detailed explanation of the background of the problem in question, its history and possible references to previous resolutions or documents on the topic.	The pre-ambulatory clauses provide an explanation of the background of the problem in question, its history and possible references to previous resolutions or documents on the topic.	The pre-ambulatory clauses provide a superficial explanation of the background of the problem in question, its history and possible references to previous resolutions or documents on the topic.	The pre-ambulatory clauses neither provide an explanation of the background of the problem in question nor possible references to previous resolutions or documents on the topic.
Operative Clauses	The operative clauses formulate precise and detailed proposals for solutions and/or statements. Demands, appeals and/or guidelines take into account the complexity of the situation. The sentences are arranged in a hierarchy.	The operative clauses formulate proposals for solutions and/or statements. Demands, appeals and/or guidelines take into account the complexity of the situation to some extent. The sentences are arranged in a hierarchy.	The operative clauses formulate superficial proposals for solutions and/ or statements. Demands, appeals and/or guidelines don't sufficiently take into account the complexity of the situation. The sentences are not clearly arranged in a hierarchy.	The operative clauses don't formulate precise and detailed proposals for solutions and/or statements. Demands, appeals and/or guidelines don't take into account the complexity of the situation. The sentences are not arranged in a hierarchy.
Formal Aspects	The formal requirements are precisely met.	The formal requirements are generally met.	The formal requirements are partially met.	The formal requirements are not met.

WORKSHEET 9.6 How to Express Yourself as a Delegate

How to Express Yourself as a Delegate?

The delegate of (member state) ...
The delegation of (member state) ...

✓ Proposing something:
  - proposes/suggests something
  - hopes for/put forward
  - likes to table
  - likes to achieve
  - recommends that ...
  - encourages the committee to ...
  - would like to state/establish
  - calls upon this meeting to ...
✓ Speaking in favour of something:
  - supports
  - affirms
  - approves
  - urges
  - endorses
  - welcomes
  - recognises
  - praises
  - acknowledges
✓ Speaking aganist something:
  - would like to contradict
  - opposes to
  - must find fault with
  - needs to criticise
  - regrets

Discussion strategies:
  - The delegation of ... agress with ... on ... but wants to warn of ...
  - This committee keeps discussing ... therefore this delegation suggests to move on to ...
  - The following statistics will show the honourable delegations that ...
  - Only very few member states share the honourable delegates' position on ...
  - In its last statement the delegation of ... put forward ... Now the delegation contradicts ...
  - The delegation will not get tired of restating that ...
  - It is deplorable that the delegation of ... fails to acknowledge the fact that ...
  - It it was true that ... Consequently, ...
  - The honourable delegate of ... is comparing apples with oranges when he ...
  - We should either ... or do nothing at all ...
  - The suggestion of the honourable delegate would inevitably lead to ...
  - As Cicero said: ...
  - In former times member states could ..., nowadays, ...
  - Please allow this delegation to return to this aspect later ...

WORKSHEET 9.7 Online Conference Outline

1) **Timetable**
2) **Lobbying**
3) **Guidelines for Procedure during Committee Debate**
4) **Procedure – Chronology**
5) **Committee Procedure at a Glance**
6) **MUN Best Delegation Award**
7) **Dress and Behaviour Code**
8) **Language**
9) **How to Be the Perfect Diplomatic Delegate**
10) **Appendix**

WORKSHEET 9.8 Model United Nations Conference

1 Timetable

Model United Nations Conference

9.00–9.30 Welcome and explanation of debating rules
9.30–10.30 Opening ceremony with opening speeches
10.30–11.00 Coffee break with lobbying
11.00–12.30 Economic and Social Council in session
12.30–13.30 Lunch break
13.30–14.30 Economic and Social Council in session
14.30–14.45 Coffee break with lobbying
14.45–15.30 Economic and Social Council in session
15.30–16.00 Closing ceremony with best delegation awards

2 Lobbying

Delegates lobby both before and during the conference. First, they read all resolutions submitted to the General Secretariat (teachers) and published via Padlet. They try to convince other delegations of their resolution, make them sign it or join other delegations, integrating their pre-ambulatory or operative clauses. The idea is to get as many co-submitters for a resolution as possible by 'advertising' them verbally via chat or video call.

Delegations can use all channels of communication to work cooperatively on resolutions and merge them. **In order to submit a merged resolution for the**

Economic and Social Council debate, the delegations need to collect the approval of the teachers' panel.

3 Guidelines for Procedure during Online Committee Debate

1. One delegate of each member state makes an opening speech of a maximum of one minute.
2. All delegates switch on their camera while speaking.
3. The Chair selects resolutions for the debate and decides on the order of the agenda.
4. Two formal debates are held, debating resolutions in committee.
5. The main submitter (i.e. the member state handing in the resolution with the most signatures in lobbying process and the approval of the chair) reads the operative clauses to the committee.
6. Delegates write their country's name in the committee chat to request time to speak for or against a resolution or amendment.
7. The statements for and against the resolution are followed by **points of information** (questions). They can be raised by writing your country's name and '?' in the chat. Tip: you can also use questions to express your opinion (e.g. by using rhetorical questions). The Chair's decision to allow questions is final.
8. **Time for**: The submitting delegation is invited to speak for two minutes in favour of the resolution or amendment plus one minute for questions or comments from the floor (including right to reply).
9. Then **time for or against**: All other delegations are invited to speak for two minutes in favour or against the resolution plus one minute for questions or comments per speaker (including their right to reply).
10. If an improvement to the resolution can be made by striking out whole clauses or parts of them or adding an operative clause or new phrasing, delegates can submit **amendments** to the Chair.
11. Amendments to operative clauses or resolutions are considered during **time against** by writing the quotation in the chat; for example, 'Turkey: "Regrets that troops have <u>not</u> been withdrawn from …"'. Any changes need to be <u>underlined</u>. If approved by the Chair, these can be debated. Each speaker has two minutes to make their case. Each amendment is then voted on.
12. Delegates can also submit new operative clauses as amendments (see **submitting an amendment** in 5. Committee Procedure at a Glance).
13. The Chair may post a speaker list in the chat to announce the upcoming speeches.
14. When the Chair decides, a vote is called for the amendment or the whole resolution to be approved or rejected by a **majority vote**.

15. **Points of Order** can be raised anytime by writing your country's name and '#' in the chat. Besides questions on procedure, timetable, etc., this includes the request to move on to vote for amendments or the whole resolution or move the debate to another amendment or new resolution. The Chair may decide to put this to a vote (a two-thirds majority of the committee is required).

16. Votes are held in the chat. Delegates therefore either respond FOR or AGAINST within ten seconds after the vote has been called by the Chair.

17. You can support other delegation's resolutions (e. g. during informal debate), submit amendments via chat to the Chair and request **time for** the debate of the amendment.

4 Procedure – Chronology

GENERAL ASSEMBLY Day 1

Chair:
• Opens General Assembly by welcoming delegations
• Asks speakers to address the General Assembly
• Asks delegations to take the floor to deliver their opening speeches

Delegates of the member states:
• Switch on their microphone and camera
• Deliver their opening speeches of maximum one minute
• Ask questions to the keynote speakers and enter informal discussion with them

ECONOMIC AND SOCIAL COUNCIL IN SESSION

Chair:
• Switches on microphone and camera
• Delivers welcome address
• Informs delegates about the order of the agenda
• Asks sponsors of the first (most successful) resolution to read out its operative clauses (delegations are expected to have read the pre-amble)

Sponsors (main submitters) in 'time for':
• Read the operative clauses to the committee
• Speak for two minutes in favour of the resolution plus one minute for questions or comments from the floor (including right to reply)

Delegations:
• Can raise points of information (questions on the resolution) by writing their country's name and '?'

(cont.)

GENERAL ASSEMBLY Day 1

- Can raise points of order (questions on procedure, timetable, etc.) by writing their country's name and '#'

Delegations in 'time for and against':
- Write their country's name in the committee chat to request time to speak for (e. g. RUSSIA +) or against (e. g. USA -) the resolution
- Speak two minutes in favour or against the resolution plus one minute for questions or comments per speaker (including their right to reply)

Chair
- Calls upon delegations to hand in amendments to the resolution
- Organises the speaker list in the chat
- Reads out amendments and presents them by sharing the screen
- Sets 'time for' and 'time against' the amendment
- Decides on votes for amendment or the whole resolution (two-thirds majority)

Delegations
- Improve the resolution by amendments striking out or adding whole clauses or parts of them or adding an operative clause or a new phrasing
- Write the quotation in the chat with any changes underlined (e. g. 'Turkey: "~~Recommends~~ Agrees that electronic waste recycling should not be carried out on the basis of child labour …"')

5 Committee Procedure at a Glance

	Write … in the Committee Chat	Example
Submitting an amendment	Country's name and quotation of the changed operative clauses '…' (with underlined changes)	Turkey: ADD/STRIKE OUT/ REPLACE '~~Recommends~~ Agrees that electronic waste recycling should not be carried out on the basis of child labour …'
Points of information	Country's name and '?'	USA?
Request time to speak for resolution or amendments	Country's name and '+'	Russian Federation +
Request time to speak against the resolution or amendments	Country's name and '-'	Federal Republic of Germany -
Points of order (questions on timetable, procedure, etc.)	Country's name and '#'	UK #

6 MUN Best Delegation Award

Passing a constructive solution is the individual goal of MUN. Never forget that, as a delegation, you must work together as a team to win the prestigious award of 'MUN-BEST-DELEGATION'.

Criteria:

- Ability to work constructively on the resolution
- Ability to cooperate with other delegations
- Authenticity of portrayal (including political position, appropriate language and style)

7 Dress Code and Behaviour

- Behave like UN delegates at all times.
- All delegates must have their camera switched on while speaking, therefore all delegates are required to wear formal clothing (shirt, tie, . . .); Jewellery and make-up should be unobtrusive, with no facial piercings.
- Make sure you ALWAYS switch off your microphone and camera if you are not talking.
- If possible, create a suitable background indicating your country (flag, traditional items or clothing, . . .)
- Please do not chew gum!
- Follow the instructions in 9 – How To Be the Perfect Diplomatic Delegate

8 Language

- In all your dealings, be courteous to everyone, especially the Chair, and always address them as 'Mr Chairman' or 'Madam Chair' during debate.
- Always use the third person while speaking. Delegates will refer to themselves as 'this delegate' and other delegates as 'the distinguished delegate of the United Kingdom . . .', using the country's official name.
- Speak of yourself as '(country's official name) thinks that . . .' or 'the delegation of (country's official name) suggests that' and address the chair and other delegates as 'Would the honourable Madam Chair please . . .' or 'Could the distinguished delegate of Israel please elaborate on . . .'
- See Worksheet 9.6 How to Express Yourself as a Delegate.

9 How to Be the Perfect Diplomatic Delegate

- The essence of MUN is to try to recreate reality. As a diplomat, therefore, you must be supremely diplomatic, creating or maintaining peace and accord, the purpose of the real UN. You should, therefore:
  - become aware of the will of your committee
  - achieve consensus for decision-making, emphasising negotiation rather than confrontation

- ◦ address the issue by defining its terms
  - ◦ never indulge in meaningless rhetoric
  - ◦ never sacrifice the country's interest to serve private motives (either your own or someone else's).
- Always speak slowly, clearly and loudly, so that people can hear and respond to your points. Always follow the rules of diplomatic language. Never use colloquial language.
- Remember: when talking on a resolution, you are a salesperson!
- Try to come up with your own ideas on how to solve the problems being debated.
- Chairs get annoyed by dilatory points and poor debate. Be prepared to speak up if the chair has the impression the country is not contributing to the debate enough.
- Always have **points of information** prepared and work as constructively as possible on all resolutions.
- Do not try to make too many points in your speech. All arguments must be as constructive as possible.
- Ensure that your arguments against others' resolutions are sensible and politely expressed.
- Follow the rules on 'How to Argue'.

REFERENCES

Denver, D., & Hands, G. (1990). Does Studying Politics Make a Difference? The Political Knowledge, Attitudes and Perceptions of School Students. *British Journal of Political Science*, *20*(2), 263–279. https://doi.org/10.1017/S0007123400005809

The Documentary Channel (2019). Blame Game – E-Waste in Africa and Solutions. Online video clip. www.youtube.com/watch?v=mrCcTiSL_Hg

Grinth, H. (2010). Sprachverwendung in der Politik. *Bpb: Bundeszentrale Für Politische Bildung.* www.bpb.de/politik/grundfragen/sprache-und-politik/42687/sprachverwendung

Sander, W. (2009). Wissen: Basiskonzepte der Politischen Bildung. In Forum Politische Bildung (Ed.), *Informationen zur Politischen BildungI*, vol. 30 (pp. 57–60). www.nibis.de/uploads/2medfach/files/30_sander.pdf

The Writing Center, University of North Carolina at Chapel Hill. (n.d.). *The Nature of Political Inquiry.* Retrieved 25 June 2021 from www.csun.edu/~cahn/inquiry.htm

Westholm, A., Lindquist, A., & Niemi, R. G. (1990). Education and the Making of the Informed Citizen: Political Literacy and the Outside World. In O. Ichilov (Ed.), *Political Socialization, Citizenship Education, and Democracy.* Teachers' College.

World Economic Forum (Ed.). (2019). *A New Circular Vision for Electronics: Time for a Global Reboot – In Support of the United Nations E-Waste Coalition.* www3.weforum.org/docs/WEF_A_New_Circular_Vision_for_Electronics.pdf

10 Modern Languages: Exploring Pluriliteracies through a Deeper Learning Episode in French Literature with Younger Beginner Learners

FREDERIC TAVEAU

10.1 Redefining Literature as Subject Teaching and Learning in French?

The complexity of rethinking language learning as a subject discipline within the formal school curriculum with its own knowledge base, skills and processes has more recently been brought into sharper focus due to an increase in bilingual education and the attention paid to the role of language learning and using. Learning languages traditionally involving disconnected language competences to be used at some point in the future or applied generically across other disciplines, which defines language learning as acquiring increasing linguistic fluency through understanding the syntax and grammar of a specific language. More recent pedagogic moves in pluriliteracies thinking have provided opportunities to experiment in building alternative experiences, especially with beginner or near-beginner learners in lower secondary school. This involves a shared exploration of the nature of a language (e.g. French) and how understanding (meaning-making) and using language to communicate appropriately and to construct dynamic, deeper knowledge based in creative, academic and 'real-world' contexts can offer purposeful and motivating learning experiences for learners. Such repositioning responds in practical ways to Kramsch's statement:

> In the last decades, [the] world has changed to such an extent that language teachers are no longer sure of what they are supposed to teach nor what real world situations they are supposed to prepare their students for. (Kramsch, 2014, p. 296)

Addressing the most fundamental question offers a useful starting point: how can we define French (or German or Spanish and so on) as an academic discipline in secondary school curricula? The centuries-old legacy of seeing 'modern languages' within the classical Western language tradition (reading Latin and Greek) still persists, translated into common classroom practices, especially in the earlier years of language learning. These practices include, for example, writing – foregrounding grammatical systems, building vocabulary and imitating models to replicate and demonstrate understanding of structural concepts; listening and speaking – predicated on repetition, non-authentic imposed 'communicative' scenarios; and reading – using simple, specifically created texts to demonstrate 'understanding' at surface level and subsequently deciphering authentic literature, shifting from explicit to more implicit understanding. This is neither adequate nor appropriate for secondary school learners in contemporary society. Despite the advent of the communicative approach, many foreign language programmes continue to use a grammatical spine to develop reading, speaking, listening and writing skills, located in set topics such as 'house and home' or 'transport' – often reducing the potential cognitive level of the thematic content to match the linguistic level, especially for younger learners. The value, therefore, of increasingly using language development as a vehicle for deepening intercultural consciousness and transdisciplinary world knowledges remains untapped – building knowledges other than linguistic ones has not been considered a priority. Consequently, teenagers may find their language experiences boring, irrelevant or disconnected. So, the processes set out in this chapter reconfigure the cognitive components of French language and literacies to reconcile working with challenging relevant *literature* (from individual and local to transnational and global knowledges) that matches student cognitive abilities with access to the language required for meaning-making and communicating or languaging their understanding appropriately. This is the subject discipline.

Two phenomena have more recently gained attention, demanding a rethink in classroom language learning: Content and Language Integrated Learning (CLIL) and the literacies movement redefine the role played by language teachers across different models of bilingual education; and pluriliteracies, particularly the pluriliteracies teaching for deeper learning (PTDL) model, provide alternative means of meaning-making and using languages purposefully to move students towards deeper learning, personal growth and enrichment in our multilingual, multicultural world. Yet, while subject educators teaching through other languages remain firmly rooted in their discipline, rethinking the teaching and learning of French as a subject discipline raises issues about what this means for language teachers who have linguistic expertise with indeterminate intercultural experiences. This sometimes leads to the misconception that language teachers are to 'serve' other subject disciplines – a contention that has been well counter-argued. Another challenge is overcoming the 'alien' concept of developing literacies skills in a language that is not the main language of schooling, especially in the lower years of secondary education. This, too, is linked to widely held views about literacies development in a first language, focusing on learning to speak and read appropriately, which is disconnected from learning other languages, and is built on the notion that languages and literature are separate entities. It seems, then, that many current language learning practices reflect the absence of dialogue until recently amongst practitioners, educators and researchers – dialogue that brings together multiple perspectives and epistemologies to reposition *languages* as an academic discipline in our contemporary educational world.

Pountain (2019) usefully describes language learning as a discipline defined by an interrelationship between language in use, linguistic structures and literature, which he defines as the *critical study* of cultural manifestations that depend on the language, that is, multimodal literary texts. He refers to these as the three Ls (language, linguistics and literature). In addition, Goldman et al.'s (2016) earlier work details two fundamental considerations for rethinking language learning as a subject discipline. The first demands a redefinition of **text** that impacts how and why text is used as a dynamic learning space. When texts – ranging from social media to literature – are used as diverse multimodal cultural tools, they open up an exploration of the human condition from social, economic, cultural, philosophical and political perspectives, not constrained by more traditional subject boundaries. Literary texts offer opportunities where learners can collaboratively and explicitly develop reading skills that investigate genres, modes, purpose and multilayered meaning-making. In turn, such understanding, when mediated and applied to learners' own composition, encourages content and age-relevant possibilities that promote agency and connectivity across languages. According to Goldman et al. (2016), this requires a shift from the traditional mono-textual reading model, which only focuses on reading one text at a time, to an intertext model, so that learners can develop the ability to detect, evaluate and resolve potential conflicts between information sources and expectations. Texts then become the currency for critical understanding and cultural consciousness rather than providing learners with surface-level comprehension exercises. Reading and reasoning using a wide range of texts leads to creative writing as learners deepen their cognitive, cultural and linguistic skills.

The second consideration follows on and focuses on **task design**. The need to shift from prioritising 'performance' tasks to rebalancing these with *learning tasks* that generate different types of knowledges along with curiosity and spontaneity for 'digging deeper' becomes clear. From this perspective, it is fundamental to demonstrate, through additional language and literacies development, an understanding of the philosophy, reasoning and purposes behind societal behaviours, lived experiences and world events. The choice of texts is guided by learners' interests, identities, creativity and critical responsiveness. The choice of texts also reflects their narrative, expository or argumentative nature, described by Hallet (2016) as macro-genres detailed according to micro-genres (such as recount, anecdote, explanation, exposition or persuasion) and modes. The goal is now to bridge 'life concepts' across other subject disciplines through developing and applying the necessary language to develop and deepen (pluri)literacies and (pluri)literary disciplinary knowledges and discourses using genre-specific tasks relating to activity domains – that is, ways of *doing, organising, explaining* and *arguing.*

Of course, there is a need to gather evidence and justify experimental practices during timetabled language lessons. The examples outlined in the chapter demonstrate evolving deeper learning episodes (DLEs) in a school context, based on practitioner thinking and cross-school dialogue, discussions with researchers and, above all, listening to learners.

The materials in this chapter focus on the development of creative and literary reading and writing in French with two strands: as language development and as a mode of discovery in cognitive and socio-cultural terms. Each strand has a knowledge base: a (pluri)literacies strand that opens the door to 'understanding the world' (Freire, 2000) by developing specific reasoning, analytical, creative and critical skills through the lens of another language, underpinned by growing linguistic competence; and the cognitive and metacognitive processes for deepening student understanding of multilingual, multicultural worlds through multimodal texts – broadly ranging from works of literature to social media. Carefully selected by the teachers and learners, texts of a social, cultural, political and historical nature offer themes and language-rich worldviews from the personal to the global, requiring multilevel analysis to understand how *language* is the conduit of interpretation and sense-making that enables learners to deepen their understanding of how working with authentic texts provides creative, reflective experiences. Carter (2007) refers to these opportunities as using the power of more contextualised and relativised theories of language and literature. In short, this requires students to develop both *textual fluency* and *linguistic fluency*, where textual fluency is the ability to critically evaluate and produce appropriate multimodal text and text types in another language (secondary discourse) building on diverse primary discourse and increasingly complex literary texts.

Hyland's (2011) knowledge domains provide practical framing for language teachers to consider the literary knowledge base in their task design:

- Content knowledge (ideas, concepts related to human condition/world themes)
- System knowledge (syntax, lexis, grammar)
- Process knowledge (strategies for text construction)
- Genre knowledge (purpose, values, meaning-making)
- Context/Cultural knowledge (communities, cultural presence)

The skills involved in developing a literary knowledge base need to be practised and progressed through both learning and performance tasks. In this example, creative writing in French embedded in developing reading and reasoning skills includes 'noticing' technical and structural moves, sense-making, interpreting and reflecting critically. Reading and reasoning skills, for example, involve synthesising, argumentation, evaluation and demonstration, which in turn require tasks to develop relevant and specific linguistic forms, functions and language use.

In this particular case, the end goal of the first year of language learning for near-beginner learners is to develop creative literary writing skills in French through modelling, analysing and exploring how meaning-making works. Throughout a series of lessons targeting creative writing in French, learners are encouraged to experience the following.

- Understand how specific features of multimodal text and layers of conceptual meaning are expressed through language (e.g. strategies, genre moves, sequencing, functions, grammatical functions and lexis) in order to enable them to demonstrate deeper understanding through applying their own skills and knowledge to their own texts.
- Build a repertoire of cognitive and metacognitive strategies to understand, analyse, interpret and construct a range of text types and genres for meaning, social purpose and context. This marks a move away from single texts used for comprehension to multiple texts for noticing, analysis and interpreting. It also signifies that, when appropriate, more than one language may be used for deepening understanding of the strategies and processes required to read and write creatively in French (i.e. translanguaging).
- Develop critical awareness of meaning-making processes, building on creative and culturally responsive tasks which seek to develop a deeper understanding, going from 'knowledge telling' (planning, drafting, revising, redrafting and editing) to 'knowledge transforming' (through social interaction, multiple perspectives and critical evaluation) (Manchón, 2011).

The following example of a DLE (Deeper Learning Episode 2) is the second in a series of three DLEs spanning one academic year. The sequencing of the three episodes is detailed in Section 10.3. Deeper Learning Episode 2 is based on a pluriliteracies-inspired theme that was co-designed with younger learners: to develop the necessary skills and knowledges (literary, historical, creative evocative descriptions and emergent ideas compared to current society) for everyone to be and feel like a (literary) creative writer (and reader) in French. Learner interest was triggered by reading multimodal texts, drawing on descriptions of Gothic landscapes and events taking place in them (learners' choice), with progression pathways over one academic year focusing on skills for deconstructing and analysing text and co-constructing creative 'literary' texts with beginner learners of French (see Table 10.1).

10.2   What is Deeper Learning in French Creative Literary Writing?

Deeper learning in the context of creative literary writing in French is not only about the construction of appropriately framed creative descriptive text (the Gothic landscape – Deeper Learning Episode 2); it is as much about the reading, 'experiencing' and drafting processes that demonstrate the development of specific literacy conventions, that is, using appropriate linguistic strategies to build and nuance

Table 10.1 Activity domains, language functions and student outputs for creative literary writing in French

Aim: Writing a creative, evocative Gothic portrait and landscape description in French in response to reading and researching different texts

Activity Domains in French	Sample Activities in French	Cognitive Discourse Functions (CDFs) and Learner Progression in French	Student Outputs in French
Doing: Constructing creative written texts involving 'scary', atmospheric' stories using descriptions, emotions, sensory experiences, reporting activity **CDF** • Describe	1. Reading and identifying key features of 'specific genre' of texts on *landscape* in Gothic literature 2. Observing and identifying landscape features through videos and geography resources 3. Researching – learners finding own texts (extracts) in L1 that they believe create a good story (i.e. 'spooky moment') 4. Small group discussions – follow-through activities focusing on specific features, such as connectives	**Novice Descriptors:** • I start my description with the two important objects I wish to describe: 'il y a une maison et un arbre' **Expert Descriptors:** • I can add unusual vocabulary and focus on more than one sense. For example, 'on remarque un arbre solitaire et mort et le hululement d'une chouette brise le silence de la nuit'	**Main:** Creative, individual written text with built-in descriptions (people and landscapes) in a story with features of nineteenth-century Gothic literature **Others include:** • Responding to stimulus texts and video resources • Demonstrating genre awareness • Making bridges with other subjects, such as arts, geography and L1 literature
Organising: Textual meaning-making, deconstructing and reconstructing textual features, refining the features and impact of texts through drafts **CDFs** • Describe • Classify • Explore	1. Progressively in-depth deconstruction of key textual features in L2 for different landscape descriptions (pastoral, spooky) 2. Creating classification visuals by prioritising the most impactful/important text features (e.g. as in a Diamond Nine) 	**Novice Descriptors:** • I can identify linguistic features (e.g. adjectives) to make my text more impressive, link up my sentences with connectives, and use 'qui' sentences, as in 'il y a une grande maison qui a l'air d'etre hantée' **Expert Descriptors:** • I include a variety of verbs to develop further, especially the use of the five senses: 'on aperçoit une grande maison qui a l'air d'être hantée et on sent l'odeur du bois pourri'	**Oral:** • Reporting • Meaning-making • Discussion • Critical analysis **Written:** • Drafting/redrafting • Application of grammatical features • Sentence building • Using literacy features • Nuancing • Presentation • Analysis

Table 10.1 (cont.)

Aim: Writing a creative, evocative Gothic portrait and landscape description in French in response to reading and researching different texts

Activity Domains in French	Sample Activities in French	Cognitive Discourse Functions (CDFs) and Learner Progression in French	Student Outputs in French
Explaining: Processes underpinning interpretation of texts **CDFs** • Define • Explain • Report	1. Analysing key textual features to evaluate earlier simple drafts 2. Increasing sophistication and emotional impact on reader concerning the senses (e.g. fear), using increasingly nuanced language 3. 'Playing' with punctuation to create ambiance 4. Using grammatical features (such as tenses) to be creative, sensitive and strategic 5. Using similes and metaphors 6. Acting on feedback following video ('Austin's Butterfly') as a trigger	**Novice descriptors:** • I can structure my description more and improve my text by adding: 'au premier plan, au deuxième plan, à droite, à gauche', etc.: 'Au premier plan on remarque un arbre solitaire et derrière l'arbre, au deuxième plan, il y a une grande maison qui fait peur.' **Expert descriptors:** • I can improve my text by adding similes and metaphors and changing the tense to tell my story in the past: 'Au premier plan, à gauche, on remarquait un arbre solitaire et mort. Son tronc paraissait tordu comme les veines d'un cou qui montreraient sa douleur. Le hululement d'une chouette brisait le silence de la nuit.' 'Derrière l'arbre, au deuxième plan à l'est, on remarquait une maison qui avait l'air d'être hantée et on sentait l'odeur du bois pourri comme la mort.'	**Digital:** • Texts • Models • Text sharing • Feedback and feed-forward • Scaffolding videos • Task magic (text manipulation)

Arguing: Justifying what the most impactful features/meaning-making are. Are some features more impactful than others? How good are individual texts on impacting the reader (and his or her emotions)?

CDFs
• Explore
• Evaluate

1. Critically appraising the use of textual techniques – graphic descriptions versus the power of suggestion, subtleties, crescendo and the 'unseen' – assessing the impact of text
2. Critically evaluating language choices (e.g. verbs, senses, emotions, metaphors, similes)
3. Taking account of different reader perspectives and interpretation (e.g. responses to landscape paintings) and engaging in critical active readership

Novice Descriptors:
• I can make my description more interesting by structuring the text into paragraphs, making my sentences longer and using comparatives rather than adjectives
• I realise I have to structure my descriptions more and improve my text by adding au premier plan, au deuxième plan, à droite, à gauche:

'Au premier plan on remarque un arbre solitaire comme un loup et derrière l'arbre, au deuxième plan, il y a une grande maison effrayante comme la mort'

Expert Descriptors:
• I can appeal more to my reader by using the language of the senses, emotion and powerful similes and metaphors:

'Même si c'était évident que la maison était toute sombre, on pouvait toutefois apercevoir que la fenêtre en haut avait de la lumière, comme si le visiteur égaré était attendu … mais le cri strident qui perçait régulièrement le silence de la nuit avertissait que cet accueil n'avait rien d'hospitalier!'

textual meaning. It also enables those literary writing conventions (pertaining to creative literary text) to be reflected upon, analysed, practised, redrafted and improved so that they can be adapted to inform subsequent creative descriptions of different genres and registers (The Travelogue – Deeper Learning Episode 3) drawing on different modes of textual construction practices. Modelling is essential, and developing reading skills through 'noticing', text analysis and reflection constitutes the inclusive elements needed for deeper learning.

Deeper learning in French, therefore, involves guiding learners to transparently develop the strategies and skills for meaning construction needed to respond to and construct text creatively at an age-appropriate level. This is crucial for motivation and challenge, supported by scaffolding and mentoring learners to make explicit progressing towards *textual fluency* and demonstrating that this is not the reserve of advanced students of French but starts at the very beginning of language learning. Content relevance is, of course, key. For near-beginner learners in more traditional language learning settings, 'content' is used *for* language learning rather than *as* language learning – typically surface or transactional content, such as daily routines, house and home or hobbies. However, when learners become involved in discussing and co-selecting broad themes for analysis, they take on increasing responsibility to develop critical enquiry skills that enable them to carry out their own research according to group and individual interests. We know that expanding any of the typical themes to include alternative texts ranging from worldviews to local events requires raising consciousness and practices for integrating intercultural, creative, ecological and ethical perspectives. These have the potential to open up new knowledge pathways that are 'owned' by learners and relevant to their own interests and lives while providing bridges to other worlds – from the real to the imaginative, from the past to near futures.

Focusing on textual fluency shifts an emphasis on decontextualised grammatical structures to understanding how the language system relates to the genre, styles and purpose of text. It involves learners in verbal reasoning, languaging their learning and demonstrating their understanding as it evolves at different times and in different ways. Simply put, learners need to access the kind of language needed to engage in these tasks.

Progression for deeper learning involves

- practising and developing literary writing practices focusing on specific reading and writing strategies and skills
- increasing different knowledges (meaning construction, linguistic functions)
- engaging in discourse, connecting core ideas and principles to support interpretive analysis
- making appropriate choices of linguistic forms or functions to express meaning
- mentoring by teachers (and peers) to provide meaningful feedback and feed-forward.

Table 10.2 Connecting Scarborough's Reading Rope (2001) and Sedita's Writing Rope (2019) with Hyland's (2011) knowledge domains for L1 literacies and Coyle and Meyer (2021) L2 literacies

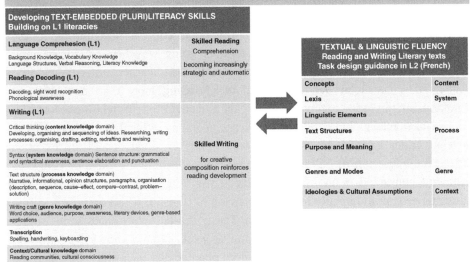

Using the four activity domains to guide task design involves learners in *doing, organising, explaining* and *arguing* their interpretations and their compositions. Tasks focus on developing critical understanding of text meaning (knowledges) and text construction (linguistic strategies) as well as building increasing understanding of task-transparent CDFs. In other words, the responsibility for the choice of textual themes and related pluriliteracies practices goes way beyond more traditional language syllabuses and promotes contextually bound learner agency and interests. In turn, this enables more personalised learning pathways to emerge. It frames language learning as *literacies using* across languages (pluriliteracies) and as a significant cognitive contributor to educating young people. Redefining literature as language learning requires shifts in rethinking epistemologies and principles for classroom practice.

Table 10.2 provides us with a useful overview linking reading and writing literacy skills, emphasising critical thinking and what Sedita calls 'writing craft', indicating alternative questions teachers need to reflect upon in their learning design. It should be pointed out that the table uses first-language literacies skills development, which form a useful basis from which to connect with and develop further those literacy skills in other languages. For example, a focus on simple written descriptions is commonplace for younger learners in their first language. This typically involves understanding, responding to and writing very simple physical 'descriptions' of places (rooms and furniture) or people (hair and eye colour) using simple subject–verb–object phrases with a few 'safe' adjectives. Yet if these practices are replicated in the second or additional language several years later – in this case, French - the learners will have advanced several years in age, cognitive development and understanding the world, making the content simplistic and irrelevant. However, when 'description' in other languages becomes *reframed* within a pluriliteracies context, descriptions act as a gateway to creative interpretation of literature going way beyond, for example, describing people and their physical attributes. Instead, learners enter the world of personalities, emotions, behaviours and beliefs using more than one language. Similarly, interpretation of physical landscape and environments relating to historical and social trends, global conditions, poverty, economy, ethical analysis and so on, develops critical consciousness along the way. This is not about an 'add-on' text about citizenship education or cultural awareness. Instead, these are ways of being and behaving embedded in multimodal texts across languages, which are age- and content-relevant and openly invite comparison or transfer, where appropriate, from first to second languages and vice versa. These task-led experiences serve to raise learner awareness of ways in which languages work, expand knowledge pathways, raise cultural consciousness and provide deep practice that melds both language and meaning processes and deepens the knowledge domains outlined.

10.3   Example of a Deeper Learning Episode

As stated in Section 10.2, in this chapter reference is made to three sequential DLEs, which together comprise one overarching year-long goal: for beginner learners to develop deeper understanding and practices of the processes and skills needed to become creative literary writers in French.

The sequence of episodes is designed to move learners from surface learning to opening minds by connecting cognitive–cultural knowledges to language and literary genre-based knowledges in order to promote the development of the academic literacies required for composing written descriptions. To do this, learners are encouraged to progressively explore a range of opportunities to integrate and deepen all core knowledge domains over time, a process that underpins the episodes. Table 10.3 sets out a design plan that summarises how learners move from simple to increasingly complex descriptions in French, raising cultural consciousness and culminating in creating alternative travel diaries (Deeper Learning Episode 3).

Deeper Learning Episode 1, illustrated in Table 10.4 is the first in the series and occurs in the early stages of literary *descriptive* writing. The aim is to encourage creativity in learners, raising their expectations by starting with simple ideas for describing physical attributes of people to guiding them along pathways leading to

Table 10.3 Progression in descriptive writing (French) across deeper learning episodes

Developing (Character) Descriptions through Episodes
Drawing on Five Knowledge Domains

Introduction: Robots	**Descriptive Vocabulary:** Colours, sizes, shapes, personalities, functions.	**Grammar:** Adjectives Modal verbs Negative and affirmative sentences Connectives Present and past tenses

Deeper Learning
Episode 1:
All About Me
	Me/You:
	• Physical description + the face+ moral portrait
	• Zodiac sign, interests, phobias
	• Relationships (family/friends)
	He/She:
	• Full literary portrait
	• Physical description, moral portrait + actions
		Opinions:
		Justification of opinions
		    using
		Because/car
		Before + imperfect
		But now + present
		Conditional:
		He/she would have gone/
		    would go …
		We would watch/go/do

Deeper Learning
Episode 2:
Gothic-Inspired
    Literary Writing
	Fictional Characters:
	Complete literary portrait:
	• Attention to facial features, tics, particular visible
	    details, such as scars and tattoos
	• Nineteenth-century printing/look/clothing
	• Interests/habits/character traits
	• Emotions: fear!
		Descriptions:
		Imperfect tense
		Actions:
		Perfect or imperfect (see
		    grammar course)

Deeper Learning
Episode 3:
The Travelogue
	Modern Character with a Mission
	• Literary portrait + CULTURE
	• Evolution of the character in landscapes + from
	    varied cultures
	• Influence of character on environment and
	    vice versa
		I/We Dialogues
		Descriptions using present
		    tense
		Actions using either present
		    and/or perfect tense

literary portraits conveying characteristics, personalities, emotions and behaviours. Moving towards 'deeper meaning' involves a series of tasks encouraging learners to gain confidence, take risks, learn genre-related linguistic features, play with words and explore new ways of working with languages at an age-appropriate level. The processes involved in creative writing from this perspective are not part of the regular language learning curriculum. Deeper Learning Episode 1 is entitled '*Tout sur Moi – All about Me!*'

Table 10.4 Planning grid for a deeper learning episode in French

Designing Deeper Learning Episodes

Planning Grid for a Deeper Learning Episode in French

What do I want my learners to know or be able to do?	How will my learners demonstrate increasingly deeper understanding at the surface, consolidation and transfer levels?	How can I support active knowledge co-construction for my learners?	How will I support my learners every step of the way?	How can I generate and sustain learner commitment and achievement?
Basic Understanding: • Different styles of composing written physical and 'moral' portraits, focusing on characterisation, thematic content • Use of basic literary conventions (language) • Use of visuals and expressions for colours, shapes, textures and materials **Foundational Skills:** • Reading texts (exemplar descriptions) • Analysing texts (for meaning and literary conventions) • Organising text construction techniques to access meaningful guidance • Applying basic literary conventions and visuals	**Preliminary Product Outcomes:** • Drafts of written text in French, presenting the physical and moral portrait of self, demonstrating appropriate and creative use of language **Main Learning Product:** • A final version of a written description of self with visuals, which has been evaluated by peers and self • A presentation of work **Transfer Task:** • Compare own text with an extract from a literary novel (Guy de Maupassant's *La Parure – The Necklace*) and present an analysis of the differences and similarities (group work)	**Construction of Knowledge:** • Make transparent and use guided tasks in *all five knowledge domains*: content, system, process, genre, context (e.g. detailed description using shapes, colours, texture in the past tense; use of adjectives and comparatives, modal verbs and connectives) • Design tasks that are inclusive, interesting and encourage confidence building and meaning-making (e.g. mind mapping ideas) • Modelling, analysis and drafting for co-construction of meaning key (e.g. engage in short	**Scaffolding:** Learning is mentored (Learning Conversations) and scaffolded in four different ways: • Cognitive scaffolding (thinking and behaving like ...); for example, how to enrich descriptions through nuancing aspects such as 'public personality' and 'in my secret garden' • Literacies scaffolding (knowing, using, applying and transferring specific literacies skills); for example, focus on register, expanding repertoire so that learners understand the difference between *je souffre d'achluophobie et de cynophobie* rather than *j'ai peur du noir et des chiens.*	**Engagement:** • Learners negotiate the thematic content of their writing with each other and the teacher • Learner confidence and sense of purpose is developed due to high expectations of their French progression, the positive ethos of the classroom and the implicit cognitive challenge • Creativity, for many, is linked to engagement and motivation (e.g. use of Proust portrait) • As younger learners, they are 'allowed' to study topics not usually associated with traditional language learning (e.g. love, ambitions, dreams, star signs)

Personal Meaningfulness/ Relevance:
- Learners carry out investigations and research into sub-themes that are of particular relevance and interest to them

Opportunities for Autonomous Learning:
- Research and inquiry to create a sense of ownership and agency
- What it means to be a creative writer in another language is openly discussed using L1 to develop a sense of self-respect and confidence
- Learners learn how to negotiate, classify, make a convincing argument
- The use of authentic materials (i.e. Francophone TV)

Reflection and Revision:
- Learners evaluate their learning
- Whole-class reflection and analysis about the unit discussed
- Use of informal videos of their own learning to participate in reflective analysis.

- Language scaffolding (increasing awareness of the role of grammar, syntax and linguistic structures); for example, the language needed to detail and make more sophisticated descriptions [*le nez busqué, des sourcils épilés*]
- Metacognitive scaffolding that impacts on learner affect (how to . . ./peer support, reflection, ownership and agency)
- Make the above four steps clear

Social Interaction:
- A mix of whole-class, group and individual tasks that focus on languaging, discussing and transparency require an interactive dialogic classroom environment
- Learning Conversations and reflections with individuals, groups and teachers are constant

Use of (Digital) Media:
Extensive exploration of digital sources to inspire creativity and provide exemplars
- Video clips to watch French-language episodes of a drama to trigger analysis of how characters are presented (e.g. *Café des Rêves*)

- Extension: My physical and moral description; likes, dislikes, phobias and nightmares; emotions and relationships – what is love to me? – dreams and ambitions

Feedback and Feed-forward:
- Using the principles for feedback demonstrated in 'Austin's Butterfly' video, conduct Learning Conversations to discuss what has been achieved (feedback) and how it can

- discussions, watch a TV drama)
- Learners encouraged to research and follow their own interests – agency, creativity and individual style

Possible Transfer:
- Research a similar text/ extract individually or in groups that has the structural and thematic elements of a literary portrait

- Composing and drafting own text with visuals
- Explaining the features of own writing
- Evaluating drafts (self and peers) using co-constructed criteria
- Researching ideas and concepts to develop creative composition (e.g. phobias, imaginative feelings)

Deeper Understanding:
- Nuancing different types of physical description
- Extending physical and moral description to include likes, dislikes, phobias and nightmares, emotions and relationships, dreams and ambitions
- Self-evaluation of texts, demonstrating critical analysis, risk-taking and creativity
- Increasing awareness of the reader

Deep Practice:
- Drafting and languaging (explaining and self-evaluation) to

Table 10.4 (*cont.*)

Designing Deeper Learning Episodes

demonstrate increasing depth of understanding and application of the five knowledge domains • Researching creative aspects of the language of fear, the language of love, etc. Transfer • Apply and adapt learning to the next learning episode focusing on literary portraits	• Drafting of text is done using iPad as well as handwriting • Research (e.g. into bizarre phobias) requires use of digital resources • Vlogs and blogs useful • Many resources to support learners are digital, including those created by teachers • Use of film recordings of learners at work to encourage analysis and celebrate achievements	be improved – next steps (feed-forward) with individuals and groups in personalised ways that respond to individual needs Assessment: • Co-constructing the rubrics for assessment criteria with learners ensures the framework acts as a heuristic • Learners also feed back to the teacher about their experiences	• Actions taken forward to inform next learning episode.

10.4   Alignment

Designing DLEs involves aligning creative writing literacies, knowledge pathways, and learner and teacher 'learning behaviours' with learner needs and interests. Making this alignment transparent for learners and teachers alike is crucial to understanding the effectiveness of adopting a pluriliteracies approach. Moreover, the creative student-directed nature of the work means that while the five *knowledge domains* provide a solid framework and the broad themes of content knowledge are designed by the teacher, the detail and direction of the content of the learning through *activity domains* is dynamic, underpinned by the scaffolded development of literary written texts – in this example focusing on creative literary *descriptions*.

Learner Strengths, Needs and Interests
Creative literary writing in an additional language opens up opportunities to increase learner motivation and commitment. First, the notion of learning to become an 'expert' writer in another language offers individuals a genuine cognitive challenge – one that treats learners respectfully, recognising them as maturing individuals and guiding them in using another language to express their thinking, creativity, experiences, new understanding and views. Second, it provides learners with a safe platform to develop self-agency by following and developing their interests while discovering alternatives. Learners are invited to suggest themes, negotiate them fairly and find ways of expanding their knowledges, both collaboratively in groups and individually, according to their strengths. We try to encourage personalising pathways by openly discussing individual learning needs through regular and reliable *Learning Conversations*, which provide languaging opportunities and 'check-ins', scaffolded as appropriate by the teacher and peers. This connects learners to their world. Deeper Learning Episode 2, for example, begins with reading, analysing and comparing extracts from Gothic literature in French and English. Learners then vote to carry out further investigations – in this example the investigation of Gothic clothing was selected. This, in turn, led to studying the social status of women in nineteenth-century industrial Europe through clothing (e.g. the wearing of corsets, the evolution of fashion) and subsequently to twentieth-century suffragettes and how Coco Chanel claimed to give 'freedom to women through clothing' in the 1930s. The sub-themes were not planned in advance but emerged to suit the students' interests and discoveries.

Disciplinary Literacy

Epistemology and Inquiry Practices
Fundamental to learning to behave like a literary reader and writer involves guidance as to how learners put themselves into the role and mindset of a writer

and become aware of the learning skills, processes and ways of thinking they need to develop. These are embedded in the different knowledge domains. Inquiry practices are based on text analysis and comparative elements across languages as learners read, analyse, compare and use multimodal 'literary' texts to build their own repertoire for writing – in this case, creative descriptions. Inquiry practices are based on broadening interdisciplinary thematic analysis. The above example opens with Gothic descriptions and is developed by learners into a social and cultural study of female liberation and conditions in the nineteenth and twentieth centuries. While the teacher plans the main strands of the learning episodes, an ecological approach encourages learner agency for progressing both textual and linguistic knowledges and understanding. In practice, this means that tasks and activities are increasingly co-constructed and co-directed by the learners.

Principles, Constructs and Themes

The premise upon which creative literary writing in French is based is as follows: *understanding and practising the principles of literary writing processes, based on reading a wide range of texts used to express different perspectives across a wide range of relevant, topical or creative themes, will enhance and deepen both textual and linguistic fluency in near-beginner learners.* As learners become increasingly aware of the use of literary conventions and genre-based principles, classroom tasks focusing on textual and linguistic features engage learners in interactive, collaborative and intercultural processing. Texts from authentic literature are used for comparative study. In this example based on Gothic descriptions, the fusion of content knowledge and literary conventions is transparent. Extracts from French and British literature include Guy de Maupassant's *La Peur, La Parure*; Theophile Gautier's *Le Chevalier Double*; Emily Brontë's *Wuthering Heights*; Robert Louis Stevenson's *Dr Jekyll and Mr Hyde* and Mary Shelley's *Frankenstein*. Comparative study enriches the potential for intercultural, critical meaning-making – the deconstruction and reconstruction of text. It also validates the use of the first language, when appropriate, which might include, for example, more than one language used for social, cultural and historical thematic content discussion, research suggestions and data gathering, yet always synthesised in French. Progression takes account of both textual and linguistic development in French, led by increasing the complexity of the literary rather than the linguistic focus – in this case, description.

Forms of Representation

Since the aim is to develop creative writing in French, learner output focuses on the composition of written text. Writing, of course, also involves careful reading and analysis of models, using a range of multimodal texts – for example, watching and analysing video extracts based on a novel, listening to conversations recorded from an audiobook or analysing speeches and multimedia representations, such as blogs or news, for thematic exploration. Genre-based approaches are used to reinforce conventions of register, style and purpose as learners are guided to construct their own texts. Practising tasks reinforces linguistic and genre-based understanding. Visual texts also play an important role in supporting learner meaning-making – especially important when learner linguistic levels are at a novice level. Analysing visual texts and encouraging learners to create criteria for the selection of visual texts alongside their writing reinforces key principles for creativity, meaning-making and coherent composition. Final drafts are celebrated and distributed.

Discourse Structures

Creative literary writing draws on reading, analysing and modelling expository, persuasive, descriptive and narrative types of discourse. The focus across all episodes is on descriptive writing – that is, composing creative and literary descriptions of people and landscapes. Discourse structures focus on the specific purpose of descriptive writing styles, including sensory imagery or evocative and emotive choice of language. These are supported by linguistic elements including the use of connectives, metaphors and similes, modal verbs, adjectives and tagging negative sentences. However, as learners language their understanding and increasingly use French to explain, question and redraft their learning, their 'metacognitive' language will typically include analysis, discussion, explanation, justification and evaluation.

Activity Domains

Using the knowledge domains (content, system, process, genre, context) as the basis for the systematic development of literacy-based tasks involves learners working across activity domains, that is, *doing* (e.g. reading, analysing text, noticing language); *organising* (e.g. increasing awareness of the language – grammar and syntax – as well as the genre-based processes and conventions required to make meaning in written descriptions); *explaining* (e.g. drafting and redrafting own text while languaging meaning construction in context and engaging in Learning Conversations); and *arguing* (e.g. textual meaning and argumentation – *thèse, anti-thèse, synthèse* reflecting appropriate cultural embeddedness). This is language learning. Learners experience increasingly demanding tasks ranging from constructing simple descriptions to having to 'argue', 'define' and so on, developing their awareness of literary reading and writing processes and the language used to express them. Critical reflection permeates all domains. This marks a significant shift in the nature and aims of tasks planned in the regular languages classroom, as outlined in Table 10.5.

Table 10.5 Activity domains for creative writing

Examples of Pluriliteracies Activity Domains Compared to Regular French Learning

Doing	Doing' is what L2 students tend to be most familiar with: reading, copying, repeating, recognising, learning, memorising and practising spelling and grammatical structures and being able to apply them to their spoken or written production. It also involves them in carrying out component tasks that prepare them for the development of reading analytical skills and writing composition.
Organising	Organising might consist of reconstructing a text in the right order, using their syntax logic, classifying words according to their gender or family association, or researching facts about a person or a country and presenting these facts in a structured and coherent manner.
Explaining	Explaining usually focuses on the question 'Why?' used to elicit learner responses starting with 'because'. This requires learners to explore linguistic structures through which to express reasoning or substantiating. In the early stages, responses are unlikely to result in deep thinking due to limited language levels and few, if any, opportunities to answer an open question in depth with meaning, sincerity and purpose. Teacher questioning has tended to focus on language rather than the cognitive potential of the utterances. To change this and deepen understanding requires scaffolded tasks and being open, as appropriate, to some discussion in two languages, especially with novice learners, to promote in-depth meaningful discussion (of a linguistic, pluriliteracies and thematic nature).
Arguing	Arguing involves, for example, expressing opinions and counter-arguing to practise the language of debating and using connectives for contrasting, qualifying or emphasising. Learners have to demonstrate how the substance of the argument or discussion and the language used to make cases for/against, for example, are connected.
Note:	Opportunities for genuine curiosity, spontaneous exploring of further ideas, understanding the philosophy behind some life events or bridging concepts with other subjects, for example, are no longer constricted by the linguistic and grammatical demands and expectations of L2 teaching and learning.

Growth Mindset, Deep Practice and Deep Understanding

In the extract from Deeper Learning Episode 1 'Tout sur Moi! – All about Me', the aim is to encourage growth mindsets by using the knowledge domains effectively. A focus on the *cognitive challenge* of creative literary writing bridges new learning potential. Transparent promotion of learner ownership and responsibility for deeper understanding not only requires consideration of the content itself but also how it links to individual and group interests. The drive is to avoid the usual surface learning of content areas, often assessed by linguistic accuracy, and instead provide dynamic creative and intercultural opportunities for students to follow and then develop a main theme collaboratively, complemented by engagement in personalising and deepening their own learning. Of course, this cannot be achieved without a shared understanding of how to nuance and use the language needed and literacies conventions practised. For example, descriptions of character require moving from simple descriptions to intricate characterisation in L2. Integrated literacy strategies are woven throughout and include elements such as the use of connectives, metaphors and similes, modal verbs and tagging negative sentences – none of these is commonplace in typical novice language classrooms. The content and contextual knowledges of the tasks remain relevant due to learner choice and developing growth mindsets, fostered, for example, by using authentic French TV dramas. While learners do not understand in entirety the language in the dramas, developing meaning-making strategies, scaffolded and guided by peers and the teacher, encourages commitment, resilience and determination to operate at a cognitively challenging level. Practice tasks, usually with a specific language or literacies focus, are contextualised in culturally relevant contexts, such as using the Chinese portrait (*portrait* chinois – a metaphorical description of oneself by a comparison with various things or elements, a tree, a flower, a film) and Proust's portrait questionnaire. Learners are guided through modelling, drafting and redrafting processes that build in deeper practice opportunities. Above all, meaning-making is at the core, so processes, tools and materials (including the use of dictionaries, experimenting with genres and styles, focusing on what makes evocative writing and so on) become normalised classroom learning. It should also be pointed out that deeper practice may involve very focused grammatical exercises or genre-based analysis. Sometimes students may well use more than language to support their meaning-making and languaging, processes that are fundamental for deeper learning.

10.5 How Do Learners Move from Surface Learning to Consolidation?

Moving from surface learning to consolidation is dynamic and challenging, requiring learners to deepen their textual and linguistic fluency, supported by scaffolding progression, task guidance and mentoring. As pathways develop in differentiated and individual ways, task design and text choice become increasingly important, especially if learners are to be encouraged to take on responsibility for progressing and deepening their own learning. Using the knowledge domains to make explicit different types of practice tasks that focus, for example, on raising cultural consciousness, deepening content knowledges or developing genre-appropriate discourse demands not only reconceptualising how tasks are designed and evaluated in the languages classroom but also the involvement of learners in those processes.

Creating supportive opportunities for learners to demonstrate, explain and evaluate their own learning requires specific attention in the following areas.

Engage the Learner

Reconciling typical surface L2 topics (e.g. transport, food, house and home) with more challenging content adopting a CLIL-style approach involves taking into account the affect of our students. Forget the 'can you describe your bedroom?' type of beginner learner tasks! Introducing the 'spooky' Gothic theme as a way to initiate twelve-year-old students into a comparative study of nineteenth-century British and French Gothic literature turns out to be a more effective way to capture their imagination and engagement. Next, experimenting ways to demonstrate and monitor progression brings a whole new dimension to the development of literary 'moves' as the catalyst for cognitive stimulation and deeper learning over one year (i.e. *describing* is the most obvious choice in L2 to monitor a shift from a typical early French-language setting to adopting a CLIL/pluriliteracies approach). Learner confidence develops as they become increasingly proficient in understanding genres, styles and registers in different modes. Broad core themes are worked on together, such as alternative more detailed and interesting descriptions of self, Gothic-inspired descriptive composition and The Travelogue, based on alternative problem-creating and problem-solving 'bespoke' travel diaries (see Section 10.6), yet these collaborative themes are always open to individual research and analysis. Student voice is highlighted through negotiating sub-themes and topics, and all learners are expected to carry out research to demonstrate their own meaning-making processes and justify their interpretations. Being treated as a 'serious' writer has a fundamental effect on L2 learners who are encouraged to dig deeper in ways that challenge their current cognitive levels. Learners feel they are being treated with respect, and their ideas, negotiations, arguments and suggestions for thematic focus and research are listened to and acted upon. Raising aspirations is a given.

Promote/Acquire Basic Understanding and Acquisition of Foundational Skills

Learners are guided through recurrent modelling of a range of literary multimodal descriptions, from factual to evocative, demonstrating their use of the protocols for creative text construction. Tasks require learners to 'notice' appropriate discourse rules in French through reading. Tasks also encourage learners to be confident 'owners' of the language they use and express meanings in ways they want. These processes are fundamental for text production. They require scaffolding learners' reading, drafting and redrafting as they develop deeper awareness of how to construct text according to disciplinary (literacy) strategies and conventions that constantly improve a previous draft (see Figure 10.1). Changing contextual stimulus encourages creativity, ranging from descriptions of robots and landscapes to Gothic

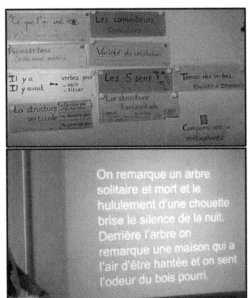

Figure 10.1 Classroom clips synthesising progression in descriptive writing

characters and contemporary workers in global settings – that is, *from physical description to fictional characters who influence their environment* (see Deeper Learning Episode 3 – The Travelogue). The starting point might be an image with the question 'What do you see?'. Early responses involve simple description – '*Il y a une maison et il y a un arbre*'; these are improved through building on textual structures and delving into 'writing craft' via manipulating, exploring and drafting to transform descriptions into composed (not cut and pasted) text. Teacher modelling of the use of literary and literacy strategies means that near-beginner learners can transform their early description into '*Gustav se tenait en face d'une grande voûte gothique c'était interminable. Un point sur la gauche il y avait un escalier central sur le dessus de l'escalier. Il y avait un portrait de la femme qui avait sept fils*'.

Language practice builds learner confidence; classroom discussion is expected, and learners are constantly required to talk about their learning, increasingly using the target language to express meaning as disciplinary protocols and practices become normalised.

Provide Feedback and Feed-Forward/Demonstrate Basic Understanding and Reflect

Two key tools are prominently used to provide learners with indicators of progress and ways to move on. **Rubrics** for assessment are co-created with learners and are used constantly as a heuristic to guide learning. They clarify expectations and learning goals. They are discussed and modified as necessary. All learners are aware of the

> ### Description d'un Intérieur Gothique par CK 7B
>
> Louise Dubois et sa soeur, Chloé Dubois, visitent le vieux manoir de leur grand - grand -oncle Monsieur Benedeit qui avait disparu, il y a 68 ans. Sa femme, Madame Benedeit, était morte dans un feu 2 mois avant. Personne ne savait ce qui avait causé le feu.......
>
> On trouvait une porche en saillie et il y avait 7 escaliers avec une énorme porte grise avec un heurtoir avec le visage d'un lion. La porte a grincé et on était frappé par un escalier central. On voyait au centre un portrait ancestral, d'un vieil homme qu'il avait l'air très riche et il avait des yeux sévère. Il y avait trois séries d'amour de chaque mur, et ils avaient l'air de vous regarder tout le temps.
>
> En haut des escaliers et vers la droite il y avait 2 colonnes massives qui tenaient un vase de chine. Au fond du couloir, il y avait une porte ouverte avec des rideaux en velours. La seule lumière était de un bougeoir sur un petite table. Dans la chambre, à gauche il y avait un gros lit à baldaquin et à côté on remarquait un tapis en velours. En face du lit, on voyait un fauteuil en cuir et derrière il y avait une bibliothèque avec beaucoup de livres. Tous les murs étaient gris ou noir, et sur le plafond on voyait une corniche. Sur la terrace, on remarquait des vignes qui poussaient partout et on était frappé par des gargouilles dont les visages grondaient de façon menaçante.

Figure 10.2 Final draft of creative writing description by novice learner

content, language and literacy goals and the ways of weaving all these together through metacognitive awareness and strategies (e.g. writing, researching, meaning-making, justifying, discourse functions). **Learning Conversations** are key to reflection and self-analysis. Sometimes these are spontaneous; sometimes they are factored into the design. Sometimes they involve the whole class; sometimes they are individual or small group events. Learners demonstrate their understanding through *languaging* their learning informally and presenting their work in groups more formally.

Facilitate/Acquire Deeper Understanding and Deep Practice

Modelling texts with and for learners draws on extracts from multimodal descriptive texts of Gothic landscapes. This immerses learners in language-rich experiences; opens minds about the power of words (reading and meaning-making); deepens understanding though expanding new ideas in creative ways; uses imagination; interconnects the local and the global; and enables the development of strategies for noticing, drafting and dealing with longer written or creative multimodal and increasingly complex text. Deep practice involves learners in the systematic and conscious analysis of different styles of descriptive text, expanding lexical families and using CDFs in order to build increasingly creative yet appropriately written descriptions. It also involves learners in practising the written language in a range of contexts. The description in Figure 10.2 was constructed and written by a near-beginner learner. Tasks require learners to demonstrate their understanding of their written product, drawing on elements of the knowledge domains – arguing, talking about the construction process and decisions made – to guard against 'cut and paste' or 'Google Translate' solutions.

Provide Feedback, Feed-Up and Feed-Forward/Demonstrate Deeper Understanding and Reflection

Enabling learners to demonstrate deeper understanding is part of the drafting process. Through mentoring learning, the drafts are used to focus discussion and raise questions. Practice activities are used to provide a learner focus on responding to the questions *What have you learned that you weren't sure of before? How can you use this to improve your next draft?* Learning Conversations are part of regular classroom routines. Using the rubrics and bespoke materials, such as table mats with literary guidance in tabular format, as well as dictionaries and digital texts and resources (e.g. websites for metaphors), contribute to creating a supportive environment for exploration and confidence building. To further build confidence, final written products can be measured, where appropriate, against internationally recognised levels, such as CEFR (The Common European Framework of Reference for Languages) and DELF (Diplôme d'Etudes en Langue Française) to demonstrate progress that can be made by near-beginner learners when alignment is carefully planned.

Facilitate Transfer/Transfer Knowledge

Deeper Learning Episode 3 – The Travelogue– is designed to facilitate the transfer of learning and provide learners with opportunities to apply what they learned in previous contexts in novel ways. Throughout the previous episodes, learners have been guided through the processes of creative literary writing. The focus has been on reading and writing descriptions of self and other characters as well as landscapes. The Travelogue might appear as an extension of describing particular geographical regions and landscapes from a tourist perspective. This is not the case. Instead, learners follow the journey of a specific character 'on a mission' who travels across different countries and encounters communities, whose experiences impact his or her decisions and who, in turn, impacts the environment and communities encountered. The mission might be a fashion designer wishing to source new textiles who discovers poor working conditions in some factories. Encouraging critical thinking in terms of world issues and real-life events, the episode requires knowledges already worked on, sustains the cognitive level of the content learning and enables transfer of some writing conventions, but also presents new challenges for further exploring style, register, humour and empathy in multicultural and multilingual contexts.

Mentor Reflection/Present and Reflect

Throughout all the DLEs, emphasis is placed on the role of mentoring and normalising the analysing, practising, drafting and redrafting processes involved in creative writing. Learning Conversations are seen as a crucial conduit for enabling individual learners to deepen their understanding, to explore how to resolve difficulties and to gain confidence in their own understanding of the five knowledge domains, which are fundamental for descriptive writing. We, as teachers, must also engage with our students in deep reflection. For example, with one particular year group in the Gothic episode, it was decided not only to describe a nineteenth-century literary character and a 'spooky' landscape but also the exterior and interior of buildings. However, interior descriptions proved problematic since it became evident that students were missing a whole specialist glossary of Gothic architecture. The issue was resolved through scaffolding. Responding to this need proved to be very popular, revealing that a group of students was fascinated with architecture and wanted to become architects but had never been exposed to thinking of this kind in any language. They started adding their own 'discoveries' to the list.

More interesting is the natural curiosity that grows. Episodes have to be open to spontaneous developments. So, for example, during research into nineteenth-century fashion, some students, on discovering the torturous process of lacing up a whalebone corset, decided to explore the conditions of women as reflected in fashion. Others wanted to dig deeper into the industrial revolution, steam inventions and Jack the Ripper! Through the study of *Around the World in Eighty Days* by Jules Verne, twelve-year-old students combined their mathematical skills to come up with a whole set of speed–distance formulae to check if Phileas Fogg's timing was indeed plausible. As one teacher described, 'It all goes right back to affect and engagement of students. If they learn in an environment that will open doors for them, they will quickly open other doors themselves.'

Another useful resource is the questionnaire that learners are asked to fill in after each episode. While learner evaluations are used by teachers and learners to guide the co-design of further episodes, they also encourage students to discuss their learning, raise their aspirations and take greater responsibility for their own learning – see Table 10.6.

10.6 The Progression Pathways for the Three Deeper Learning Episodes: Creative Literary Descriptions in French

In this section, the progression of the three deeper learning episodes is laid out. Table 10.7 describes the first stage, which explores physical and personal descriptions.

The second stage (Table 10.8) looks into subject-specific literacy and the necessary scaffolding to give learners access to a high cognitive content.

The third stage (Table 10.9) explores ways to make deeper learning more frequent, authentic and transferable to different contexts or subjects.

The final stage gives learners more time and greater opportunities to reflect on their learning, not with the usual 'in this unit, I have learned ..., I need to improve

Table 10.6 Learner questionnaires for episode evaluation and reflection

My Thoughts on Learning Activities in This Class

In this course, I was really pushed to think (Circle)	Not at All	A Little	Moderately	Much

Classify each statement as follows:

#1 what we have spent a lot of time doing

#2 what we have spent some time doing

#3 what we have spent less time doing

> Examine things closely, describe them, notice details or detect patterns
>
> Build our own explanations, theories, hypotheses or interpretations
>
> Reason with evidence and support our ideas with facts and reasons
>
> Raise questions and be curious about what we are studying
>
> Establish connections between different things, with the world or with our own lives
>
> Look at things from different angles and points of view to see things in a new way
>
> Identify central ideas, draw conclusions or grasp the essence of things
>
> Dig deep into a subject to uncover mysteries, complexities and challenges
>
> Organise and gather ideas, information, notes and experiences to understand them
>
> Reflect on where we are in our learning and understanding to determine where to go next
>
> Use and apply what we have learned to solve new problems or create something original
>
> Review and revise information from previous readings or class work
>
> Read, listen or get new information on the topic we are studying
>
> Practise the skills and procedures that the class has already learned

As a learner, it would have helped me if I had . . .

As a learner, it would have helped me if the teacher had . . .

on . . .', but rather to introduce new, more visible thinking routines. Simultaneously, we, as teachers, have to reconsider how we give feedback to our students and see if we could provide comments and strategies that enhance true learning and progression (see Table 10.6).

10.7   Conclusion and Outlook

The DLEs in this chapter are built on principles, ideas, guides and encouragement to reconceptualise language learning as an emergent subject discipline. This means finding ways of offering learners a solid knowledge base as well as a linguistic base that is cognitively challenging, linguistically purposeful, learner-centred and relevant. In other words, creating with learners a means of deepening their critical understanding of life experiences and the world at an age-appropriate level while increasing their understanding of the ways in which languages and literacies are

Table 10.7 Deeper Learning Episode 1

Moving From a Traditional French L2 Language-Focused Approach to a Disciplinary-Oriented Pluriliteracies Approach

From the physical description to the fictional character who influences his or her environment

Step 1: 'All About Me'

CDFs: describe, classify, explain, evaluate, persuade, influence

Sections	Brief Summary	Visual and Literary Support	Remarks
Section 1: 'Physical and moral portrait"	Basic physical descriptions There are different types of portraits (portrait-robot, Chinese portrait …) Personality by the sign of the Zodiac, by numbers The other's gaze: what do my friends think of me? The Chinese portrait The portrait of Proust	TV series *Café des Rêve (The Café of Dreams* – available on YouTube); Guy de Maupassant's short story *La Parure – The Necklace* Unit plan: 'Physical and moral portraits'	Each teacher uses their own approach to develop: Classic theme of physical description, but focusing on the face, for example, becomes much more detailed (a hooked nose, arched eyebrows depilated …) For personality, learners need exposure to much more sophisticated vocabulary before classifying the vocabulary between, for example, personality traits visible in public and those that stay in one's 'secret garden'
Section 2: 'What I don't like, my fears, my phobias, my nightmares'		See unit plan Top weird phobias https://www.youtube.com/watch?v=CIPKQRf8NQw The guests of a TV show share their phobias: https://www.youtube.com/watch?v=3vR0DQvfNMI	More motivating to provide a list of phobias and read 'I suffer from achluophobia and cynophobia' rather than 'I am afraid of the dark and dogs' (See Appendix 1: List of Phobias)
Section 3: Emotions and relationships; 'What is Love?'	Work on the language of feelings and emotions 'Diamond Nine activity' in groups to classify, negotiate, convince and create a hierarchy of what constitutes love or friendship	Discuss the affectionate relationships of the characters in *Café des Rêves* (the Café of Dreams) Useful resource: http://www.bbc.co.uk/languages/french/mafrance/flash/interactive_popup.shtml	Can introduce dreams and ambitions into the frame as necessary; individual and group research

Appendix 1: List of Phobias

Ablutophobia – Fear of bathing (this phobia is more a fear of drowning than a fear of water)

Acerophobia – Fear of what tastes sour (acidic)

Achluophobia – Fear of darkness

Algophobia – Fear of pain

Climacophobia – Fear of using stairs, especially going down them

Coulrophobia – Fear of clowns

Cyclophobia – Fear of getting on a bicycle or other two-wheeled vehicles

Fumiphobia – Fear of smoke (tobacco, for example)

Gephyrophobia – Fear of bridges (or crossing bridges)

Gerascophobia – Fear of getting older

Osmophobia – Hypersensitivity to odours

Phonophobia – Hypersensitivity to sound

Photophobia – Hypersensitivity to light

Animal phobias

Acarophobia – Fear of skin parasites, mites

Chiroptophobia – Fear of bats

Cuniculophobia – Fear of rabbits

Cynophobia – Fear of dogs

Entomophobia – Fear of insects

Herpetophobia – Fear of reptiles or amphibians

Hippophobia – Fear of horses, equines

Ichthyophobia – Fear of fish

Musophobia – Fear of mice or rats

Myrmecophobia – Fear of ants

Table 10.8 Deeper Learning Episode 2

Step 2: The Literary Portrait

In this unit, students apply what they have learned about physical and psychological descriptions to a nineteenth-century context.

Transferring what they may also do in their first language, they learn how to profile a character for their story with examples drawn from nineteenth-century French and British literature. The characters come alive through in-depth work on appropriately describing emotions and perceptions and how a specific environment can affect a character.

Progression	Remarks
2.1 Extension of the vocabulary of the portrait	Vocabulary extension tasks for descriptions of characters in literature
2.2 'The look'	The impression given by the character, the role of the attitude, clothes and voice; importance of detail in the eyes, hands …
2.3 Clothing in the nineteenth century	See support resources for this highly specialised language field
2.4 Vocabulary of Emotions 2: Fear	In preparation for Gothic unit
2.5 Study of character descriptions in nineteenth-century literature	See work on Victor Hugo, Guy de Maupassant, Jules Verne, Emily Brontë, Mary Shelley, H. G. Wells …
2.6 The character of the novel: habits, interactions …	Learners work on the profile of their character: past, habits, dreams and ambitions, fears …; to transfer the linguistic aspects learned in the previous step through literacies development
2.7 Gothic unit	The character is positioned in a Gothic-style story (which also requires a thorough study of the description of Gothic interiors and landscapes) See unit plan 'Gothic Unit'

needed to make meaning. Identifying reading and writing as a conduit for learning fits with Manchón's view that 'the exploration of writing as a site for language learning is a newcomer to the fields of second language acquisition (SLA) and second language (L2) writing' (2021, p. 1). Adopting a pluriliteracies approach requires a shift in teacher mindset and a shift in learning design. In particular, the need to develop textual fluency as well as linguistic fluency makes sense. The outcomes of the student learning so far suggest that levels of attainment in French writing are well in advance of what would be expected in the regular language classroom – some learners have reached an unprecedented B1 level for writing as near beginners. In other words, creative literary writing offers ways of substantially increasing the knowledge and language skills base required to read and compose creative literary text in French through focusing on specific elements of literacies and pluriliteracies.

This series of DLEs has foregrounded developing *description* as a conduit for learning and a means for benchmarking progression.

Table 10.9 Deeper Learning Episode 3

Step 3: Ethics and Empathy
A study of reciprocal influences between a character and a 'working' environment, raising cultural consciousness.

This final stage is part of a unit on 'Le Voyage et le Carnet de Voyage' (travel diaries): students choose a character who will travel through all five continents, including at least three francophone countries.

As well as the work to be completed on a 'travel diaries' style of writing, students must move away from typical tourism language scenarios towards researching cultures, problems, aspirations of the local population/communities encountered and demonstrate a change of attitude of their character as they discover more about local culture.

The very colourful and multicultural context of this unit integrates notions of humour and empathy in the character's profile, as in L1 advanced lessons. Learners must demonstrate not only how the environment influences the character but also how the character can influence their environment.

Examples:
- A businesswoman in charge of finding new exotic locations for her chain of luxury hotels discovers the social and ecological impact of her industry on the local communities.
- An aid worker travels through disaster/war-torn countries for the first time and tries to raise awareness of poverty and suffering.
- A big fashion designer wants to find new textiles and discovers the working conditions in some textile factories.
- A French DJ goes around the world in search of inspiration and discovers a whole new francophone musical experience. Will he or she create a sound fusion and create a new style of music?
- Francophone *MasterChef*: let all your senses explode!

The main pedagogical implications of the available theory and research on writing as a site of language learning relate to issues in task selection, design, and implementation, on the one hand, and feedback provision and processing, on the other. Regarding the selection of tasks, the more problem-solving, meaning-making challenges a task represents, the more chances of fostering the kind of deep linguistic processing associated with writing that is deemed to lead to language learning. (Manchón; 2011, p. 64)

In addition to Manchón's claim, another crucial implication is that of developing a serious content and cultural knowledge base that usefully comes together in Hyland's (2011) five knowledge domains. There is a great deal more work to be done with colleagues and researchers, and it is essential to stress that this is an ongoing process, full of trials and errors and that, along the way, some compromises have to be made. There are tensions. For example, the sole use of the target language is brought into question – transforming classroom practices suggests that translanguaging is more likely to grow a positive environment where deeper learning thrives – especially with near-beginner learners, as in this case. A language teacher must be willing to endorse the role of being and behaving as a deeper learning coach or mentor while addressing the demands of a language national curriculum. Most importantly, in the design of DLEs teachers should be prepared to take risks, to question traditional practices, to accept that not everything works for students and to keep working at it – we know it is going in the right direction when our learners say so.

REFERENCES

Carter, R. (2007). Literature and Language Teaching 1986–2006: A Review. *International Journal of Applied Linguistics*, *17*(1), 3–13. https://doi.org/10.1111/j.1473-4192.2007.00130.x

Coyle, D., & Meyer, O. (2021). *Beyond CLIL: Pluriliteracies Teaching for Deeper Learning*. Cambridge University Press.

Freire, P. (2000). *Pedagogy of the Oppressed* (30th anniversary ed.). Continuum.

Goldman, S. R., Britt, M. A., Brown, W. et al. (2016). Disciplinary Literacies and Learning to Read for Understanding: A Conceptual Framework for Disciplinary Literacy. *Educational Psychologist*, *51*(2), 219–246. https://doi.org/10.1080/00461520.2016.1168741

Hallet, W. (2016). *Genres im fremdsprachlichen und bilingualen Unterricht: Formen und Muster der sprachlichen Interaktion*. Klett/Kallmeyer.

Hyland, K. (2011). Disciplines and Discourses: Social Interactions in the Construction of Knowledge. In D. Starke-Meyerring, A. Paré, N. Artemeva, M. Horne, & L. Yousoubova (Eds.), *Writing in Knowledge Societies*. Parlor Press/WAC Clearinghouse, pp. 193–214

Kramsch, C. (2014). Teaching Foreign Languages in an Era of Globalization: Introduction. *The Modern Language Journal*, *98*(1), 296–311. https://doi.org/10.1111/j.1540-4781.2014.12057.x

Manchón, R. M. (2011). Writing to Learn the Language: Issues in Theory and Research. In R. M. Manchón (Ed.), Learning-to-Write and Writing-to-Learn in an Additional Language, vol. 31. John Benjamins, pp. 61–82. https://doi.org/10.1075/lllt.31.07man

Manchón, R. M. (Ed.) (2021). *The Routledge Handbook of Second Language Acquisition and Writing*. 1st Ed. Routledge.

Manchón, R. M., & Cerezo, L. (2018). Writing as Language Learning: Framing the Issue. In J. I. Liontas, T. International Association, & M. DelliCarpini (Eds.), *The TESOL Encyclopedia of English Language Teaching*. John Wiley & Sons, pp. 1–6. https://doi.org/10.1002/9781118784235.eelt0530

Pountain, C. J. (2019). Modern Languages as an Academic Discipline: The Linguistic Component. *Language, Culture and Curriculum*, *32*(3), 244–260. https://doi.org/10.1080/07908318.2019.1661153

Sedita, J. (2020). We Need a Writing Rope [Blog Entry]. *Keys to Literacy*. https://keystoliteracy.com/blog/we-need-a-writing-rope/

11 Religious Education: Exploring Pluriliteracies through a Deeper Learning Episode on Modern-Day Prophets

STEFAN ALTMEYER & JOHANNES KERBECK

11.1 Competences and Literacy in Religious Education

Religious Education (RE) in European countries varies significantly in terms of organisational form, content and educational goals and does so even more worldwide (Rothgangel, Danilovich & Jäggle, 2014–2020). Despite the partially substantial differences, we can nevertheless assert for many of these concepts that they concordantly focus the task of RE on the learnable ability to deal reflectively with religion as it occurs (or may occur) in one's personal life and in society. In most fundamental terms, RE thus pursues the goal of enabling students to think and act responsibly in matters of religion, in particular by providing structured and life-relevant basic knowledge, exploring forms of lived religion and developing the ability to engage in inter-religious or worldview dialogues (Altmeyer, 2010; Meyer, 2021). Hence, the basic concern is to enable learners to gain reflexive and relevant orientational knowledge from contact with religious traditions. How far this reflective approach extends and of what it exactly consists, can – depending on context – be interpreted in very different ways (Hannam et al., 2020): from a 'neutral' comparative understanding of religions or a 'critical' evaluation of religious claims to a 'positional' empowerment of individual decisions and identity development regarding religion.

With each different approach to RE, the concept of what deeper learning means necessarily differs as well. In this chapter, we would like to proceed from an understanding that is primarily related to the German school context but also shares a high degree of connectivity with many other contexts. From our point of view, deeper learning can be defined as the process of 'bringing religion and lifeworld or religious traditions and current experiences into a lively dialogue with each other' (Englert, Hennecke & Kämmerling, 2014, p. 12, own translation). On this basis, deepening can be modelled in terms of the level reached at both critically and productively, linking elementary content structures and elementary lifeworld perspectives (see Section 11.2). Competences to be acquired in RE therefore refer to cognitive abilities and skills in dealing with religion in its various dimensions (experience, cognition, practice, ethics) as well as to the motivational and volitional

capacity to relate these productively and critically to questions of lifeworld orientation and to arrive at a reflected judgement. In other words, competence in RE refers
to students' ability 'to evaluate their understanding of religion in personal terms and
to evaluate their understanding of self in religious terms' (Miedema, 2017, p.133).
Consequently, learning processes in RE go hand in hand with two fundamental
deepening movements: a constant change of perspective (learning about/from
religion) as well as an associated continuous, student-oriented evaluation of the
relevance of what has been learned.

In this context, deeper learning in RE possesses a basic linguistic dimension and
goes hand in hand with the development of religious literacy since subject and
language learning are inseparably linked. To promote deeper learning, not only the
subject language of 'religion' must be acquired but at the same time the ability to
communicate the gained knowledge and procedures appropriately in a personally
meaningful way (Coyle & Meyer, 2021; Meyer et al., 2018). The corresponding
didactic question of how to teach the linguistic skills corresponding to content
and lifeworld structures can be clarified with the help of the following model
(Table 11.1; Altmeyer, 2021b).

The model suggests thinking of literacy in RE in a two-dimensional manner, with
two basic distinctions being crucial. The first lies between 'religious language' and
'language of religion' and reflects the insight that religion can become the topic of
learning in a subjectivising or an objectivising approach, meaning by investigating
personal religious orientations (religiosity) or materialised religion (religious tradition). Being able to switch between the two perspectives and to draw relations
between them coincides with person-centred goals in RE and the corresponding
question of relevance construction mentioned above. The second distinction
looks at the speaker's positioning in relation to religion and distinguishes along
an inside/outside line between 'talking religiously' and 'talking about religion'.
Being able to distinguish between these two poles and change perspectives entails
the competence of critical reflection upon the positionings inherent in different
linguistic approaches to religion.

Insofar as RE in general pursues the goal of enabling students to deal with
religion in a responsible and mature manner, four inter-connected literacy tasks
arise, namely that learning in RE intends to open up elementary forms of religious
traditions ('language of religion'), to deal with personal forms of religious expression ('religious language'), to address the question of life-relevant orientation
through religion ('talking religiously') and to promote religious judgement and
dialogue ('talking about religion'). The model overview shows in detail which
linguistic competence expectations are associated with this (italics in Table 11.1)
and which approach of didactic modelling they correspond to (terms in brackets in
Table 11.1).

Table 11.1 Literacy in religious education

	Talking Religiously	Positioning Inside and Outside	Talking about Religion
Religious Language	*Learning to talk*: being able to communicate on relevant religious issues (Exploring religion)	*Reflecting language use*: being able to distinguish different standpoints of religious speakers	*Learning to reflect*: being able to recognise, name and evaluate religious claims (Arguing religion)
Subjective ↑ **Reference** → **Objective**	*Assessing relevance*: being able to relate subjectivised and traditional forms of talking religiously	Changing perspectives	*Assessing relevance*: being able to relate evaluative and interpretative forms of talking about religion
Language of Religion	*Learning to perceive and express*: being able to discover and express elements of one's own religiosity by entering the religious language game (Experiencing religion)	*Reflecting language use*: being able to distinguish different standpoints relational to religion	*Learning to understand*: being able to interpret linguistic forms of religious traditions (Explaining religion)

11.2   Deeper Learning in Religious Education

As already formulated above, we want to connect deeper learning in RE with the subject-specific question: *at which level does a lively dialogue between the lifeworld perspective on religion and the acquisition of exemplary knowledge about religion take place?* In German RE research, this is classically referred to as the so-called correlative or dialogical principle of religious learning (Englert, Hennecke & Kämmerling, 2014; Roebben, 2021). This principle states that religious knowledge should always be developed in dialogue with the questions, experiences and convictions of the students and therefore through personal communication. What follows from that central concern of religious learning is that RE must develop both cognitive academic language proficiency and basic interpersonal communicative skills (Cummins, 2000). Unlike in other subjects, the linguistic learning progress in RE can therefore not be focused solely on the development of academic language competences. On the contrary, competences in ordinary language for personal communication remain of fundamental, irreplaceable importance in RE (Altmeyer, 2019).

Connecting general deeper learning strategies (see Part I) with specific competences in religious learning processes and corresponding basic modes of didactic modelling (see Table 11.1), we want to distinguish four levels of deeper learning in RE as follows.

1. *Basic knowledge about religion.* At this level, the focus lies on basic understanding and foundational skills related to a particular topic of RE. According to 'explaining religion' (Englert, Hennecke & Kämmerling, 2014, pp. 59–60), it is about understanding a religious phenomenon and being able to approach and articulate it appropriately.

2. *Elementary religious knowledge from original encounters with religion.* A first step into deeper understanding can be achieved where learning about religion turns into learning from religion – that is, where authentic religious tradition is explored in the mode of 'experiencing religion' (Englert, Hennecke & Kämmerling, 2014, p. 61) through different media or personal encounter and examined in a student-centred way.

3. *Applied religious knowledge with a focus on actuality.* The level of deep understanding can be reached when religious knowledge is questioned for its relevance to the present. This is 'arguing religion' (Englert, Hennecke & Kämmerling, 2014, p. 60): obstacles of religious traditions, claims and convictions, as well as their potential problem-solving capacity, are critically examined and insights communicated.

4. *Deepened religious knowledge with completed construction of relevance.* The fourth level, related to transfer, focuses on the level of an individual evaluation and, if appropriate, positioning (Heimbrock, 2017). The question of relevance is not only posed abstractly but, in the sense of 'exploring religion' (Englert,

Hennecke & Kämmerling, 2014, pp. 58–59), it is brought into connection with one's own personal convictions, whereby this personal construction of relevance and its articulation is intended to be made possible by the teachers but is in no way to be influenced or directed or predefined by them.

We want to briefly illustrate this understanding of deeper learning levels by means of a classical topic of (Christian) RE, choosing the example of prophets. *Basic knowledge about religion* can be found in questions such as: *What is understood by a prophet in biblical tradition, other religions, or history? Which central prophetic figures do we know? Which concerns can be linked to their messages?* When students get to know a specific prophet in more detail, in the various facets of his or her life, the historical setting, the tradition of his or her calling, or examples of his or her message and history of influence, *elementary religious knowledge from original encounter with religion* comes into play. *Applied religious knowledge with a focus on actuality* can be introduced, for example, by formulating question such as *Are prophets only a phenomenon of the past and of religious traditions or might there be present day prophets* as well? Or *Where might women and men be needed to perform in a prophetic sense?*

Finally, the level of a *deepened religious knowledge with completed construction of relevance* can be achieved through questions like this: *If I were allowed to give a speech to humanity right now, what would I say?* Through such a task, prophets are no longer merely spoken about in a detached way, but a prophetic role is directly taken on in a playful and experimental way, which challenges deeper cognitive, emotional and action-oriented experiences and insights from an inner perspective (Altmeyer, 2015).

The example may already clarify how deeper learning might be realised in RE and how it can be didactically modelled, but it also points out that the four levels mentioned need by no means be interpreted in the sense of a linear sequence. A specific teaching project on prophets could certainly start with a very challenging task like the one mentioned above (writing a speech to humanity). In that case, fundamental religious knowledge about prophets might be acquired at a later stage of the project. The crucial point of deeper learning in RE is not when and in which order a certain depth of learning is reached, but that there exists the conscious intention of the teacher to create opportunities for learners to touch all of the four levels of deeper learning in the course of a specific learning episode.

11.3   A Model Deeper Learning Episode in Religious Education

With our model episode (see Table 11.2), we pick up on a current and overarching topic that we piloted in project teaching. The project was developed in cooperation with the Public Climate School, a Germany-wide initiative of the 'students for future' movement, which aims to raise cross-disciplinary awareness of the climate crisis in schools and offers alternative teaching activities as part of an annual campaign week (https://publicclimateschool.de/). In this context, our learning episode for RE was developed for upper-secondary students in years 10-13 and implemented in May 2021. It centred on an inter-religious panel discussion with experts from Buddhism, Judaism, Islam and Christianity, which was centrally hosted and recorded and provided students with interactive opportunities for participation. Teachers across Germany were able to participate with their RE classes as the panel discussion was available via a streaming service and the lesson planning and teaching materials were accessible online.

Thematically, the learning episode focuses on the question of what contribution the four world religions can collectively make to promote climate justice (Altmeyer, 2021a; Grelle, 2018; Tomlinson, 2019). The topic is particularly suitable for deeper learning in RE as it is highly relevant both from the students' point of view and in terms of subject matter. After all, there is no doubt that climate change is one of the epochal challenges of our day. What a decade ago might have been seen as one political issue among many, or as the concern of a few environmental activists, has now become a key social and global issue, the urgency of which is being pointed out not least by the younger generation with clarity and insistence. Some scholars even argue that climate change is perhaps even *the* religious issue of our day since it fundamentally concerns the relationship between humans and the natural order, as well as the question of responsibility for global justice, the future and humanity (Gardner, 2006; Jenkins, Berry & Kreider, 2018; Tomalin, Haustein & Kidy, 2019). Insofar as corresponding cosmological, anthropological and ethical questions belong to the core of all religious traditions, the question arises whether these traditions can also make a substantial contribution to solving the climate crisis at present. Consequently, the thematic focus lies on the field of environmental ethics, and an inter-religious learning approach has been chosen that fits into the global goals of education for sustainable development. Major goals of the learning episode can be located within the competence spectrum of the Orientation Framework for Global Development (Ständige Konferenz der Kultusminister der Länder in der Bundesrepublik Deutschland, Bundesministerium für wirtschaftliche Zusammenarbeit und Entwicklung, & Engagement Global, 2016, pp. 272–284) and specified for religious learning as follows:

- Recognising diversity: Students will be able to recognise natural and socio-cultural diversity and name different religious approaches to sustainable development.
- Change of perspective and empathy: Students can become aware of, appreciate and reflect on their own and other people's religious orientations in terms of their significance for a sustainable way of life and social order.

Table 11.2 Planning grid for model deeper learning episode in religious education

Designing Deeper Learning Episodes

Planning Grid for Model Deeper Learning Episode in Religious Education

What do I want my learners to know or be able to do?	How will my learners demonstrate increasingly deeper understanding at the surface, consolidation and transfer levels?	How can I support active knowledge co-construction for my learners?	How will I support my learners every step of the way?	How can I generate and sustain learner commitment and achievement?
Basic Understanding: • Basic approaches to climate justice in Buddhism, Judaism, Islam and Christianity • Basic awareness of potential impacts of religious orientations on climate justice	**Preliminary Learning Products:** • Tweets from panel discussion on statements and beliefs about the connection between climate and religion	**Construction of Knowledge:** () Inquiry-based learning () Problem-based learning () Experimenting (X) Original encounter (X) Project-based learning	**Scaffolding:** • Twitter scenario with clear, focused observation tasks and linguistically reduced text production challenge	**Engagement:** Personal meaningfulness/ relevance: • Reference to pre-experiences in opening phase • Representation of relevant content through original encounter with authentic people • Addressing of personal positioning
Foundational Skills: • Recognising religious diversity with empathy	**Main Learning Product:** • Tweet on shared concerns of four religious panellists • Tweet engaging with critical counter-position	**Social Interaction:** • Original panel discussion with the possibility of interactive participation • Intensive interaction in group work and presentation in plenary session	**Feedback:** • By peers in group discussion and final plenary **Feed-Up:** • Teacher advice during group work	Opportunities for autonomous learning: • Independent and creative learning in group phase • High proportion of discussion and exchange through Twitter scenario that encourages pointed expression
Deeper Understanding: • Exploring an inter-religious contribution to solving the climate crisis • Change of perspective between different worldview perspectives	**Transfer Task:** • Brief personal positioning at the beginning and end of the episode (correlative framing)	**Use of (Digital) Media:** • Opening picture collage, worksheets with Twitter scenario • Live panel discussion via stream and interaction via mobile devices	**Feed-Forward:** • Targeted step by step tasks in phased group work • Teacher advice during group work **Assessment:** • Not explicitly intended in this episode, but might link to the written tweets	**Reflection and Revision:** • Various possibilities for follow-up and more in-depth learning in supplementary material
Deep Practice: • Evaluative self-positioning in the face of a critical counter-position • Consider solidarity and co-responsibility				
Transfer: • Relating critically and being open-ended to own lifeworld orientation				

- Solidarity and co-responsibility: Students can identify areas of personal co-responsibility for people and the environment and review and develop their own basic orientation in dialogue with others.

The structure of the learning episode can be roughly divided into three sections: a motivating introduction to the topic (approx. 20 minutes), the inter-religious panel discussion, during which the students work on targeted observation tasks and can also participate interactively (approx. 45 minutes), and a concluding consolidation phase (approx. 30 minutes). Optionally, additional material was provided for further work in class after the learning episode.

In the motivating introduction, the aim is to enable the students to personally connect to the problem. For this purpose, a visual impulse is given by means of a picture collage (see Material No. 2) and discussed with the students with regard to *which thoughts and/or emotions the pictures trigger in them, which connections they perceive and where they would finally position themselves.* In a second step, the collage is expanded to include a reference to religions so that, for the first time, the world's religions become the focus of the question about climate protection. This gives the students the opportunity to activate and express pre-conceptions and pre-experiences about the relationship between religion and the climate crisis or climate protection.

Phase 1 is followed by the inter-religious panel discussion, which is streamed into the classroom. In this panel, four people from the world's major religions discuss the question of motivation, opportunities, and specific examples of why and how their religion is committed to climate protection and how the religions can work together to become an important voice in sustainability transitions. Students observe the discussion in groups of four (see Material No. 4), with each student being responsible to follow one person on the panel more closely, given the following scenario for observation: 'Imagine you are reporting on Twitter about your participation in the panel discussion. To do this, you want to capture the key statements of a discussant in short and concise sentences'. Accordingly, the task is given to write three tweets during the panel discussion: *why climate concern is important to the respective religion, which examples for engagement the person names,* and *what his or her most important statement is.* In a group of four students, all four panellists are observed in this way. In addition to the observation tasks, there are several opportunities to interact with the panel through digital media channels.

After the panel discussion, the in-depth phase begins with group work in which the groups of four engage in conversation about their observations, for which they are provided with targeted tasks. First, they might talk about what was important to the people on the podium and what, if any, differences there were. Then the group is asked to write a joint tweet about what views the discussants have in common. Afterwards, a very critical tweet is to be discussed and answered, in which a fictitious user expresses the opinion that religions always lead to conflicts and war and will therefore never find a common solution against climate change. In the final step of the consolidation phase, which returns to the plenary, the teacher asks some students to present their group tweets, which can be briefly commented on or discussed. The episode ends with a short concluding question about how the students now evaluate a possible contribution of religions to a more climate-just world.

For further work following the learning episode, a second, closer look at the group's tweets is important, in which the individual results are discussed and advice is given for further development. For this follow-up work, three additional material suggestions are available (see Material No. 6). Two of them include an explanatory video and corresponding tasks. The topics are Christian environmental ethics and a biblical theology of creation. A third suggestion leads to an online response tool that deals with an everyday ecological dilemma (Altmeyer & Dreesmann, 2020; 2021) and the question of how one would act in this situation and for what reasons. This way, students can learn more about their attitudes towards climate protection in everyday life and discuss the question which (potentially religious) orientation is important for them personally.

Public Climate School on Climate and Religion (Years 10–13)

11.4   Alignment of the Deeper Learning Episode

In the following discussion, we aim to demonstrate how the model learning episode is intended to facilitate deeper learning related to religion. We will first analyse this didactically with regard to the suggested learning path and then elaborate on teacher and student activities.

How Is Deeper Learning Didactically Modelled?

The learning episode clearly focuses on an original encounter with religion, from which *elementary religious knowledge* can be gained. This becomes particularly evident in the panel discussion, in which the students come into contact with authentic voices on the climate crisis from four religious backgrounds. Through the observation tasks, the students also gain *basic knowledge about religion* ('explaining religion'), but above all they pay attention to what the panellists personally stand for and what is particularly important to them from their religious orientation. Thus, the didactic mode of 'experiencing religion' stands clearly in the foreground. With regard to literacy, this means that the students are confronted with the language of religion from an inner perspective of religious speakers and are challenged to switch between and relate to both an inside and outside positioning towards religion. They are specifically guided to do this in the observation tasks of writing short tweets: On the one hand, they report in factual (i.e. objectivising) language about the central statements of the religious speakers in relation to the climate issue, but they also focus on the question of how they personally position themselves in relation to the articulated values and orientations.

The latter perspective especially comes to the fore when the students share their observations after the panel discussion, find out what the discussants stand for together and respond to a critical tweet. This is where the level of deep practice comes into play, because by guiding the students to independently address a critical objection about religion – namely, that religions per se cannot be expected to contribute to solving the climate crisis or even any social issue – the didactic focus shifts to 'arguing religion', and the focus is on *applied religious knowledge with focus on actuality*. Here, the students are forced to undertake a further change of perspective on the language level, namely from an interpretative approach to an argument that can take into account different evaluative stands and develops in the direction of a reflective personal positioning.

This last level, which aims at deepening religious knowledge in the direction of *establishing relevance* or *exploring* religion, is addressed by the way the learning episode is framed. As early as in the introduction, personal standpoints and pre-concepts are activated, which are kept virulent throughout the entire learning episode and are made explicit once again at the end, namely when the students are asked for a personal conclusion and evaluation of the significance of religious orientation in the context of the climate crisis. However, this level of deeper learning is only briefly addressed explicitly in our learning episode but is implicitly present through the framing and the entire didactic modelling. It seems to be important to continue working on that dimension by using our supplementary in-depth materials. But even apart from this, statements from the evaluation of our teaching project show that the intended level of deepening can already be touched in our episode. The following students' statements show that before the learning episode, the students had hardly seen any connection between the climate issue and religion but have now discovered it quite positively. The first one speaks of exciting and inspiring discoveries:

> The topic was very exciting! Combining climate and religion is something you might not otherwise think about. Above all, I learned a lot about the different religions, and I was inspired by how harmoniously the different views complemented each other and agreed with each other. (Student, Year 12)

The second feedback even goes one step further and reports lasting effects on the participant's own everyday orientations:

Before this lesson, I didn't really think that religion and climate could somehow be connected. However, the panel discussion made me think otherwise [...] and in fact, since the discussion, I try to reflect more on my impact on the environment and be more in the moment. Because of that, I think these discussions can make a difference and are a really good concept to bring students closer to the environment on different levels. (Student, Year 12)

11.5 How Do Learners Move from Surface Learning to Consolidation to the Transfer Stage?

To show how our didactic modelling affects the practice dimension of teacher and student activity, we refer to the elements of a deeper learning episode as described in Part I, Figure 4.1.

Engage the Learner

The cognitive and volitional activation of the students at the beginning of the learning process is initially ensured by the topic – the climate crisis being a highly relevant but also controversial matter. The opening picture collage, which is to be introduced by the teacher with open and motivating questions, serves to give the students a chance to bring up their pre-experiences and to activate pre-concepts. The link between climate and religion given in the second step is likely to be somewhat surprising for most students but at the same time motivating due to the prospect of an interactive panel discussion. It is important to make clear that personal positioning is significant for the entire learning episode – that is, beyond the acquisition of abstract knowledge, the question of everyday orientation is also addressed.

Promote/Acquire Basic Understanding and Acquisition of Foundational Skills

Basic knowledge is introduced via the four panel members, and the students' focus on relevant knowledge perspectives is ensured by the targeted observation task during the panel discussion. The fictitious Twitter format makes this motivating for the students and at the same time linguistically simplified. The tasks focus on two central literacy aspects, namely the objectivising articulation of significant content as well as the perception and expression of subjectivised viewpoints and orientations. Since the learning process is designed for independent learning in groups, the teacher must ensure a clear understanding of the tasks and an adequate grouping.

Provide Feedback, Feed-Up and Feed-Forward/Demonstrate Basic Understanding and Reflect

The students first demonstrate and reflect on their learning outcomes from observing the panel discussion independently in groups, for which they are provided with a clear task. The teaching material uses the Twitter format as a media framework that serves as a scaffold to facilitate informed discussion. The teacher is available as a contact person in this phase to provide online feedback.

Facilitate/Acquire Deeper Understanding and Deep Practice

In the second part of the group work, the students take two steps towards a deeper understanding. First, they bring the four different religious voices into conversation with each other and articulate what they perceive as their common concerns. Second, they independently engage with a critical interjection that might be expressed in a similar way in current social discourses. These steps towards a more complex in-depth level are set out in writing in the task sheet, so that the teacher is primarily confronted with clarifying understanding and maintaining a productive working atmosphere.

Provide Feedback, Feed-Up and Feed-Forward/Demonstrate Deeper Understanding and Mastery of Skills

After completion of the group work, selected students present their group results in the plenary followed by short comments and discussions. If organisationally possible, this phase should be given sufficient time so that all students can participate and an intensive exchange can be stimulated. In this case, more students could participate, and a more intensive exchange could be stimulated. The role of the teacher at this point is primarily that of a moderator who should, however, also give helpful hints with regard to the central learning task, which, with regard to literacy, consists of clearly distinguishing evaluative and interpretative approaches to religious positioning on climate issues and interweaving the perspectives pointing to a reflected evaluation competence.

Facilitate Transfer/Transfer Knowledge

Transfer of learning is targeted throughout the entire learning episode: when students can take their own position at the beginning of the episode, when they experience authentic voices from the inside perspective of four religions, when they present these with reference both to objectivising and subjectivising approaches, or when they finally respond to a critical interjection by arguing independently. The transfer loop finally closes at the end of the episode, where in a short plenary communication the students are once again invited to a personal interim conclusion. In all of this, the transfer performance consists of multiple changes of perspective regarding the topic of climate and religion, which requires and promotes corresponding linguistic activity in each case.

Mentor Reflection/Present and Reflect

Presentation and reflection of the transfer level takes place only very briefly in our model learning episode. It is the task of the subsequent, more in-depth learning process to go into more detail and to create space for consolidation and reflection of the learning success. The supplementary materials provide various possibilities for this, which the teacher can use depending on the interests and level of competence of the learning group.

11.6   Conclusion and Outlook

At the end of this attempt to relate the concept of deeper learning to RE and to develop a model learning episode, there stands a straightforward conclusion. Subject and language learning are to be regarded as deeply intertwined in the field of religious learning as well, so that the goals and processes of religious learning can be fruitfully reformulated and specified within the framework of deeper learning. In RE, too, the conditions, goals, objects and communicative forms of teaching are to be questioned with regard to inherent language requirements, and the students are to be offered targeted support according to their literacy skills. When planning deeper learning processes in religion, teachers must also take into account the (linguistic) pre-conditions of the learners and reflect on the language of teaching; they must integrate linguistic requirements into planning and design, support transitions between everyday and academic communication and create a variety of occasions for linguistic action. In this regard, the planning grid (see Table 11.2) for deeper learning episodes serves as a helpful tool. When implementing the planning grid, the teacher is confronted with a twofold task: first, to plan a deeper learning path didactically, taking into account the levels of subject-specific deepening and didactic modelling typical for religious learning, and second, to translate these into appropriate teacher and student action. If this is successful, RE in the deeper learning framework can develop its very specific literacy profile, which envisions itself in teaching language skills that really serve all students to achieve religious maturity and to develop a healthy personality.

11.7   Learning Materials

Overview

　　No. 1: Short planning phase of the learning episode (Table 11.3)
　　No. 2: Picture collage (activation)
　　A copy is available on request from the authors.

No. 3: Panel discussion (personal encounter/basic understanding)

A recording of the panel discussion (in German) is available on request from the authors.

No. 4: Observation task to panel discussion (preliminary learning products) – Worksheet 11.1

No. 5: Tasks for in-depth group work after panel discussion (main learning products) – Worksheet 11.2 (see Table 11.4)

No. 6: Follow-up tasks to continue after the learning episode (transfer task)

These materials also include an assessment grid (Table 11.5) dealing with religious language and the language of religion.

No. 1: Short Planning Phase of the Learning Episode
Section 1: Preparation and Introduction to Topic

Table 11.3 Section 1 – Preparation and introduction to topic

Phase	Activity	Setting	Media/Materials
Preparation	*Teacher prepares the technology, materials and livestream.*		For the complete episode: Smartboard or PC with projector Students: portable device
Greeting	The teacher greets the class and outlines the framework for the learning process.	Plenary	
Creating motivation through images	The teacher presents a collage with five images. After a short and quiet phase of looking at the image, the following questions prompt a discussion: • What do you see in the images? How do they belong together? Which ones are more fitting, which ones less so? In regard to what and for which reason? • Where would you position yourself within the collage? It is possible but not necessary to create a bridge between nature and religion. Most important is that the students get the opportunity to start	Plenary	Collage (Material No. 2)

Table 11.3 (*cont.*)

Phase	Activity	Setting	Media/Materials
	engaging thematically and personally with the unit.		
Transition	The collage is completed; by doing so the world religions are placed into the centre of the question of climate justice. The teacher can make the topic more concrete by asking the following questions: • In your opinion, what are the connections between climate justice and religion? • Have you heard of projects that connect religion and climate justice? The teacher explains that there will now be a discussion panel, by which there will be the opportunity to learn what four different religious people think about climate justice.	Plenary	Collage (Material No. 2) now complete
Organisation of panel discussion	The students are split up into groups of four. The teacher hands out the worksheets to every group. The task is to write three tweets about one of the people from the panel. These notes will be the foundation for the task after the discussion panel.	Group work	Worksheet 11.1 in four variations (Material No. 4)

Section 2: Panel Discussion (Material No. 3)
Section 3: Consolidation

Table 11.4 Section 3 – Consolidation

Phase	Activity	Setting	Media/Materials
Transition	The teacher explains the further procedure: The students remain in the groups from the beginning of the unit and complete Worksheet 11. 2, which is handed out by the teacher.	Plenary	Worksheet 11.1 Worksheet 11.2 (Material No. 5)
Elaboration stage	The students interchange their thoughts on the debate. They take notes on differences and similarities and give reasons and examples. 1. Exchange and discussion about the panel discussion, based on the students' notes: What was most important to the person? Where are differences and similarities between the different positions? 2. The students write two short texts in their group (see Worksheet 11. 2).	Group work	Worksheet 11.1 Worksheet 11.2
Presentation	The teacher asks different groups to present both their tweets. The students present their results; time is offered for commentary and discussion. The teacher invites students to a personal interim conclusion: How do you know how evaluate a possible contribution of religions to a more climate-just world?	Plenary	
Closing	The teacher closes the unit.	Plenary	

WORKSHEET 11.1 Observation of the Panel Discussion

No. 4 Observation task to panel discussion (preliminary learning products)

There are four simultaneous worksheets: in place of #Name the name of one of the panellists is added. Each group is given four different observation tasks.

Observation of the panel discussion

Task 1 – Statements by #Name

Imagine you are reporting on a panel discussion on Twitter. To do so, you want to note down the central statements by #Name in short and concise sentences. To do, so complete the tweets listed below.

Student @student

For @#Name climate justice is question of her religion because ...

Student @student

@#Name states ...

as an example, why people of her religion work towards climate justice.

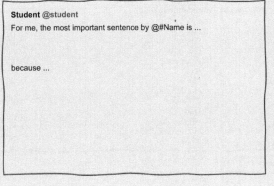

Student @student

For me, the most important sentence by @#Name is ...

because ...

WORKSHEET 11.2 In-Depth Group Work after the Panel Discussion

No. 5 Tasks for in-depth group work after panel discussion

Tasks after the panel discussion

Task 2 – Similarities and Differences

Exchange your thoughts on the panel discussion, using your notes: What was important to the panelists? Where do you see similarities and differences in their positions?

As a group, write a tweet concerning the positions on which the panellists agreed.

Now write an answer to the user @provocative_Pete, who offers a critical response: Do you believe that religious people can work towards climate justice despite their differences? Give reasons for your answer.

Students group @student_group

@#Name1, @#Name2, @#Name3 and @#Name4 represent the same opinion on the relationship between religion and climate justice, namely ...

Provocative Pete @provocative_pete

@student_group, a likely story! Religion leads to conflict and war. They will never find a collective solution aganist climate change!

Student group @student_group

Here is our response to @provocative_pete:

WORKSHEET 11.3 Follow-Up Tasks to Continue after the Learning Episode (Transfer Task)

No. 6 Follow-up tasks to continue after the learning episode (transfer task)

Bonus material

Bonus Video 1: More information on why the movement towards climate justice could benefit from a religious motivation (video in German)

The climate crisis is evident – and still only little is done against it. How can we establish that climate justice is a commandment of social justice?

The social ethicist **Gerhard Kruip** from the University of Mainz answers the question in following video:

Task:
- Task notes on why it is difficult for people to take responsibility for the future.
- How does the argument of the 'chain of love' work? Where are the weaknesses?
- In the end, the Chrisian perspective of a 'triple-commandment' is brought up: What is new about this – and what is your opinion on this concept?

Bonus Video 2: More information on climate justice and theology of creation (video in German)

The following quote from the creation narrative in the first book of the Bible is famous and infamous. God blesses the humans he created and speaks:

"Be fruitful and increase in number; fill the earth and subdue it. Rule over the fish in the sea and the birds in the sky and over every living creature that moves on the ground." (Gen 1:28 NIV)

The biblical scholar **Thomas Hieke** from the University of Mainz explains how this quote has to be understood.

Task:
- Write down the most important argument. How do you feel about it?
- Compare Gen 1:28 to the translation in The Message Bible (search online). What was changed and why?

Bonus Material 3: More information on your own attitude towards climate justice

 The QR Code will bring you to a questionnaire (15 minutes). In the end, you will be given a number from one to five and a code word.

You want to know what the number means? Scan the QR Code and enter the code word (after the discussion task!)

Task:
- Form groups with students who have the same number.
- Discuss the question: What would a just solution to the dilemma look like?
- Compare the solutions of each group and discuss your arguments. Can you find one solution with the whole class?

Table 11.5 Assessment grid: Religious language and language of religion

Assessment Grid Religious Language and Language of Religion	Well done!	OK	You're not quite there yet.
Religious Language			
Learning to talk: Being able to communicate on relevant religious issues (Exploring religion)	You precisely describe the religious position and the argument used to support the position.	You correctly describe the religious position and the argument used to support the position.	You don't describe the religious position and/or the argument used to support the position comprehensibly.
Learning to perceive and express: Being able to discover and express elements of one's own religiosity by entering the religious language game (Experiencing religion)	You can express your own religiosity explicitly by relating to a religious statement and by stringently expressing the reasons for your choice.	You can express your own religiosity by relating to a religious statement and expressing the reasons for your choice.	You have difficulties in relating to a religious statement and/or are not or not comprehensibly expressing the reasons for your choice.
Language of Religion			
Learning to understand: Being able to interpret linguistic forms of religious traditions (Explaining religion)	You can interpret the religious statements stringently and explain precisely in what way they are similar.	You can interpret the religious statements and explain in what way they are similar.	Your interpretation of the religious statements does not clearly say in what way they are similar.
Learning to reflect: Being able to recognise, name and evaluate religious claims (Arguing religion)	You can conclusively evaluate a religious claim based on well-founded religious reasoning.	You can evaluate a religious claim based on religious reasoning.	Your evaluation of a religious claim is not based on religious reasoning.

REFERENCES

Altmeyer, S. (2010). Competences in Inter-Religious Learning. In K. Engebretson, M. de Souza, G. Durka, & L. Gearon (Eds.), *International Handbook of Inter-Religious Education*, vol. 4. Springer, pp. 627–640.

Altmeyer, S. (2015). The Aesthetic Dimension of Believing and Learning. In M. T. Buchanan & A.-M. Gellel (Eds.), *Global Perspectives on Catholic Religious Education in Schools*. Springer, pp. 61–72.

Altmeyer, S. (2019). Sprachhürden erkennen und abbauen: Wege zu einem sprachsensiblen Religionsunterricht. In S. Altmeyer, B. Grümme, H. Kohler-Spiegel, E. Naurath, B. Schröder, & F. Schweitzer (Eds.), *Reli: Keine Lust und keine Ahnung?* vol. 35. Vandenhoeck & Ruprecht, pp. 184–196.

Altmeyer, S. (2021a). Religious Education for Ecological Sustainability: An Initial Reality Check Using the Example of Everyday Decision-Making. *Journal of Religious Education*, *69*(1), 57–74. https://doi.org/10.1007/s40839-020-00131-5

Altmeyer, S. (2021b). *Sprachsensibler Religionsunterricht: Grundlagen und konzeptionelle Klärungen. In Sprachsensibler Religionsunterricht*, vol. 37. Vandenhoeck & Ruprecht, pp. 14–29.

Altmeyer, S., & Dreesmann, D. (2020). The Importance of Religion for the Evaluation of Everyday Ecological Decisions by German Adolescents: A Case Study with Students in Biology and Religious Education Classes. *Worldviews: Global Religions, Culture, and Ecology*, *24*(3), 285–307. https://doi.org/10.1163/15685357-20203001

Altmeyer, S., & Dreesmann, D. (2021). 'The Tree Was There First' – Using an Everyday Ecological Dilemma to Explore the Personal Orientations of Secondary School Students in Environmental Decision-Making. *Environmental Education Research*, *27*(1), 67–87. https://doi.org/10.1080/13504622.2020.1853062

Coyle, D., & Meyer, O. (2021). *Beyond CLIL: Pluriliteracies Teaching for Deeper Learning*, 1st ed. Cambridge University Press. https://doi.org/10.1017/9781108914505

Cummins, J. (2000). *Language, Power, and Pedagogy: Bilingual Children in the Crossfire*. Multilingual Matters.

Englert, R., Hennecke, E., & Kämmerling, M. (2014). *Innenansichten des Religionsunterrichts: Fallbeispiele, Analysen, Konsequenzen*. Kösel.

Gardner, G. T. (2006). *Inspiring Progress: Religions' Contributions to Sustainable Development*. Norton.

Grelle, B. (2018). Worldviews, Ethics, and Ecology: 'Sustainability' as a Context for Religious Education. In J. Astley, L. J. Francis, & D. W. Lankshear (Eds.), *Values, Human Rights and Religious Education: Contested Grounds*, vol. 14. Peter Lang, pp. 189–206.

Hannam, P., Biesta, G., Whittle, S., & Aldridge, D. (2020). Religious Literacy: A Way Forward for Religious Education? *Journal of Beliefs & Values*, *41*(2), 214–226. https://doi.org/10.1080/13617672.2020.1736969

Heimbrock, H.-G. (Ed.). (2017). *Taking Position: Empirical Studies and Theoretical Reflections on Religious Education and Worldview*. Waxmann.

Jenkins, W., Berry, E., & Kreider, L. B. (2018). Religion and Climate Change. *Annual Review of Environment and Resources*, *43*(1), 85–108. https://doi.org/10.1146/annurev-environ-102017-025855

Meyer, O., Coyle, D., Imhof, M., & Connolly, T. (2018). Beyond CLIL: Fostering Student and Teacher Engagement for Personal Growth and Deeper Learning. In J. Martínez Agudo (Ed.), *Emotions in Second Language Teaching: Theory, Research and Teacher Education*. Springer, pp. 277–297. https://doi.org/10.1007/978-3-319-75438-3_16

Meyer, K. (2021). *Religion, Interreligious Learning and Education* (edited and revised by L. Philip Barnes). Peter Lang.

Miedema, S. (2017). Position, Commitment and Worldview from a Pedagogical Perspective. In H.-G. Heimbrock (Ed.), *Taking Position: Empirical Studies and Theoretical Reflections on Religious Education and Worldview*, vol. 33. Waxmann, pp. 127–138.

Roebben, B. (2021). Religious Educational Leadership in Times of Upheaval: How to Build Sustainably on Insights from the Past? *ET-Studies*, *12*(2), 357–367.

Rothgangel, M., Danilovich, Y., & Jäggle, M. (Eds.). (2014–2020). *Wiener Forum für Theologie und Religionswissenschaft: Religious Education at Schools in Europe*, vol. 10. Vandenhoeck & Ruprecht.

Ständige Konferenz der Kultusminister der Länder in der Bundesrepublik Deutschland, Bundesministerium für wirtschaftliche Zusammenarbeit und Entwicklung, & Engagement Global (Eds.). (2016). *Orientierungsrahmen für den Lernbereich globale Entwicklung im Rahmen einer Bildung für nachhaltige Entwicklung*, 2nd ed. Cornelsen.

Tomalin, E., Haustein, J., & Kidy, S. (2019). Religion and the Sustainable Development Goals. *The Review of Faith & International Affairs*, *17*(2), 102–118. https://doi.org/10.1080/15570274.2019.1608664

Tomlinson, J. (2019). Ecological Religious Education: New Possibilities for Educational Practice. *Journal of Religious Education*, *67*(3), 185–202.

12 Music: Exploring Pluriliteracies through a Deeper Learning Episode on 'The Wellerman'

VALERIE KRUPP

12.1 Introduction

In every school subject, acquiring skills and knowledge is strongly linked to the development of the learners' general and subject-specific language skills. This is also the case for the aesthetic subjects, be it the arts, music or drama. Although artistic practice often relies on non-verbal communication and interaction, all kinds of artistic practice, especially in educational contexts, are also linked to language production and reflection: artistic practice and products can be described, evaluated and reflected on; creative processes in all stages need inter- and intrapersonal reflection; and subject-specific genres, such as the analysis of musical pieces or aesthetic argumentation, highly rely on the availability of subject-specific knowledge and language. Often, however, too little attention is paid to the close integration of subject learning and language acquisition in the arts subjects (Bossen, 2019). While the music curricula specify that students should learn the technical terms of the subject, the question of how these terms should be used in specific discourses or genres often remains open. However, the competent use of subject-specific language in school and, finally, in everyday communication is very important to promoting participation in musical culture, even beyond a student's school career.

Just as people dance differently to different types of music, they also talk about them differently as this is part of a specific habitus connected to specific cultural phenomena. Consequently, music teaching and learning should be complemented by opportunities for language learning and reflection that decipher codes and symbols connected to specific musical practices and genres. However, language learning should in no way override the acquisition of subject-specific skills. Rather, it can be argued that language is a central element of culture and cultural capital because language transmits culture and is therefore an indispensable tool that facilitates students' ability to access every musical practice (Weininger & Lareau, 2018).

With this in mind, it is also important to consider aspects of educational inequality. A student's academic language acquisition is highly dependent on the cultural capital and educational background of his or her family. As a result, major differences can be seen between the academic and everyday registers of students across social classes, which can be misrecognised as a gift or talent in more privileged students (Weininger & Lareau, 2018). In music, this has particular weight since social standing determines to a large degree one's ability to access the subject matter. For example, classical music is particularly distinctive and might only be accessible to a relatively small number of people. However, it is this kind of music that represents a central component of music education, which means less privileged students enter the music classroom at a disadvantage.

In order to address this language problem in the music classroom, teachers can use the pluriliteracies teaching for deeper learning (PTDL) model (Coyle & Meyer, 2021), which offers ways of integrating content and language learning through a distinct focus on the development of subject literacies for deeper learning. In this chapter, I seek to apply the approach to the context of music education and give an example of what a deeper learning episode, as proposed by Coyle & Meyer (2021) could look like.

12.2   Musical Competence and Musical Literacy

While musical participation and musical agency can be seen as the overarching goals of all music education, a plurality of goals exist that can guide music educational efforts in the classroom (Kranefeld, 2021; Krupp, 2021). The reason for this is the variety of pedagogic approaches to teaching music that have emerged since the 1970s (Kranefeld, 2021). Whereas earlier approaches focused on the analysis and interpretation of classical music, today's focus is rather on the exploration of a variety of musical–cultural practices as well as on the students' own music-making (Jank, 2021). Music education, from a constructive perspective, can be seen as musical meaning-making through processes of intra- and interpersonal negotiation and reflection (Krause-Benz, 2014), related to the acquisition of subject-specific knowledge, skills and methods. *Doing, organising, explaining* and *arguing* music are key components of the learning process and rely not only on subject-specific knowledge (i.e. music history, music theory, musical genres) but also on general linguistic skills, the proper use of genres and registers and the ability to understand and use technical terms (Bossen, 2019).

In recent years, competency models that describe different dimensions of overall musical competence have been developed and empirically validated in the context of German music education research. Those dimensions refer to (1) perceiving and understanding music (Jordan, 2014; Jordan et al., 2012; Knigge, 2010); (2) practical musical competences (singing, rhythm production, playing an instrument [Hasselhorn, 2015]); and (3) argumentation competence (Ehninger, Knigge & Rolle,

2021; Knörzer et al., 2015; Rolle, 2013)[1]. It is quite obvious that perceiving and describing music as well as *arguing* about music are highly interrelated with adequate use of language, not only with respect to technical terms but also with respect to genre conventions, style (i.e. scientific or colloquial) and mode (oral or written). Aesthetic discourses like these provide a challenge since they involve subjective perceptions and preferences as well as their justifications and thus leave the realm of objective assessment.

However, the linguistic requirements needed to exercise these competences are addressed rather implicitly, and the question of how they can be promoted is only discussed at the content level, not at the linguistic level. And yet, all models assume that the students have acquired a certain level of academic language literacy. The approaches modelling aesthetic argumentation competence that have been developed (Ehninger, Knigge & Rolle, 2021; Gottschalk & Lehmann-Wermser, 2013; Major, 2007; Major & Cottle, 2010) are restricted to certain age groups.

Although Bossen (2019) emphasises the relevance of language teaching and learning in the music classroom, the concept of music literacy has hardly been elaborated on. Based on a general definition of cultural literacy as 'being competent in a number of [...] modes of discourse – verbal and nonverbal', Levinson (1990) describes a narrow concept of music literacy that refers to 'all sorts of factual information *about* music that a common reader is expected to possess and which enable him or her to understand discourse which takes music or musicians as its *subject*' (p. 18). This definition is, in fact, too narrow as it solely focuses on the understanding of music based on theoretical music knowledge while neglecting all forms of active communication and interaction occurring during musical practice.

The pluriliteracies approach defines subject literacy in a wider sense as the ability not only to participate successfully in increasingly complex subject discourse but also to communicate acquired subject knowledge adequately across cultural and linguistic boundaries. Citing Beacco et al., Coyle and Meyer (2021) interpret this process as a 'path towards critical thinking and knowledge application as well as towards social participation' (p. 40). Understood in this wider sense, music literacy encompasses all other aspects of musical competence and refers to the students' ability to use adequate language and expression across different subject-specific genres and communication contexts (e.g. music analysis, recensions, aesthetic argument, comments on music or music explanations), requiring specific modes and styles of communication. Music literacy becomes visible in the growing ability to successfully navigate the four activity domains that PTDL promotes (i.e. *doing, organising, explaining* and *arguing* music). It doesn't develop automatically but rather progressively over time (see Shanahan & Shanahan, 2008, cited in Coyle & Meyer, 2021).

---

[1] These three dimensions of musical competence have also found their way into the German music education curricula.

To some degree, most pupils already have some degree of music literacy as they spend time discussing their music (e.g. favourite artists or favourite songs) among their peers. It can be taken for granted that colloquial communication about music plays a major role in their social activities. The task of music education is, then, not only to appreciate the multiple ways in which young learners already do communicate about music but to also bring their music literacy to a higher level by teaching them to decipher and encode specific cultural codes that may be hidden to learners in communication about music. Integrating the development of musical competence and musical literacy in this way would also contribute to inclusion and social equality (Coyle & Meyer, 2021; Weininger & Lareau, 2018).

12.3   Deeper Learning in Music

Pluriliteracies teaching defines deeper learning as 'the successful internalization of conceptual content knowledge and the automatization of subject-specific procedures, skills and strategies.' (Meyer & Coyle, 2017, p. 1). It includes 'the ability to adequately communicate and negotiate knowledge, as well as the ability to apply knowledge and skills not only in different subject contexts but also to real world issues' (Coyle & Meyer, 2021, p. 40). Deeper learning finally becomes visible, among other things, through the learners' subject-specific literacy performance. The approach 'aims to facilitate deeper learning through an explicit focus on disciplinary literacies. [...] This will encourage successful communication across cultures' (p. 41).

The concept of deeper learning as such is not directly present in current music education discourse. Nevertheless, there are approaches and concepts to music teaching and learning, designed around key assumptions similar to those of PTDL, that promote constructive approaches to learning, the importance of meaning-making (Krause, 2008; Krause-Benz, 2014), problem solving (DreÔler, 2016), cognitive activation (Gebauer, 2013) and the development of different areas of musical competence. The shared assumption is that learning takes place through participation in learning activities that require different forms of engagement (i.e. cognitive, aesthetic, emotional and social). Within those activities, meaning-making plays a crucial role and is closely linked to broader, overarching educational goals, especially against the background of a transformational understanding of education that is central to the aesthetic subjects: *Bildung* takes place when a subject's self- and world-relations undergo fundamental changes (Biesta, 2012; Krause, 2008; Rolle, 2011). This includes the development of musical competences as well as a critical reflection of culturally situated practices and how they are 'mediated by language and other symbolic systems embedded in cultural contexts' (Coyle & Meyer, 2021, p. 158)

Strategies to Enhance Deeper Learning

Coyle and Meyer (2021) define eight strategies to enhance deeper learning, which they adapt for the language classroom. The following section provides examples of what an adaptation for music education might look like, although it is important to note that any strategy would first need to be empirically examined with respect to its effectiveness.

Deepening Textual Understanding

For the context of music education, the term 'text' has to be applied in a wide sense as it can refer not only to texts from journals or textbooks but also to written music. There are many ways to write down music that are interrelated with specific musical genres, conventions or epochs. Reading written music and carrying out a musical analysis requires not only subject-specific methods and technical terms but also the capacity to place the music within specific historical or social contexts and to develop a deeper understanding of the ways and contexts in which music is written and the ways meaning emerges from the music and how that knowledge can be applied to understanding other music.

Increase Content Relevance

Music is relevant in most people's lives, but the same doesn't hold true for music education. The role of content relevance has been discussed in music education with varying foci: in the U.S. context, there is a huge opposition between advocates of the 'aesthetic arts education' paradigm and the 'praxial music education' paradigm (see Regelski, 1998), the first promoting the introduction and analysis of classical music in the light of aesthetic theory, the latter promoting a strong integration of the students' musical practices. In the German discourse, there has been a prominent discussion on the question of real-world relevance (*Lebensweltbezug*), which can be established by referring to a particular topos and its realisation in music (Ehrenforth, 1993; Richter, 1993). DreÔler (2016) revives the discussion of problem-oriented learning within the music education discourse. She states that a deeper understanding of music can only occur when the problems learners are supposed to solve have personal relevance and therefore initiate deep engagement. Thus, the quality of the learning task and its design become central: any content can be relevant for students if there is a 'problem' that affects and motivates them to engage in meaningful learning processes.

Develop Critical Cultural Consciousness

Critical cultural consciousness, as defined in Coyle & Meyer (2021), refers to reflecting and understanding oneself in relation to other cultures. This is the goal of many approaches to so-called intercultural music education (Barth, 2012; Knigge, 2012). Though Western classical music and its history is still much more prominent than anything else, musical practices from all over the world now play an important role in the music classroom. A major objective of music education is the development of cultural understanding and intercultural competence based on a very broad conception of culture. This understanding can be fostered by getting to know various musical cultures and reflecting on similarities and differences between them, but it should be extended to any engagement with music. Critical cultural consciousness means not only acknowledging but also valuing differences 'that are inherent in cultural identities and experiences that are forever present in any classroom' (Coyle & Meyer, 2021, p. 172). It also means understanding mechanisms of power, gender or other identity issues and social inequalities that have influenced the creation of musical practices and texts.

Developing critical cultural consciousness starts with the teacher's decision as to which texts and music to bring into the classroom and depends on the use of a critical cultural lens on the reading and interpretation of the materials presented (Coyle & Meyer, 2021). This is similar to an approach formulated by Geuen and Stöger (2016, 2017): They develop the idea that music education means understanding music as a condensation of cultural signs that offers special possibilities for understanding and expression and fostering the ability to analyse culture through understanding.

Increase Agency and Accountability

Musical agency is a central goal of music education, and theories referring to Aristotelian ideas of *praxis* also deal with questions of ethics and accountability (Kaiser, 2010; Karlsen, 2011; Krupp-SchleuÔner, 2016; Vogt, 2014). An increase in agency and accountability results from growing musical competence, literacy and critical cultural consciousness. Not only will students be empowered to engage in music class due to their own preferences and goals, they will also be aware of cultural differences and their relevance for shaping musical identities. By including self-regulated and cooperative learning methods in the music classroom, agency and accountability can be fostered. A prominent example of this is the creation of a composition combined with a justification of aesthetic decisions that have been made during the composition process. Another example is the examination of comments for TikTok or YouTube music videos, which can be rather objective but also very insulting or disrespectful. Creating awareness that one's own actions always have consequences for others is central here.

Differentiating and Individualising Learning Pathways

Differentiating and individualising learning pathways includes integrating multiple means of representation, means of action and expression and means for meaning-making and languaging (Coyle & Meyer, 2021). Also, the alignment and the design of the learning tasks are crucial. As music itself is a very multimodal phenomenon, there are manifold ways of accomplishing differentiation and individualisation in the music classroom (i.e. connected to practising musical pieces). Teachers can allow students freedom regarding the way in which they practise a piece, their text choice, their text interpretation, their written realisation of a composition or their presentation of results in a final product (e.g. a podcast).

Deep Practice

Deep practice has to be offered on a regular basis, especially when it comes to playing music on instruments. It is often overlooked that students have to learn how to practise musically and that, especially, those students who play an instrument at home are privileged in that regard. Deep practice needs time, but it also requires knowledge about how to practise (meta-cognitive strategies). That is, practice needs to be practised. And just as it is for the notation of music, depending on the music that is played, there are different possible ways of practice and skill acquisition (Green, 2012). Not only do different types of music require different types of practice, but different practice contexts call for different skills and methods: the way students practise alone at home is quite different from the way they practise at school when musically accompanied by their peers. These different practice scenarios in the music classroom need further research.

In addition to the practice of music-making, time for deep practice also needs to be allocated for other modes of expression: students must be given the time to learn how to understand and make meaning in discourse about music. This means practising the many subject-specific genres that follow specific genre conventions (e.g. describing music, aesthetic argument, analysis and interpretation of a musical piece, formulating aesthetic arguments . . .). Coyle and Meyer (2021) argue that if students are to be become confident in those genres, practice and reflection are important prerequisites for building mental models that help them solve the respective tasks more and more independently. Thus, practising not only refers to practising music, but also to practising language and reflection.

Scaffolding Development

Individualisation, differentiation and deep practice very often require scaffolding, which means that the teacher and students enter a feedback process that eventually results in the adaptation of a given task (van de Pol, Volman & Beishuizen, 2010; van Geert & Steenbeek, 2005). With respect to the development of music literacy, language scaffolding (e.g. vocabulary lists, text examples, guided dialogues) is a very helpful tool, but there is an important distinction between supporting students in the short term (in the sense of bypassing difficulties for the moment) and an effective promotion of learning and personal development in the long term. Although bypassing difficulties is sometimes important, teachers should always be aware that in this case, deeper learning cannot take place as real learning opportunities are not provided (Prediger & Buró, 2021).

An approach to music learning that integrates content, musical practice and language learning as described above places high demands on the design and formulation of learning tasks. Here, a combination of methods that are based on oral or written expression is important. Taking the approach seriously, the planning of each task should comprise a reflection on linguistic requirements and, if necessary, the development of language scaffolding measures (see Hardy, Hettmannsperger & Gabler, 2019; Tajmel & Hägi-Mead, 2017).

The following section presents an example of a deeper learning episode that takes into account the design principles for deeper learning as presented in Meyer and Coyle (2021). Such episodes are 'not limited to specific timetabled lessons' (p. 128) and focus on a well-designed arrangement of tasks and activities that enable students to progress from shallow to deeper learning by applying the above-mentioned strategies and principles. They need to comprise the four prototypical activity domains (*doing, organising, explaining* and *arguing*), to meet learner strengths, needs and interests and to be aligned with disciplinary competences and literacy.

12.4   A Model Deeper Learning Episode in Music: Why Does Everybody Sing 'The Wellerman'?

In December 2020, a Scottish postman named Nathan Evans shared his version of the 150-year-old sea shanty 'The Wellerman' on TikTok. Within a very short time, the video went viral and got thousands of views, likes and comments, as well as thousands of remakes and remixes: duets, choirs, text adaptations, dances, instrumental versions and parodies. There is an endless number of videos that can be found, and many people got involved. Everybody was singing 'The Wellerman'. But why did this short video become such a success? This is what students are supposed to figure out in the presented model episode (see Tables 12.1, 12.2 and 12.3). Specifically, the episode requires students to research the shanty genre, analyse user comments on the piece and compose their own comments. More generally, the episode is about classifying musical and social media phenomena and developing a critical perspective on them. Consequently, the episode could also be used with or extended to other prominent music examples.

This episode doesn't require students to perform their own rendition of the shanty[2]. In contrast, it aims at promoting meaningful and critical inquiry of a musical piece as well as its social and cultural meaning and context. Only playing the music without

---

[2] However, some educators might find that practising the piece in class is a very good starting point for the whole project. If this be the case, a published arrangement can be found in the *mip-Journal* (Höfer, 2021).

Table 12.1 Planning grid for a deeper learning episode in music

Designing Deeper Learning Episodes

Planning Grid for a Deeper Learning Episode in Music

What do I want my learners to know or be able to do?	How will my learners demonstrate increasingly deeper understanding at the surface, consolidation and transfer levels?	How can I support active knowledge co-construction for my learners?	How can I support my learners every step of the way?	How can I generate and sustain learner commitment and achievement?
Basic Understanding/ Knowledge and Foundational Skills: Students • Acquire basic knowledge about the shanty/sea shanty genre • Develop basic understanding of mechanisms around musical practice on social media platforms, especially with respect to evaluative spaces **Deeper Understanding:** Students • Develop consciousness of historical and social context of musical genres and their emergence via example of shanties • Develop understanding for how meaning is made through music	**Preliminary Learning Products:** • Mind map on shanty genre • List of evaluation criteria **Main Outcome Products:** Encyclopaedia Entry • Genre: description, explanation, definition • Mode: written • Style: academic **(Aesthetic) Argument** • Genre: discussion • Mode: oral • Style: colloquial and academic **Comment** • Genre: music magazine article • Mode: written • Style: academic **Transfer Tasks:** Comparison to other work songs	**(Co-)Construction of Knowledge:** (X) inquiry-based learning (X) problem-based learning ( ) experimenting (X) project-based learning **Social-Interaction:** (X) solo work (X) pair work (X) group work **Use of (Digital) Media:** • TikTok scenario • Online research • Online mind map • Etherpad (shared documents) • Video editor	**Scaffolding:** • Different forms of language scaffolding (oral and written) in all modules with respect to formulating evaluations and personal statements **Feedback** • By peers for own 'The Wellerman' version • By teacher for written encyclopaedia entry and written comment **Feed-Up** • Teacher advice during group work **Feed-Forward** • Step-by-step development of definition and evaluation **Assessment:** • Summative: Can be performed on	**Engagement:** **Personal Meaningfulness/ Relevance:** • Setting: internship at the *Rolling Stone* magazine • Reference to a common musical practice in a social media environment • Reference to a well-known TikTok phenomenon • Claiming evaluation and self-positioning **Opportunities for Autonomous Learning:** • Combination of solo, pair and group work • Self-directed research activities and music production • High level of discussion and exchange in pair and group work **Reflection and Revision:** • Various opportunities to reflect on content, language

Table 12.1 (cont.)

Designing Deeper Learning Episodes

Planning Grid for a Deeper Learning Episode in Music

• Reflect critically on the aesthetic quality of musical products on social media platforms

Deep Practice:
Students
• Carry out inquiry into musical phenomena/practices and their historical and social contexts
• Practise aesthetic judgement and critical evaluation with respect to (social) media phenomena in different linguistic modes and styles
• Develop critical cultural consciousness

Transfer:
Students
• Compare the emergence and meaning of shanties to the emergence and meaning of work songs (optional)
• Apply evaluation and critical judgement to a similar musical media phenomenon/practice

Self-made 'The Wellerman' version (video optional)
Comparison to other viral TikTok videos (optional)

encyclopaedia entries and written comments
• Formative: Can be performed during oral discussions and during group work

and learning processes by comparison of results
• Development of formal, aesthetic and creative criteria
• Optional modules allow for critical reflection on similar or other cultural phenomena
• (Self-)assessment based on assessment grid

going further might be fun and promote musical playing skills but would also mean squandering an opportunity for deeper learning with respect to the content and context of the musical phenomenon under question.

12.5   Alignment of Deeper Learning Episode

In the case of this episode, high task fidelity (Coyle & Meyer, 2021) is achieved for several reasons: the *personal and practical relevance* of the project is very high as a musical phenomenon in a widely used social media platform is at the centre of the activities. Research on the topic (shanty as a genre) is combined with digital modes of presentation and oral and written production of text. Working with comments on music videos (analysing and writing) develops music literacy in the domain of aesthetic argumentation, including an increasing awareness of context-specific language styles and register. By doing so, knowledge about the shanty genre is constructed and critical reflection on an actual phenomenon is accomplished.

Learner Strengths, Needs and Interests

Internet and social media phenomena like 'The Wellerman' are highly present in students' daily lives. Consequently, a high motivation for the topic can be expected. Producing their own video adaptation of 'The Wellerman', as well as commenting on other people's versions, requires students to actively engage in thinking about the music, its function and its quality. While Modules 1–4 are mandatory, Modules 5–9 are optional so that students can choose to engage in ways of learning that correspond with their individual strengths. These modules vary in difficulty and complexity, so teachers can decide which modules they choose to provide.

Musical Competences and Musical Literacy

With respect to musical competences, the episode focuses on the perception and critical understanding of musical social media phenomena. Using the example of 'The Wellerman', students discover ways of researching and explaining such phenomena and thus develop their critical cultural consciousness: they acquire knowledge on the shanty genre, listen carefully to different versions of 'The Wellerman', verbalise the differences between those versions and reflect on their quality by applying evaluation criteria. They furthermore reflect on the functions that music can have in different social and historical contexts.

Musical literacy is developed in two genres: the description of the videos and the presentation of the shanty genre requires factual texts in which description and explanation are dominant. The evaluation of videos requires arguing and discussing. Oral and written modes of text production are combined. Furthermore, the use of different registers (academic and colloquial) is necessary.

Activity Domains

Students collect information on the shanty genre, which they need to produce their presentation and to work on the evaluation of the videos (*doing* music). Furthermore, students who choose to do so *do* music by producing their own 'The Wellerman' video, which combines the original with either singing, dancing or rhythm patterns.

They *organise* music through the development of a mind map with information on the shanty genre and *explain* the different functions that shanties have in their original context. Furthermore, they develop evaluation criteria for TikTok music videos and apply them by formulating their own comments in academic and colloquial register.

Finally, they write a comment on the guiding question: Why does everybody sing 'The Wellerman'? A wider transfer can be realised by applying the whole project to another viral music video or by comparing sea shanties with the work songs that were sung by African slaves in the U.S. and elsewhere.

Surface Learning – Consolidation – Transfer Stage

How do learners move from shallow processing to deep learning and the transfer stage? The episode focuses on a phenomenon that students already know but on which they probably haven't reflected any further. They already possess surface knowledge about the song and its origin. In this episode, deeper learning is promoted through the intense work on a genre definition and through a conscious confrontation with comments and feedback as a reaction to social media videos. The most important aim lies in the development of critical cultural consciousness with respect to online music cultures. By empowering students to formulate their own comments based on knowledge and on objective evaluation criteria, they will, in the future, be able to read online comments in a more reflective way. They will also be able to express their own opinion using an appropriate style and register.

Feedback, Reflection and Assessment

Feedback and reflection are of high relevance within this episode. There are several opportunities for feedback (teacher feedback and peer feedback).

Modules 1 and 2 result in a mind map and in an encyclopaedia entry. Both products can be subject to peer or teacher feedback. The evaluation criteria and the comments that result from Module 3 should be discussed in class. Here, the opportunity should be used to discuss comment and feedback culture in social media contexts and reflect on the quality and moral appropriateness of such comments. Furthermore, there should be some reflection on language style and register typical for internet comments. A more academic comment should emerge from Module 8.

Also, peer or teacher feedback is possible here and should focus on the linguistic quality of the comments. The last mandatory module is Module 4, which results in a plenary discussion. Here, learners should be encouraged to assess the quality of their arguments with the help of an assessment grid that the teacher provides so that the most convincing arguments can be identified. Feedback should also be provided for the products of the other modules, if selected. For each product it is important to also reflect and give feedback on the linguistic quality of student products with respect to style, register and genre conventions.

Assessment

There is hardly any empirical evidence on reliable assessment of musical competence or musical literacy as defined above. The assessment of oral or written statements on music is generally based on criteria derived from the three cognitive discourse functions. A good example of this can be found in the music subject curriculum of the state of Baden-Württemberg. Here, operators are defined specifically for music and can be used as a basis for evaluation. Those operators are specified linguistically with respect to content typical of the subject of music (Ministerium für Kultus, Jugend und Sport Baden-Württemberg, 2016, p. 33 ff).

A general model for music literacy as defined in this chapter has not been developed so far. Consequently, the assessment grid for this episode (see Table 12.4) is aligned with linguistic specifications that can be found in the school curricula. It focuses on the requirements arising from the tasks and can be used flexibly or adapted to specific ages depending on the module selection. The levels are specified for Grade 8/9 for the following criteria.

- **Describe:** Engage with a musical phenomenon and describe it using technical language terms.
- **Explain:** Put a phenomenon into context using musical terminology and pointing out backgrounds and causes.
- **Evaluate:** Evaluate a musical product on the basis of self-selected formal, aesthetic and creative criteria.
- **Discuss:** Discuss the quality of a musical product and reflect on varying perspectives.

12.6 Conclusion and Outlook

Under the assumption that music education in schools should put more emphasis on the integration of content and language learning and that the development of musical literacy goes hand in hand with an increase in critical cultural consciousness, this chapter tries to apply PTDL and the concept of deeper learning to the context of music education. Although many assumptions and theoretical accounts have to be complemented by empirical classroom research, there is evidence from other subjects that points to the relevance of the language of deeper learning to educational success in all subjects. Nevertheless, I propose conceiving music literacy as an overarching dimension that is relevant to all other dimensions of musical competences and has to be taken into account for all music educational designs. In conclusion, not only subject learning but also inclusion and educational inequality are addressed.

12.7   Learning Materials

Student Material

Overview

Do you know 'The Wellerman'? Last year a short version of the song went viral on TikTok and, suddenly, everybody was singing 'The Wellerman'.

Imagine the following situation: *You have an internship at* Rolling Stone *magazine and are supposed to write an article explaining to the readers why the video of 'The Wellerman' is so successful.*

In this project you will be asked to write an article for a music magazine using appropriate language by following the modules. The process starts with research on the shanty genre and gradually asks you to develop and use evaluation criteria for TikTok music videos. You will be given language tools to structure and formulate comparisons to put the success of 'The Wellerman' into context. As a self-experiment, you can also include your experiences attempting to make a viral shanty video yourself.

Table 12.2 Overview

Module No.	Title	Mandatory (Y/N)
1	Getting Started	Y
2	Exploring the Genre: What Is a 'Shanty'?	Y
3	Shanty and Work Song: A Comparison	N
4	Nathan Evans' 'The Wellerman': Why Do People Like It?	Y
5	What Makes the Difference? Comparing Versions of 'The Wellerman'	Y
6	Your Own Version of 'The Wellerman'	N
7	Finding Another Example	N
8	Writing an Article for *Rolling Stone* magazine	Y

WORKSHEET 12.1 Modules 1–2

Module 1

Getting Started

Let's get started:

1. Watch the original from Nathan Evans on YouTube (QR Code No. 1).
2. Listen to a full version of 'The Wellerman' by The Longest Johns on YouTube (QR Code No. 2).
3. Read the article 'Shanty-Boom. Die Sehnsucht singt zuletzt.' (Stefan Kruecken, *Der Spiegel*, QR Code No. 3).

1	2	3

Module 2

Exploring the Genre: What Is a 'Shanty'?

In this module, you will explore the shanty genre. Based on a *mind map*, you will find a definition of the genre and describe its characteristics.

1. *Create a shared mind map* and collect everything you already know about shanties.
   👥 3–4 ⏳ 10 minutes.
2. *Do research* on the internet (e.g. search the terms 'shanty' or 'sea shanty'). Collect as much information as possible about the questions below and *fill in your mind map*. Write down the sources (you can create a list of links).
   a. What are shanties and when/how did they develop historically?
   b. What is the content of shanties?
   c. By whom were they sung? When and where?
   d. What function(s) did shanties originally serve?
   e. When and where are shanties sung today?
   f. What are the musical characteristics of shanties?
   g. What are famous shanty examples?
   👥 3–4 ⏳ 30 minutes.
3. *Partner Interview:* Walk around the classroom and find an interview partner. Let your partner explain to you what a shanty is using his/her notes collected during the research phase. Change roles after approximately three minutes.

Your teacher will give you a sign (two rounds). Does your partner like shanties? Why (not)?

👤 👤 ⧗ 10 minutes.

4. *Write a short encyclopaedia entry* that sums up the most important information about the genre in academic style.

👤 or 👤 👤 ⧗ 15–20 minutes.

Useful phrases

A **sea shanty**, **chantey** or **chanty** is a genre of . . .

The term *shanty* refers to . . .

The shanty genre is typified by . . .

The lyrics are often . . .

Shanties were sung in . . . contexts and functioned as . . .

Module 3: Shanty and Work Song – A Comparison

Shanties do have some things in common with the work songs that were invented by African slaves to accompany their work.

1. *Compare:* What do the two genres have in common, and what distinguishes them? Refer to musical characteristics and to the functions the music served.

👤 👤 ⧗ 15–20 minutes.

Similarities	Shanties	Work Songs Invented by African Slaves
Musical Characteristics:		
Function:		
Differences:	**Shanties**	**Work Songs Invented by African Slaves**
Musical Characteristics:		
Function:		

Useful technical terms

Musical characteristics:

Call-and-response format, melody, polyphony, punctuated rhythm, multiple
  rhythmic patterns, improvisation, percussive sounds (like shouts or moans)

Functions:

Reminding of home, raising morale, passing down information about life
  experience, synchronising work in rhythm

Module 4

Nathan Evans' 'The Wellerman': Why Do People Like It?

1. *Watch* Nathan Evans' original video on TikTok and *write down a description* of the characteristics of 'The Wellerman' version and its rendition.

👤 or 👤 👤 ⧗ 10 minutes.

2. *Read* the comments below the video and *write down* any comments that justify or illustrate what was (or was not) particularly well done.

   👤 or 👤 👤 ⏳ 15–20 minutes.

3. *Create a table:* What kinds of criteria are mentioned in the comments? Distinguish between musical and non-musical criteria. Add some more criteria that are, in your opinion, important to judge the quality and success of a song video on TikTok.

   👥 3–4 ⏳ 30 minutes.

4. How would your comment sound? *Write a short comment* that you could post on TikTok. Use appropriate 'TikTok comment language' (including emojis and using expressions like 'being CEO of sth.','extra', 'fire' or 'lit', 'flex', etc.) and use at least two of the criteria from your table in Task 3.

   👤 1 ⏳ 5 minutes.

5. Present the criteria you identified in class and read out your comments. *Discuss* whether or not your comments are appropriate with respect to the criteria and give reasons.

   ⏳ 15–20 minutes.

6. Why did Nathan Evans' 'The Wellerman' video go viral? On the internet, you will find a variety of articles and comments on 'The Wellerman' and the *Shanty-Tok* phenomenon. *Take some reading time* and try to find out why people like and sing 'The Wellerman' and other shanties. *Take notes* on your findings. Don't forget to make a list of links for the websites you used.

   👤 1 ⏳ 10 minutes.

7. *Discuss* your results with your partner. *Formulate and write down two or three hypotheses* about why people have recently liked 'The Wellerman' and shanties. What functions do the music or the video editing have? Compare your hypotheses to what you found out about the function of the original shanty genre (Module 2)

   👤 👤 ⏳ 15-20 min.

Module 5

What Makes the Difference? Comparing Versions of 'The Wellerman'

There are countless arrangements of Nathan Evans' version of 'The Wellerman'.

1. Take 8–10 minutes and *watch* as many arrangements as possible.
2. *Choose two arrangements*, one that you like and one that you don't like. Write down who did the arrangement and save the video in your app.
3. *Compare the two arrangements* in academic writing style and following the instructions for comparing song videos.
   - *Write an introduction* describing the two arrangements and giving reasons for your choice.

- *Use the criteria* you elaborated in Module 4 as aspects of comparison and give evidence for them by referring to elements of the arrangements.
- *Structure your text* by using paragraphs and linking words.
  a. Connectives for comparison:
     in the same way, similarly, likewise, like, also, equally, as with
  b. Connectives for contrast:
     however, but, yet, otherwise, on the one hand ... on the other hand, even though, unlike, instead of, alternatively, in contrast, whereas
- In your conclusion, *evaluate* which arrangement you like better and give reasons.

  👤 1 ⏳ 40 minutes.

Module 6

Your Own Version of 'The Wellerman'

Create your own version by video recording your own singing or by adding a second voice, rhythm, choreography, etc. to Nathan Evans' video. Use the criteria from Module 4 to check on the quality of your work and to assess the work of other groups.

👥 3-4 ⏳ 30 minutes.

Module 7

Finding Another Example

'The Wellerman' went viral in a very short time. You surely know other musical phenomena/examples that went viral in a similar way on TikTok or on another social media platform.

1. Choose one example. What does it have in common with 'The Wellerman', and what distinguishes it? Include all your findings about 'The Wellerman' and prepare a short presentation (2.5–4 minutes) for your classmates, including a structured comparison. Use the structure and language help given in Modules 3 and 5.

   👤 👤 ⏳ 15-20 minutes.

Module 8

An Article for *Rolling Stone* Magazine

Now you are ready for your article for *Rolling Stone* magazine! Explain to the readers why 'The Wellerman' video is so successful by taking the following steps.

- Write a headline/title that captures your readers' interest.

Introduction

- Try to maintain the readers' interest with an opening sentence that might intrigue music lovers or people interested in social phenomena.
- You can include interesting numbers, provoking questions, etc. to highlight your point.
- Clearly define the topic, focusing on the purpose of your article, which is to explain a music phenomenon among young people to older people.

Main part

- Write in a way that suits the purpose of your article, putting 'The Wellerman' into the context of the genre and other TikTok videos that have gone viral.
- If you base your article on available texts, refer to general ideas from the material. You are not expected to give evidence from the text.
- Explain 'The Wellerman' phenomenon in detail.
- Follow a clear and logical structure and use paragraphs using the criteria from Modules 3 and 4 to formulate convincing reasons for its success.
- Give examples and evidence, referring to important facts, statistical information or your own personal musical experience to back up your arguments.
- Make clear which reasons for success are the most important ones.

Conclusion

- Indicate that you are coming to a conclusion, using phrases such as *in conclusion*, *on the whole*, *finally*, *as a result*, etc.
- Sum up your position and your main arguments. Do not, however, use the same phrasing as you used to introduce your arguments.
- You can also give an outlook for the future, speculating about other music genres going viral.

Throughout your text

- Write clear sentences. Use linking words, especially those for comparing different versions of 'The Wellerman' and different music genres.
- Write in a way that appeals to your target group of music lovers, who are likely to be older than yourself.
- Use vocabulary specific to music that is appropriate for your target group and purpose.

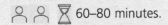 60–80 minutes.

Additional Information and Material for Teachers

Music

An a capella version of *The Wellerman* can be found on this album:

- The Longest Johns (2018). *Between Wind and Water.* Bristol: Thekla.

The original TikTok Video (Nathan Evans) can be found here:

- Nathan Evans (2020). 'The Wellerman'. Original TikTok Video on YouTube: https://www.youtube.com/watch?v=Ji1ODjzKn6E&ab_channel=tufcat13

Articles

Hunt, E. (2021) The true story behind the viral TikTok sea shanty hit. *The Guardian*, 15.01.2021. https://www.theguardian.com/world/2021/jan/15/shantytok-how-a-19th-century-seafaring-epic-inspired-a-covid-generation

Kulen, Y. (2021). Viraler Trend auf TikTok: Warum jetzt alle Seemannslieder singen. *Der Stern*, 17.01.2021. https://www.stern.de/digital/online/trend-auf-tiktok—warum-jetzt-alle—sea-shanties—singen—30003442.html

Kruecken, S. (2021). Shanty-Boom. Die Sehnsucht singt zuletzt. *Der Spiegel*, 25.01.2021. https://www.spiegel.de/geschichte/shantys-auf-tiktok-warum-the-wellerman-eine-riesenwelle-macht-a-2cd19d96-8a29-4b2b-99e1-978be4468ee6

Vahland, K. (2021). Nathan Evans. *Sueddeutsche Zeitung*, 25.02.2021. https://www.sueddeutsche.de/meinung/sea-shanty-wellerman-nathan-evans-tiktok-1.5218156

Vinter, R. (2021). How a Scottish postie's simple sea shanty struck a global chord. *The Guardian*, 16.01.2021. https://www.theguardian.com/music/2021/jan/16/how-a-scottish-posties-simple-sea-shanty-struck-a-global-chord

Organisation, Methods and Additional Comments

For each module, it is suggested whether students should work alone, with a partner or in groups. This can be handled very flexibly, depending on what the learning group is used to.

Also, depending on the learning group, a sample solution for all tasks should be prepared in advance to identify possible linguistic difficulties and to decide where language scaffolding might be useful.

Table 12.3 Modules 1–8: Organisation, methods and additional comments

No.	Titles	Mandatory (Y/N)
1	Getting Started	Y
2	Exploring the Genre: What Is a 'Shanty'?	Y

- Modules 1 and 2 can be treated as a unit.
- For the mind map, online tools like *Mindmeister* or *Flinga* can be used.
- An online document (i.e. Etherpad, available as Moodle integration) should be provided to create lists of links for each group.
- The partner interviews provide an opportunity to internalise conceptual knowledge and to practise talking about music.
- The encyclopaedia entry could be given as homework. To help formulate this, another encyclopaedia entry can be provided additionally as an example.

Table 12.3 (*cont.*)

No.	Titles	Mandatory (Y/N)
3	Shanty and Work Song: A Comparison	N

- This transfer module can be provided if work songs and spirituals have already been dealt with and students can be expected to already possess the necessary knowledge. The comparison can be prepared in oral or written mode.

4	Nathan Evans' 'The Wellerman': Why Do People Like It?	Y

- A table with evaluation criteria should be discussed in class. It might include the following criteria: image of the artist, instrumentation, voice, atmosphere or feeling conveyed, quality of production, coordination of video and music, authenticity with regard to genre, creativity and innovation, choreography.
- The students' comments can be collected in an online document (i.e. Etherpad)
- The final discussion is the core of this module. All students should get a chance to speak up in this phase. The discussion can be held in different formats, such as *fishbowl* or conversation carousel, depending on how much the teacher wants to guide the discussion.
- The discussion provides an opportunity to practise discussions about music that include students expressing their own opinions and eventually convincing others of these opinions.
- Language scaffolding could be provided by handing out a list of typical sentence starters or by briefly reflecting on what a good argument looks like.

5	What Makes the Difference? Comparing Versions of 'The Wellerman'	Y

- In this module, the quality of the comparison is important as there should be progress towards a more academic style of writing. Teacher feedback is very important here.
- Suggestion: Choose 2–3 very good comparisons and provide them to all students as examples. This should be accompanied by a brief discussion on why these comparisons are especially good.

6	Your Own Version of 'The Wellerman'	N

- In this module, the evaluation criteria from Module 4 can be used as an assessment grid to decide on the best version.
- The videos can be created directly in TikTok or using iMovie or Windows Media Maker.
- The videos should be uploaded to a shared folder so that they can be accessed by all students.
- Possible discussion in class: Which version would go viral and why? (think–pair–share)

7	Finding Another Example	N

- This transfer module should be highly motivating as it allows students to choose their own examples and present them to others.
- The evaluation criteria should be used to prepare the presentation.
- A presentation template could be provided.
- The presentation could be held in a format similar to Pecha Kucha (20 slides with 20 seconds each), which is fun and trains students' presentation skills.

8	An Article for *Rolling Stone* Magazine	Y

- Writing a magazine article on a topic is demanding as it requires reorganising the necessary information and taking into account different perspectives on a topic. It is also a very creative task as students can decide freely how the article is composed.
- For language scaffolding, a basic text structure could also be provided.

Assessment Grid

Table 12.4 Assessment grid

	☺	😐	☹
Describe	You precisely describe a musical phenomenon and correctly put to use technical terms.	You correctly describe a musical phenomenon and put to use technical terms from time to time.	You don't describe the musical phenomenon correctly and don't use technical terms yet.
Explain	You precisely explain how a musical phenomenon is situated historically and socially by referring to your research results.	You correctly explain how a musical phenomenon is situated historically and socially by partly referring to your research results.	You don't explain correctly how a musical phenomenon is situated historically and socially and don't refer to your research results yet.
Compare and Evaluate	You can conclusively compare and evaluate the quality of TikTok videos based on formal, aesthetic and creative criteria.	You can compare and evaluate the quality of TikTok videos by partly using formal, aesthetic and creative criteria.	Your comparison and evaluation of TikTok videos doesn't refer to formal, aesthetic and creative criteria yet.
Discuss	You elaborately discuss the success of TikTok videos such as 'The Wellerman', underpinning your opinion with factual knowledge and evaluative criteria.	You discuss the success of TikTok videos, such as 'The Wellerman', partly underlying your opinion with factual knowledge and evaluative criteria.	You are only partly successful in representing your opinion on the success of TikTok videos, such as 'The Wellerman', in a discussion. Factual knowledge and evaluation criteria are used only a little for justification.

REFERENCES

Barth, D. (2012). Musik-Kulturen im Klassenzimmer – Musik und Menschen in interkulturellen Situationen. In C. Wallbaum (Ed.), *Perspektiven der Musikdidaktik: Drei Schulstunden im Licht der Theorien.* Olms, pp. 201–220. https://nbn-resolving.org/urn:nbn:de:bsz:14-qucosa-87604

Beacco, J.-C., Fleming, M., Goullier, F., Thürmann, E., Vollmer, H. J., & Sheils, J. (2016). *The Language Dimension in All Subjects: A Handbook for Curriculum Development and Teacher Training.* Council of Europe. https://rm.coe.int/a-handbook-for-curriculumdevelopment-and-teacher-trainingthe-languag/16806af387

Biesta, G. J. J. (2012). Giving Teaching Back to Education. *Phenomenology & Practice, 6*(2), 35–49.

Bossen, A. (2019). *Sprachbewusster Musikunterricht Problematisierung sprachdidaktischer Ansätze und Perspektiven einer Sprachbildung im Fach.* Waxmann.

Coyle, D., & Meyer, O. (2021). *Beyond CLIL: Pluriliteracies Teaching for Deeper Learning.* Cambridge University Press.

DreÔler, S. (2016). Was genau ist (d)ein Problem? In S. DreÔler (Ed.), *Zwischen Irritation und Erkenntnis: Zum Problemlösen im Fachunterricht.* Waxmann, pp. 13–29.

Ehinger, J., Knigge, J., & Rolle, C. (2021). Musikbezogene Argumentationskompetenz: Ein Werkstattbericht über die Entwicklung von Testaufgaben. In A. Budke & F. Schäbitz (Eds.), *Argumentieren und Vergleichen Beiträge aus der Perspektive verschiedener Fachdidaktiken.* LIT Verlag, pp. 93–112.

Ehrenforth, K. H. (1993). Musik als Leben: Zu einer lebensweltlich orientierten ästhetischen Hermeneutik. *Musik und Bildung, 25*(6), 14–19.

Gebauer, H. (2013). 'Beschreibt doch mal die Form, die wir gerade gemacht haben.' Kognitive Aktivierung im Musikunterricht. In A. Lehmann-Wermser & M. Krause-Benz (Eds.), *Musiklehrer (-bildung) im Fokus musikpädagogischer Forschung.* Waxmann, pp. 61–79.

Geuen, H., & Stöger, C. (2016). Lesarten entwickeln: Eine kulturwissenschaftliche Perspektive auf Lernen und Lehren im Musikunterricht. In S. DreÔler (Ed.), *Zwischen Irritation und Erkenntnis: Zum Problemlösen im Fachunterricht,* vol. 1. Waxmann, pp. 63–82.

Geuen, H., & Stöger, C. (2017). 'Spielarten' – Musizieren im allgemeinbildenden Musikunterricht aus Perspektive der Cultural Studies: Ein Gedankenexperiment. In A. Cvetko & C. Rolle (Eds.), *Musikpädagogik und Kulturwissenschaft,* vol. 38. Waxmann, pp. 57–71.

Gottschalk, T., & Lehmann-Wermser, A. (2013). Iteratives Forschen am Beispiel der Förderung musikalisch-ästhetischer Diskursfähigkeit. In M. Komorek & S. Prediger (Eds.), *Der lange Weg zum Unterrichtsdesign: Zur Begründung und Umsetzung fachdidaktischer Forschungs- und Entwicklungsprogramme,* vol. 5. Waxmann, pp. 63–78.

Green, L. (2012). Musical 'Learning Styles' and 'Learning Strategies' in the Instrumental Lesson: Some Emergent Findings from a Pilot Study. *Psychology of Music, 40*(1), 42–65. https://doi.org/10.1177/0305735610385510

Hardy, I., Hettmannsperger, R., & Gabler, K. (2019). Sprachliche Bildung im Fachunterricht: Theoretische Grundlagen und Förderansätze. In J. Ziehm, B. Voet Cornelli, B. Menzel, & M. GoÔmann (Eds.), *Schule migrationssensibel gestaltet: Impulse für die Praxis.* Beltz, pp. 31–61.

Hasselhorn, J. (2015). *Messbarkeit musikpraktischer Kompetenzen von Schülerinnen und Schülern: Entwicklung und empirische Validierung eines Kompetenzmodells*, vol. 2. Waxmann.

Höfer, F. (2021). Nathan Evans: Wellerman. *Mip-Journal, 61*, 12–18.

Jank, W. (Ed.). (2021). *Musik-Didaktik: Praxishandbuch für die Sekundarstufe I und II*, 9th ed. Cornelsen.

Jordan, A.-K. (2014). *Empirische Validierung eines Kompetenzmodells für das Fach Musik: Teilkompetenz 'Musik wahrnehmen und kontextualisieren'*, vol. 43. Waxmann.

Jordan, A.-K., Knigge, J., Lehmann, A. C., Niessen, A., & Lehmann-Wermser, A. (2012). Entwicklung und Validierung eines Kompetenzmodells im Fach Musik. *Wahrnehmen und Kontextualisieren von Musik. Zeitschrift für Pädagogik, 58*(4), 500–521. https://doi .org/10.25656/01:10392

Kaiser, H. J. (2010). Verständige Musikpraxis: Eine Antwort auf Legitimationsdefizite des Klassenmusizierens. *Zeitschrift Für Kritische Musikpädagogik* www.zfkm.org/10-kaiser .pdf

Karlsen, S. (2011). Using Musical Agency as a Lens: Researching Music Education from the Angle of Experience. *Research Studies in Music Education, 33*(2), 107–121. https://doi .org/10.1177/1321103X11422005

Knigge, J. (2010). *Modellbasierte Entwicklung und Analyse von Testaufgaben zur Erfassung der Kompetenz 'Musik wahrnehmen und kontextualisieren'*. Unpublished doctoral dissertation, University of Bremen. http://elib.suub.uni-bremen.de/diss/docs/00012006.pdf

Knigge, J. (2012). Interkulturelle Musikpädagogik: Hintergründe – Konzepte – Befunde. In A. Niessen & A. Lehmann-Wermser (Eds.), *Aspekte interkultureller Musikpädagogik: Ein Studienbuch*. WiÔner, pp. 25–26.

Knörzer, L., Rolle, C., Stark, R., & Park, B. (2015). '. . . er übertreibt und das macht mir seine Version zu nervös' – Einzelfallanalysen musikbezogener Argumentationen. In A. Niessen & J. Knigge (Eds.), *Theoretische Rahmung und Theoriebildung in der musikpädagogischen Forschung*. Waxmann, pp. 147–162. www.pedocs.de/frontdoor .php?source_opus=12619

Kranefeld, U. (2021). Der Diskurs um Unterrichtsqualität in der Musikdidaktik zwischen generischen und fachspezifischen Dimensionen. *Unterrichtswissenschaft, 49*(2), 221–233. https://doi.org/10.1007/s42010-021-00113-y

Krause, M. (2008). *Bedeutung und Bedeutsamkeit: Interpretation von Musik in musikpädagogischer Dimensionierung*, vol. 7. Olms.

Krause-Benz, M. (2014). 'Musik hat für mich Bedeutung' – Bedeutungskonstruktion im Musikunterricht als Dimension musikbezogener Bildung. *Art Education Research, 5*(9), 1–8.

Krupp-SchleuÔner, V. (2016). *Jedem Kind ein Instrument? Teilhabe an Musikkultur vor dem Hintergrund des Capability Approach*. Waxmann.

Krupp, V. (Ed.). (2021). *Wirksamer Musikunterricht*. Schneider Verlag.

Levinson, J. (1990). Musical Literacy. *The Journal of Aesthetic Education, 24*(1), 17–30.

Major, A. E. (2007). Talking about Composing in Secondary School Music Lessons. *British Journal of Music Education, 24*(2), 165–178. https://doi.org/10.1017/S0265051707007437

Major, A. E., & Cottle, M. (2010). Learning and Teaching through Talk: Music Composing in the Classroom with Children Aged Six to Seven Years. *British Journal of Music Education, 27*(3), 289–304. https://doi.org/10.1017/S0265051710000240

Meyer, O., & Coyle, D. (2017). Pluriliteracies Teaching for Learning: Conceptualizing Progression for Deeper Learning in Literacies Development. *European Journal of Applied Linguistics, 5*(2), 199–222. https://doi.org/10.1515/eujal-2017-0006

Ministerium für Kultus, Jugend und Sport Baden-Württemberg (2016). *Musik. Gemeinsamer Bildungsplan der Sekundarstufe I.* Kultus und Unterricht.

Prediger, S., & Buró, S. (2021). Selbstberichtete Praktiken von Lehrkräften im inklusiven Mathematikunterricht: Eine Interviewstudie. *Journal für Mathematik-Didaktik, 42*(1), 187–217. https://doi.org/10.1007/s13138-020-00172-1

Regelski, T. A. (1998). The Aristotelian Bases of Praxis for Music and Music Education as Praxis. *Philosophy of Music Education Review, 6*(1), 22–59.

Richter, C. (1993). Lebensweltliche Orientierung des Musikunterrichts: Eine Komposition Mozarts als Verkleidungs- und Rollenspiel. *Musik Und Bildung, 5,* 24–29.

Rolle, C. (2011). Wann ist Musik bildungsrelevant? In H.-U. Schäfer-Lembeck (Ed.), *Musikalische Bildung – Ansprüche und Wirklichkeiten. Reflexionen aus Musikwissenschaft und Musikpädagogik.* Allitera, pp. 45–55.

Rolle, C. (2013). Argumentation Skills in the Music Classroom: A Quest for Theory. In A. de Vugt & I. Malmberg (Eds.), *Artistry,* vol. 2. Helbling, pp. 137–150.

Shanahan, T., & Shanahan, C. (2008). Teaching Disciplinary Literacy to Adolescents: Rethinking Content-Area Literacy. *Harvard Educational Review, 78*(1), 40–59.

Tajmel, T., & Hägi-Mead, S. (2017). Prinzipien des sprachbewussten Unterrichts. In T. Tajmel & S. Hägi-Mead (Eds.), *Sprachbewusste Unterrichtsplanung. Prinzipien, Methoden und Beispiele für die Umsetzung.* Waxmann, pp. 72–103.

van de Pol, J., Volman, M., & Beishuizen, J. (2010). Scaffolding in Teacher–Student Interaction: A Decade of Research. *Educational Psychology Review, 22*(3), 271–296. https://doi.org/10.1007/s10648-010-9127-6

van Geert, P., & Steenbeek, H. (2005). The Dynamics of Scaffolding. *New Ideas in Psychology, 23*(3), 115–128. https://doi.org/10.1016/j.newideapsych.2006.05.003

Vogt, J. (2014). Schwierige Gleichheit: Vom Nutzen gerechtigkeitsphilosophischer Überlegungen für die Musikpädagogik. In S. Gies & F. HeÔ (Eds.), *Kulturelle Identität und Soziale Distinktion.* Helbling, pp. 45–58.

Weininger, E. B., & Lareau, A. (2018). Pierre Bourdieu's Sociology of Education: Institutional Form and Social Inequality. In T. Medvetz & J. J. Sallaz (Eds.), *The Oxford Book of Pierre Bourdieu.* Oxford Academic, pp. 253–272. https://doi.org/10.1093/oxfordhb/9780199357192.013.11

13 Deeper Learning Mathematics

The case of algebraic questions

SUSANNE PREDIGER AND ANNA-KATHARINA ROOS

Avoiding superficial learning and engaging students in deeper learning has been a crucial goal of mathematics educators for many decades. In mathematics, deeper learning particularly refers to developing conceptual understanding and drawing connections between formerly unconnected knowledge pieces (Hiebert & Carpenter, 1992). Within the last years, mathematics education research has increasingly investigated the role of language for reaching these goals of deeper learning (Moschkovich, 2010; Pimm, 1987; Prediger, 2019b). In this chapter, we report on this subject-specific research on language and mathematics teaching and learning, and we relate it to the ideas of pluriliteracy teaching (Coyle & Meyer, 2021), with concrete examples from algebra learning.

13.1 Mathematical Literacy and Academic Literacy in Mathematics

Three Conceptualisations of Literacy

Literacy is a word with multiple meanings in mathematics education discourses:

- Mathematics education specialists talk about the major aims of mathematics learning as *mathematical literacy* (*Mathematische Bildung* in German; see, e.g. OECD [2007] or Jablonka [2003]), even if they do not explicitly think about the role of language.
- In language education, *disciplinary literacies* for different subjects are considered as important components of pluriliteracies (Coyle & Meyer, 2021, p. 49) and characterised as involving 'the use of reading, reasoning, investigating, speaking and writing required to learn and form complex content knowledge appropriate to a particular discipline' (McConachie, Petrosky & Resnick, 2010, p. 16).
- In a similar approach, mathematics education researchers focusing on language for mathematics learning suggested to extend narrow definitions of academic language proficiency to the wider construct of *academic literacy in mathematics*, involving mathematical proficiency, mathematical practices and mathematical discourse (Moschkovich, 2015).

In this chapter, we explain what we consider the core of mathematical literacy and academic literacy in mathematics and how this relates to Coyle and Meyer's (2021) suggestion to characterise subject-specific literacy by *doing, organising, explaining and arguing* mathematics (according to Polias, 2016).

Many people have experienced *doing* mathematics only in a very procedural sense, with a strong focus on calculating arithmetic tasks or transforming algebraic equations. In the recent TALIS study, only 18 per cent of German teachers' explanations referred to deep content, but in Japan, this figure was 55 per cent (Grünkorn et al., 2020).

The dominantly procedural, inner-mathematical focus on transformational activities is far away from the normative aim of developing *mathematical literacy* in students, which was conceptualised in consensus between all OECD states as '...an individual's capacity to identify and understand the role that mathematics plays in the world, to make well-founded judgements and to use and engage with mathematics in ways that meet the needs of that individual's life as a constructive, concerned and reflective citizen' (OECD, 2007, p. 304).

The cited conceptualisation of mathematical literacy mainly emphasises the role of mathematics for *describing and organising* phenomena, according to which *doing* mathematics genuinely includes

- structuring context situations so that the mathematical structure underlying the situation can be captured
- mathematising everyday situations by mathematical models such as arithmetic operations or algebraic equations
- inner-mathematical transformations
- interpreting mathematical models or results in the context situation
- validating the mathematisation process and its results (Blum & Borromeo Ferri, 2009).

Narrowing down the conceptualisation to the particular field of algebra, holding mathematical literacy in *algebra* includes the ability to use algebra as a powerful language for (1) organising phenomena and (2) exploring their mathematical structures (Bednarz, Kieran & Lee, 1996). Both algebraic activities are considered an integral part of *doing* mathematics in addition to purely transformational activities.

For the processes of *learning algebra* in such a mathematical literacy perspective, however, a second kind of literacy is crucial that we distinguish from the mathematical literacy as defined above, namely the academic language practices and academic language means needed to learn algebra and to engage in meaning-making processes for developing conceptual understanding of arithmetic operations and algebraic concepts, such as equations or equivalence of equations (Prediger & Krägeloh, 2016; Usiskin, 1988).

As many empirical studies on the role of language in developing conceptual understanding in mathematics have shown, two discourse practices are crucial in the processes of developing conceptual understanding (Moschkovich, 2015; Prediger, Erath & Opitz, 2019). Specifically,

- not *reporting* procedures, but
- *explaining* meanings of mathematical concepts and
- *arguing* how symbolic and graphical or contextual representations are connected to each other.

For specifying in detail what *literacy for learning algebra* might entail, we give examples for two of Coyle's & Meyer's (2021) five core constructs: (1) target concepts and forms of algebraic reasoning and (2) forms of representations.

Target Concepts in Algebra and Forms of Algebraic Reasoning

Many students and adults think about algebra as a game of meaningless transformations conducted according to transformation rules learnt by heart, as in the following example.

$$3x + 5 = 11 \Leftrightarrow 3x = 11 - 5 = 6 \Leftrightarrow x = 2$$

The rules are as follows: we can transform an equation by adding or multiplying the same numbers on both sides; for example, adding -5 on both sides eliminates the 5 on the left side and makes -5 occur on the right side of the second equation. Then, multiplying by 1/3 or dividing by 3 realises the second transformation.

In students' thinking, transformation rules that are not underpinned with meaning can easily become arbitrary, so typical errors have often been documented, such as the error $3x + 5 = 11 \Leftrightarrow 3x = 16$ (Malle, 1993). Additionally, students who cannot make sense of the meaning of the variables and equations are not able to use equations to structure everyday situations (i.e. to generalise mathematical relations).

Algebra education research has therefore distinguished typical forms of algebraic reasoning, all of them being important in school (Bednarz, Kieran & Lee, 1996; Kieran, 2004):

- *transformational activities* (i.e. manipulating algebraic expressions and equations according to procedural transformation rules without interpreting the symbolic letters)
- *operational activities* (i.e. using algebraic expressions and equations mainly for evaluating them for concrete numbers)
- *generational and relational activities* (i.e. using variables, expressions and equations to express general structures or conditions in everyday situations or inner-mathematical situations)

Table 13.1 Four algebraic target concepts and their meanings in different forms of reasoning

Four Concepts	Operational Activities	Generational and Relational Activities	Transformational Activities
Variable	Variable as letter to be evaluated by numbers (i.e. place holder)	Variable as unknown or generalised number	Variable as symbol without interpretation
Equation	Equations as statements with place holders to be evaluated	Equation describes the condition of a situation with unknown or generalised numbers	Equation as chain of symbols without interpretation
Solution of an Equation	Numbers belong to the set of the solutions of the equation if the equation turns into a true statement after evaluating the place holders by the number	(Formerly unknown) numbers belong to the set of solutions of the equation if they fulfil the condition described by the equation. Equations with generalised numbers describe relations which are true for all numbers	Solution of equation as result after transformation process
Equivalence of Two Equations	Two equations are equivalent if they have the same set of solutions	Two equations are equivalent if they describe the same condition/situation (e.g. given in a figure)	One equation is equivalent to a second when it can be transformed into the second by the transformation rules
Meta-Level Activity: Justifying the Rules	The transformation rules for equations guarantee that an equation is really transformed into a condition with the same set of solutions		

(Malle, 1993, p. 47; Prediger, 2020, p. 163)

- *meta-level activities* (i.e. to justify the transformation rules with respect to the meaning of variables and the relational activities).

Whereas transformational and operational activities mainly focus on procedural aspects of algebra, generational activities and meta-level activities are key for developing conceptual understanding and thereby deeper learning.

For these activities, the four target concepts are *variable, equation, solution of equation* and *equivalence of equation*. Table 13.1 presents the algebraic target concepts with their meanings in the different forms of reasoning. Some of them will be explained in further detail in the following sections. Even if not all concepts are explained in detail in the table, the overview shows that the algebraic target concepts form a network of concepts with strong connections that need to be built by students. Furthermore, Table 13.1 depicts that the meta-level activity of justifying the transformation rules includes and connects the three activities of algebraic reasoning.

The list of highly complex meanings sheds a first light as to why the two most important discourse practices are also challenging with respect to subject-specific literacy: *explaining meanings* of these four algebraic target concepts requires a highly elaborated language and their highly condensed articulation in Table 13.1 is not at all accessible for students in the first approach. That is why algebra education researchers regularly work with multiple representations, as reported in the next subsection.

Multiple Representations for Understanding Equations and Their Equivalence

Understanding the meaning of equations can be supported by the use of multiple representations for algebra concepts, usually the symbolic–algebraic representation, the symbolic–numeric representation, different graphical representations and the textual representation, often of context problems (Friedlander & Tabach, 2001; Kaput, 1998). Figure 13.1 illustrates the representations in a (simplified, thereby not authentic) example.

The translation from the textual representation of the context problem into the symbolic–algebraic representation is a typical generational activity that requires the interpretation of the variable as unknown (see Table 13.1). Once the algebraic equation is found, it can be solved by transformational activities, that is, by transforming the equation into $x = 2$.

However, before students are able to find the equation, they need to have developed the conceptual understanding of variables (as unknown numbers) and equations (as symbolising conditions for unknown numbers). These meanings can be constructed by the graphical representation in the bar model and by trial and

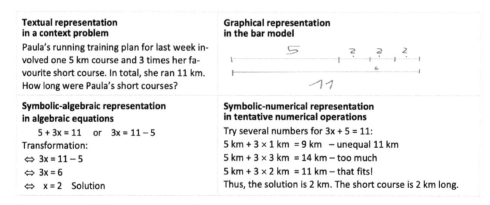

Textual representation in a context problem	Graphical representation in the bar model
Paula's running training plan for last week involved one 5 km course and 3 times her favourite short course. In total, she ran 11 km. How long were Paula's short courses?	
Symbolic-algebraic representation in algebraic equations	**Symbolic-numerical representation in tentative numerical operations**
$5 + 3x = 11$ or $3x = 11 - 5$ Transformation: $\Leftrightarrow 3x = 11 - 5$ $\Leftrightarrow 3x = 6$ $\Leftrightarrow x = 2$ Solution	Try several numbers for $3x + 5 = 11$: 5 km + 3 × 1 km = 9 km − unequal 11 km 5 km + 3 × 3 km = 14 km − too much 5 km + 3 × 2 km = 11 km − that fits! Thus, the solution is 2 km. The short course is 2 km long.

Figure 13.1 Multiple representations for algebraic equations

error for evaluating the equation by several numbers. As the example shows, numerical operations and the bar model are crucial language means for developing the meaning of variables.

The bar model is a variant of the Singapore bar model, which is used in many countries as a graphical model that can support even primary students in solving algebraic context problems without any variables and equations (Fong Ng & Lee, 2009). Malle (1993) has suggested its use (not for avoiding algebraic equations, but) for a deeper learning goal, namely making sense of the transformation rules for algebraic equations: in the generational activity context, two equations are equivalent if they describe the same condition or same situation. In Figure 13.1, the equations $5x + 3x = 11$ and $3x = 11 - 5$ describe the same bar, and looking at the bar makes their equivalence immediately visible.

In the following sections, we report on design experiments in which we tried to explore Malle's (1993) bar-model-based approach towards meaning-making for the equivalence of equations. We will show that the instructional approach bears further language challenges as students struggle to argue concisely how the representations are connected.

13.2   Initiating Progress in Meaning-Making: Connecting Multiple Representations and Engaging Students in Rich Discourse Practices

Malle's (1993) bar-model-based approach to meaning-making for the equivalence of equations suggests engaging students in constructing the meaning of equivalence by connecting the symbolic (algebraic and numerical) equations to the graphical representation of the bar model.

Figure 13.2 shows the connection of symbolic and graphical representations for numerical and algebraic equations and their parallelism for the elementary transformation of addition/subtraction and multiplication/division. The general form with A, B, C indicates that it can be used for every subexpression, such as $B = 3x + 5$.

Whereas Malle (1993) implicitly assumed that juxtaposing the representations might be sufficient for students to construct the meanings of equivalence and to justify the transformation rules within these figures, later empirical research (e.g. Amit and Fried, 2005; Prediger and Wessel, 2013) suggested that representations need not only be juxtaposed, but their connections need to be articulated and discussed explicitly in order to make sure that students see the relevant mathematical structures in them.

From this state of research, we draw the conclusion that a learning environment designed for initiating deeper learning on algebraic equivalence needs to engage students in the following rich discourse practices for articulating how the bar model

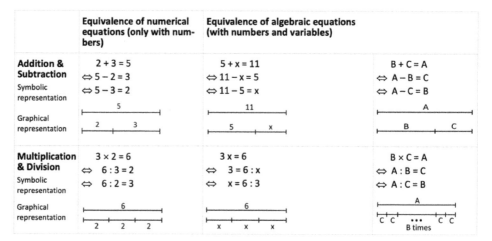

Figure 13.2 Bar-model-based approach to meaning-making for the equivalence of equations (adapted from Malle, 1993, p. 220f)

and the equations are connected as this is the intended learning trajectory towards the targeted discourse practices:

- explaining the meaning of equivalence of the depicted equations
- arguing why the transformation rules apply for all equations by referring them back to generic suitable bar models.

Deep practice of such discourse practices is the result of learning episodes designed using three principles. (1) Connecting multiple representations and languages as well as (2) engaging students in rich discourse practices belong to the key design principles of language-responsive mathematics instruction (e.g. Prediger, 2020; or research survey Erath et al., 2021). The third design principle, (3) macro-scaffolding, calls for sequencing and combining mathematics and language learning opportunities in a dual learning trajectory (Gibbons, 2002; Pöhler & Prediger, 2015). The realisation of macro-scaffolding requires topic-specific empirical research to identify the language demands in students' learning processes (Prediger & Zindel, 2017). This will be described in the next section.

13.3   Typical Obstacles on Students' Pathways towards Deep Understanding

Methodological Background
In order to determine typical obstacles on students' pathways towards deep understanding of algebraic equations and their equivalence in the bar-model-based

approach, we used a *design research methodology* (Cobbet al., 2003; Gravemeijer & Cobb, 2006). Based on an initial specification of the mathematical learning content (relevant target concepts, forms of reasoning, relevant representations and their connections according to Table 13.1 and Figures 13.1, 13.2), we designed a learning environment encompassing four sessions of 45 minutes each for the target group of low-achieving tenth graders in remedial mathematics classes aiming to pass their Grade 10 exam in a pre-vocational setting (called 'Berufsfachschule 1' in Germany, a Level 2 (pre-)vocational programme in the European framework). In this way, design research iteratively combines the repeatedly refined design of learning environments with the empirical, mostly qualitative investigation of the initiated teaching–learning processes in design experiments so that dual aims can be combined, achieving research-based design products and design-based research results, namely, insights into typical pathways and obstacles. In this process, the language demands occurring in the mathematical learning pathways are empirically identified and inform the construction of language learning goals and language scaffolds for the next design experiment cycles (Prediger & Zindel, 2017).

The data-gathering in our design experiments is still ongoing, but revisions between the mini cycles have already been completed. Design experiments have been conducted with four students in pair or individual settings. Since the experiments were conducted amidst the Covid-19 pandemic and resulting school closures, some of them were conducted via video conferences. In total, 675 minutes of video data have already been collected and partially transcribed.

In the current paper, we present five episodes, chosen with respect to their potential of providing insights into typical challenges also found in earlier design research studies on deep algebra learning (Prediger & Krägeloh, 2016). Following these episodes, we show how the design of the learning environment was enriched with respect to language.

Episode 1 and 2: Frank's and Vivien's Surface Strategies Rather than Deeper Learning

The brief Episodes 1 and 2 stem from the first design experiment session, one with Frank and one with Vivien, two 18-year-old students placed in remedial mathematics courses due to earlier struggles. Both students were born and educated in Germany. Frank's family only speaks German, Vivien's family German and Polish.

Episode 1. Frank works on Task 1b printed in Figure 13.3. When asked to find equations for the second bar model in Task 1b in Figure 13.3, he immediately writes the correct answers (also printed in Figure 13.3). However, when the design experiment leader (the second author of this paper) asks him to explain his thoughts, his surface strategies become apparent:

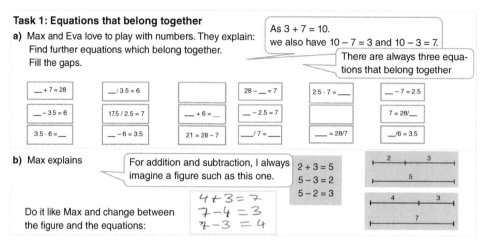

Figure 13.3 Initial task in first design experiment sessions for connecting the bar model to the equations 'that belong together' (together with Frank's correct handwritten answer)

48 DE leader:	And does this figure have anything to do with it [*pointing at the equations*]?
49 Frank:	Yes, actually it does, because it makes clear what kind of numbers you can or have to use for it.
50 DE leader:	Oh, actually you only need it [*the bar model*] to know the numbers or what?
51 Frank:	I think, as well for seeing which number is smaller or bigger. So, I wouldn't see anything more in it or take anything out of it.

Although Frank's equations are correct, he articulates that the bar model only serves as a provider of numbers (Turn 49). This surface strategy does not refer to the mathematical relational structures of the operations, which are also depicted in the bar model. Furthermore, the surface strategy does not unfold what it means that the equations belong together.

Episode 2. The same surface strategy of solely focusing on numbers and not on structures is applied by Vivien in another design experiment, when asked to draw the bar model to the given equations in Task 2 (see Figure 13.4). This time, it leads to a non-adequate bar.

74 DE leader:	Can you explain to me what the 'plus' indicates in the drawing?
75 Vivien:	I would say again, the line that is in between. You can see that it is definitely a plus. Or it could also be a minus. But it could not be 3 + 12, because I see immediately that x is 9. Thus, a minus. That x is in any case a 9.
76 DE leader:	How did you know where to put the 3, the x, the 12 in the drawing?

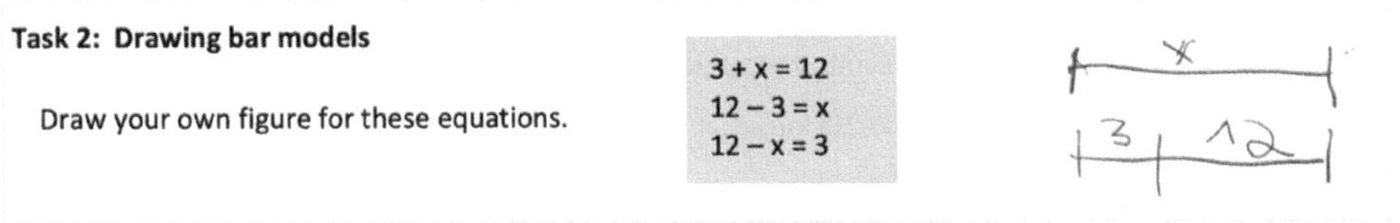

Task 2: Drawing bar models

Draw your own figure for these equations.

$3 + x = 12$
$12 - 3 = x$
$12 - x = 3$

Figure 13.4 Vivien's wrong connection of a bar model to the equation – focus solely on the numbers, not on the relations

77 Vivien: Because I've already seen that on the next one on this sheet [*pointing at the bar model on the next task for 3.2 + 4.5 = u*], the next drawing of it.

78 DE leader: But couldn't you write the 3 in the place where 12 is written or 12 where the x is written?

79 Vivien: I don't think so. You would get mixed up. It was the same with the other sheets: the exact number of centimetres was at the bottom and 2 and 3 at the top, so . . .

70 DE leader: And where do you see $3 + x$ in the drawing?

71 Vivien: Nowhere.

Similar to Frank, Vivien's focus is solely on the numbers, not on the additive structures expressed in the equations (Turn 75). In Turn 77, she makes a second typical surface strategy explicit, building syntactical analogies to other tasks and inferring from there. As the other task had a different structure (3.2 + 4.5 = *u* with the variable being the sum rather than a summand in 3 + *x* = 12), her analogies are false, but she does not recognise it because she does not focus on the additive structure (Turn 79). Instead, she proposes that the vertical line in between 3 and 12 must mean minus, rather than interpreting that two line segments are put together (Turn 75).

From these two brief Episodes 1 and 2, we learnt that juxtaposing representations is not enough as the design must make sure that students also focus their attention on the additive structures expressed in the bar model and in the equation, rather than only the numbers. The phenomenon has often been documented for younger children but persists in the thinking of low-achieving adolescents who have not learnt to talk about mathematical structures and operations (Prediger, 2019a; Prediger & Zindel, 2017).

More in general, the episode resonates with the findings by Amit and Fried (2005), which state that we need 'not just the presence of different representations said to be connected but "connectors" as well' (Amit & Fried, 2005, p. 63).

Episode 3: Vivien's Limited Language Means for Expressing Multiplicative Structures

As a consequence from the findings in the first and second design experiment sessions, we redesigned the learning environment for the third session by starting

New Task:
Three different running programmes and their drawings

- John goes running every Saturday to train for a half marathon. He runs 21 km every time.
- Eva runs 7 km three times a week.
- Max runs 3 km every day from his place to his grandparents.

Assign Eva, Max and John's runs to the matching drawings.

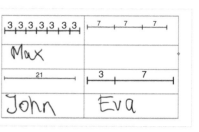

Figure 13.5 Newly designed Task 0 for connecting different bar models to the context situations (together with Vivien's handwritten answers)

with a context problem to support students' meaning-making processes for the additive and multiplicative structures in the bar model. Figure 13.5 shows the newly introduced task that connects four bar models to the textual representation of context situations with different running programmes.

Episode 3. Episode 3 stems from a follow-up design experiment, again with Vivien. The transcript starts when Vivien explains why she chose to assign John's running programme to the bar of 21 and Eva's running programme ('three times a week 7 km') to the bar that mathematicians would interpret as signifying 3 + 7:

21 Vivien: John's run fits to [*lower left bar of New Task*] because he states he 'runs the 21 km every time'.
              Thus, the one where 21 is written belongs to Max, not John.
22 DE leader: That means, we can write John beneath the 21?
23 Vivien: [*Nods*] Um, um. And Eva beneath the one next to it [*refers to the lower right bar*].
              Where there is written 3, then the middle line and then 7.
24 DE leader: And can you explain how you came up with that or why?
25 Vivien: Because it says, 'Eva runs three times a week 7 km'.
              And then I would say, the 3 stands for 'three times a week' and the 7 for '7 km'.

Similar to Episodes 1 and 2, in which students only focused their attention on the numbers while connecting the graphical and symbolic representation without taking into consideration the structure of the operation, Vivien uses the same surface focus for connecting textual and graphical representations in this transcript. Rather than expressing the additive structure of 3 and 7 in this bar, she only articulates the numbers, not joint lengths: 'Where there is written 3, then the middle line and then 7' (Line 23).

Here, it is worth analysing the lexical details and their connection to deeper thinking: 'and then' is the only connective between 3 and 7 that she uses, which does not allow her to distinguish an additive structure from a multiplicative structure.

Some minutes later, the design experiment leader guides her to discover that also the upper right bar (with three segments of 7 km) can be assigned to Eva's running programme

45 Vivien: Actually, we could also write Eva for the picture above this one.

46 DE leader: Why can we write Eva also here?

47 Vivien: Because, um, it, it is even easier, um, than, this. Because there 'Eva runs three times a week 7 km' is written and here *[refers to the bar with three segments of 7]* are, thus, three sections, and there above, it is 7.

Even when Vivien discovers the more adequate match of the bar with three segments of 7 km as matching to 'three times a week 7 km', her language for arguing the match is still very limited, as her hesitations in Turn 47 indicate. Although she correctly refers to three segments of 7 with her gestures, the logical connective she uses between the two factors is still restricted to 'and there above, it is 7' and does not adequately express multiplication as counting in larger units (which might have been expressed, for example, as 'in each section, there are 7').

Episode 3 shows that context problems can reveal the didactical potential for supporting students to grasp the multiplicative structure. These first and tentative insights might stay restricted if the students do not get access to any mediating language means; specifically, in Vivien's case, language means for expressing the key multiplicative structure by expressing the unitising.

Summary of First Empirical Findings

From the qualitative analysis of these three (and many other) episodes in our ongoing design experiments, we conclude that low-achieving students' processes of meaning construction in the bar model can be substantially hindered by limitations in *focusing, identifying and articulating the additive or multiplication structures relevant in the textual, symbolic and graphical representations*. It seems these observed adolescents in our sample have already completed ten years of schooling without actively participating in discourse practices involving deeper learning with the bar models, although the bar models were already introduced in Grade 1 (perhaps in slightly different representations).

The connection between thinking the corresponding discourse practices and the language means to articulate them is striking: whereas the sole focus on numbers only requires limited language means, such as deictic means ('here, there, above') and one single logical connective ('and then'), a deeper conversation about the mathematical structures in each of the representations requires many more connectives for expressing the different meanings of the operations. Although these conceptual (and underlying language-related) challenges are well known from Grades 1–3 (Götze & Baiker, 2021; Kuhnke, 2013) and Grade 5 (Prediger, 2019a), we had not expected to also find them in tenth-grade students with limited access to mathematics and its language. Apparently, if students never get the opportunity to overcome them, the challenges persist.

13.4   Consequences for the Instructional Design

Identified Mathematically Relevant Language Demands for Meaning-Making

What consequences can we draw from the first design experiments? The bar-model-based approach to meaning-making for the equivalence of algebraic equations (Malle, 1993) tries to exploit the connection of graphical, symbolic–algebraic and symbolic-numerical representations (see Figure 13.2). The equations $5 + 3x = 11$ and $3x = 11 - 5$ are called equivalent as they describe the same bar. Understanding this meaning of equivalence allows students not only to deal with algebra on the surface level but also to reach deeper learning. However, to fully understand and work with this characterisation of equivalence, students need to develop and articulate strong connections between the textual, graphical and symbolic representations (Friedlander & Tabach, 2001; Malle, 1993; for language learners in general Moschkovich, 2013). Dealing with multiple representations can have different degrees of depth (Kuhnke, 2013; Prediger & Wessel, 2013):

- only juxtaposing the representations
- only identifying the numbers in each representation
- identifying also the relevant mathematical structures in each representation
- arguing how the relevant mathematical structures correspond between the representations.

The design experiments revealed that, even in Grade 10, low-achieving students do not necessarily master all language demands occurring on students' pathways towards meaning-making at the deeper levels. In the discursive dimension, these language demands particularly include two discourse practices:

- *explaining* meanings of mathematical concepts and representations (in particular, additive and multiplicative structures in textual and graphical representations)
- *arguing* how symbolic and graphical or contextual representations are connected to each other.

In the lexical dimension, these discursive demands require the use of connectives and chunks for expressing additive and multiplicative structures, for the equal sign (connectors for the two expressions in each equation and the two bars in the bar model), the equivalence (connectors for the equations as conditions describing the bars) and the connection of representation (connectors for the graphical, textual and symbolic representation).

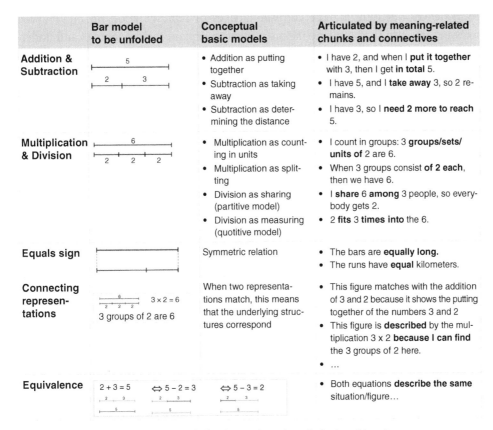

	Bar model to be unfolded	Conceptual basic models	Articulated by meaning-related chunks and connectives
Addition & Subtraction		• Addition as putting together • Subtraction as taking away • Subtraction as determining the distance	• I have 2, and when I **put it together** with 3, then I get **in total** 5. • I have 5, and I **take away** 3, so 2 remains. • I have 3, so I **need 2 more to reach** 5.
Multiplication & Division		• Multiplication as counting in units • Multiplication as splitting • Division as sharing (partitive model) • Division as measuring (quotitive model)	• I count in groups: 3 **groups/sets/ units of** 2 are 6. • When 3 groups consist **of 2 each**, then we have 6. • I **share** 6 **among** 3 people, so everybody gets 2. • 2 **fits** 3 **times into** the 6.
Equals sign		Symmetric relation	• The bars are **equally long**. • The runs have **equal** kilometers.
Connecting representations	3 groups of 2 are 6	When two representations match, this means that the underlying structures correspond	• This figure matches with the addition of 3 and 2 because it shows the putting together of the numbers 3 and 2 • This figure is **described** by the multiplication 3 x 2 **because I can find** the 3 groups of 2 here. • …
Equivalence	2 + 3 = 5 ⇔ 5 − 2 = 3 ⇔ 5 − 3 = 2		• Both equations **describe the same** situation/figure…

Figure 13.6 Lexical language demands for deeper learning of algebra: Meaning-related connectives and chunks for expressing additive and multiplicative structures

From the analysis of the design experiments, we identified a list of essential topic-specific language as summarised in Figure 13.6.

Turning the analytic findings into consequences for the redesign of the learning environment, this list in Figure 13.6 reveals the potential scaffolds needed for students with limited language proficiency on their learning pathway. As Prediger and Krägeloh (2016) have emphasised for other parts of algebra, these meaning-related chunks and connectives play the role of *epistemic mediators* between students' everyday language and the technical language referring to the symbolic representation (factor, product, quotient, equivalence, . . .). The technical language is less relevant for supporting the meaning-making processes than these meaning-related chunks and connectives.

Restructured Mathematical and Language-Related Learning Goals

The first design experiments thus led us to restructure the mathematical and language-related learning goals: for deeper understanding of algebraic equations and their equivalence. Not only are the correspondences of representation (in Figure 13.2) relevant, but also the language means needed to explain their meanings and underlying structures in Figure 13.6. Deeper learning here means to connect the algebra learning contents from Grade 8 explicitly to the additive and multiplicative structures from Grade 2 and to provide meaning-related chunks and connectives for articulating them, in the sense of language for learning (Coyle & Meyer, 2021, p. 349)

Macro-Scaffolding by Combining Mathematical Content and Language Learning Trajectory

For the new design experiments in Cycle 2, we decided to restructure the learning trajectory as depicted in Figure 13.7. According to the design principle of macro-scaffolding (Gibbons, 2002; Pöhler & Prediger, 2015), we have now sequenced the mathematical content trajectory and combined it with the corresponding language trajectory: the construct of learning trajectories was introduced in socio-constructivist mathematics education design research in order to structure learning opportunities along hypothetical steps (Gravemeijer, 1998). It can be aligned with Gibbon's language trajectories since the mathematical content trajectory is also

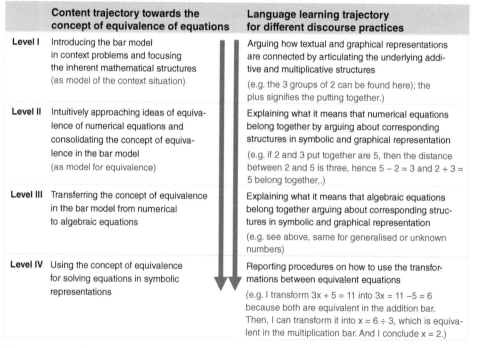

	Content trajectory towards the concept of equivalence of equations	Language learning trajectory for different discourse practices
Level I	Introducing the bar model in context problems and focusing the inherent mathematical structures (as model of the context situation)	Arguing how textual and graphical representations are connected by articulating the underlying additive and multiplicative structures (e.g. the 3 groups of 2 can be found here); the plus signifies the putting together.)
Level II	Intuitively approaching ideas of equivalence of numerical equations and consolidating the concept of equivalence in the bar model (as model for equivalence)	Explaining what it means that numerical equations belong together by arguing about corresponding structures in symbolic and graphical representation (e.g. if 2 and 3 put together are 5, then the distance between 2 and 5 is three, hence $5 - 2 = 3$ and $2 + 3 = 5$ belong together,.)
Level III	Transferring the concept of equivalence in the bar model from numerical to algebraic equations	Explaining what it means that algebraic equations belong together arguing about corresponding structures in symbolic and graphical representation (e.g. see above, same for generalised or unknown numbers)
Level IV	Using the concept of equivalence for solving equations in symbolic representations	Reporting procedures on how to use the transformations between equivalent equations (e.g. I transform $3x + 5 = 11$ into $3x = 11 - 5 = 6$ because both are equivalent in the addition bar. Then, I can transform it into $x = 6 \div 3$, which is equivalent in the multiplication bar. And I conclude $x = 2$.)

Figure 13.7 Combining the mathematical content and language learning trajectory towards equivalence of equations

shaped by tasks and support means designed to leverage students' progress along and between these steps, without assuming unitary pathways, of course.

To adapt the macro-scaffolding principle for mathematics education needs, Pöhler and Prediger (2015) drew upon typical *content trajectories* as established in the Realistic Mathematics Education approach (Gravemeijer, 1998). The trajectory starts from imaginable context problems that allow students to reinvent mathematical concepts, thereby allowing them to mentally construct their meanings in a guided process of emergent modelling, first as *models for* context problem situations, which are later used as *models of* abstract mathematical concepts. Only in a last step of the formal level are purely symbolic transformations introduced.

Level I: Introducing the Bar Model and Arguing How Representations Are Connected

Rather than directly starting at Level II, as in the first design experiment sessions, the restructured content trajectory now starts on Level I with introducing the bar model in context problems and by explicitly directing students to focus on its inherent mathematical structures. Figure 13.8 shows the redesigned task in which the focus is directed more explicitly at the inherent additive and multiplicative structures. As the context problem directly reveals lengths, their representation by line segments is very direct. In later tasks, abstract quantities are to be represented by line segments as well. This is the typical shift from a visual model of context situation to a model of an abstract operation (Gravemeijer, 1998). Here, the equality is represented by three running programmes of equal length in total. Later, it will represent other kinds of equalities (e.g. equally expensive).

Task on Level I with stronger focus on the structures:
Three different running programmes and their drawings

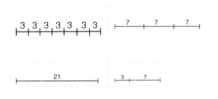

John goes running every Saturday to train for a half marathon. He runs 21 km every time.
Eva runs 7 km three times a week.
Max runs 3 km every day from his place to his grandparents.
- Which of the bars can best describe the runs of Eva, Max and John?
  Be aware that the bar will not only show the numbers but also how the numbers are combined and the result.
- One bar describes an addition, two bars describe a multiplication. How are the operations expressed in the bar?
- How are the operations expressed in the text?
  How would other operations be expressed in the text?
  Find your own examples.

Additional scaffold (provided orally)
- I see 3 × 7 because I see three segments with 7 km each
- 3 | 7 does not fit because we do not see the 'times' in the bar, it would be described by 3 + 7. The 3 in Eva's run is not a line segment.

Figure 13.8 Level I task with a stronger focus on the structures

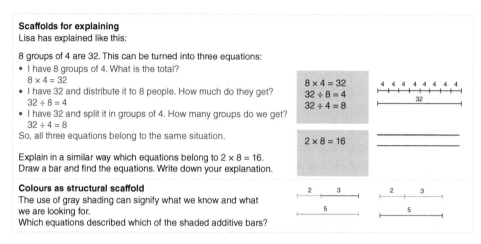

Scaffolds for explaining
Lisa has explained like this:

8 groups of 4 are 32. This can be turned into three equations:
- I have 8 groups of 4. What is the total?
  $8 \times 4 = 32$
- I have 32 and distribute it to 8 people. How much do they get?
  $32 \div 8 = 4$
- I have 32 and split it in groups of 4. How many groups do we get?
  $32 \div 4 = 8$
So, all three equations belong to the same situation.

Explain in a similar way which equations belong to $2 \times 8 = 16$.
Draw a bar and find the equations. Write down your explanation.

Colours as structural scaffold
The use of gray shading can signify what we know and what we are looking for.
Which equations described which of the shaded additive bars?

Figure 13.9 Unpacking Task 1b in Figure 13.3 and providing scaffolds

Level II: Approaching Equivalence of Numerical Equations and Explaining the Meaning

The major task of Level II is printed in Figure 13.3; in the restructured learning environment, the prompt 'Do it like Max and switch between the figure and the equations' is broken down into smaller units with refined prompts:

- Explain how the three equations describe the same bar. How can you see the different operations in the same bar?
- Explain now how these equations belong together.

After this very open, initial explanation task, the next task (shown in Figure 13.9) provides an example explanation that can be adopted by the students. The teachers then discuss how this explanation relates to the students' own explanations in the earlier task.

Also, the visual scaffold by gray shades in the lower part of Figure 13.9 has been designed to direct students' attention to the structures and the subtle differences in interpreting the bars.

Level III: Transferring Equivalence from Numerical to Algebraic Equations and Explaining the Meaning

Level III is a transfer stage when students make the transition from numerical to algebraic equations, involving not only numbers but also variables and signifiers for complete subexpressions (using the analogies depicted in Figure 13.2). In this step, the reasoning with variables is explicitly connected to the reasoning with numbers, a very important focus on the transition from arithmetic to algebra (Kieran, 2004;

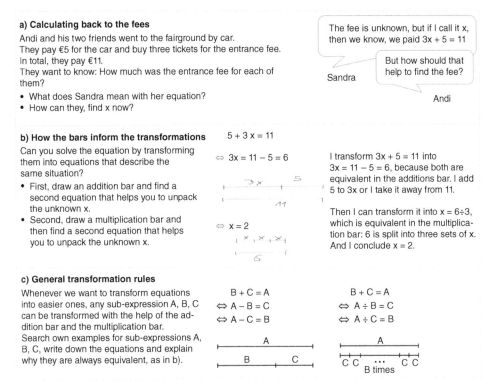

Figure 13.10 Unpacking Task 1b in Figure 13.3 with visual scaffolds and explanation scaffolds

Malle, 1993; Warren, 2003). Episode 2 above shows that once the additive structures were articulated, the variable was not the central obstacle for Vivien.

The design experiments indicate that when the deeper learning for numerical equations is accomplished successfully, this transfer is not too challenging.

Level IV: Using Equivalence for Solving Equations and Reporting Procedures

In the last step (see Figure 13.10), the developed conceptual understanding is used to introduce the corresponding procedures of transforming equations in order to solve them. In these tasks, the bar model is used to justify why the equation can be transformed. It is the argumentative warrant for the transformation rules, which are generalised in two steps. Task b) provides the explanation scaffolds of Task c).

Episode 4: Scaffolding with Relevant Meaning-Related Chunks

On each of the four levels presented above, scaffolding with meaning-related chunks and connectives (listed in Figure 13.6) is provided to support students in explaining differences. In the following episode, Vivien was asked to find the corresponding equation to the given bar model. Firstly, she assigns the expression 2×6 to the model: ⊢__2__⊢_____6_____⊣

81 DE leader: How can you see now that this corresponds to 2×6?

82 Vivien: With the 2, this middle line, and then 6.

83 DE leader: Yes, but isn't it different from the task before [referring to the expression 3 × 4]? There we had 3 times 4, for example, and then we also had **three groups of four**. And do we have **two groups of six** here now?

84 Vivien: No, so, then I must apparently have 2 plus 6.

85 DE leader: Yes. But do you know why?

86 Vivien: Because in the first one [task before] there are 4 plus 4 plus 4, and here there are only 2 and 6. Because I think if there were 'times', it would always be the same [refers to groups of equal size].

87 DE leader: Exactly, because if we would have times, then we would have here [points to the drawing] also **two groups of six**. But we don't have **two groups of six**. We have a 2 and a 6. And that's like running again: if we run 2 km and 6 km, we have a total of 8 km.

When Vivien assigns a non-adequate additive bar to 2×6, the design experiment leader elicits her articulation of the underlying multiplicative structures (Turn 81); as Vivien still restricts to the connector 'and' (in Turn 82), the design experiment leader provides scaffoldings for expressing the multiplicative structures '2 groups of 6' (Turn 83). This helps Vivien to delineate the additive structure of the bar (Turn 84) and give a first vague articulation of the multiplicative structure (Turn 86). The design experiment leader revoices her utterance by offering the '2 groups of 6' again (Turn 87).

13.5   Pushing Students from Surface Learning via Consolidation to the Transfer Stage

By sequencing the learning opportunities systematically in a combined content and language trajectory, students can successively grow along the learning trajectory. For many students, this requires not only the sequence of tasks but also targeted nudges by the teacher to guide them to the next level. The following Episode 5 illustrates such a nudge. Students are asked to correct another (fictitious) student's errors in a bar model task (Figure 13.11), guided by teacher prompting (in the transcript).

Tasks for explaining errors

Max made an error. Find the error and explain to Max
what went wrong and how he could do it correctly.

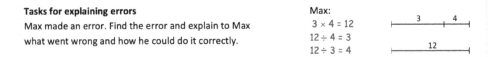

Max:

$3 \times 4 = 12$

$12 \div 4 = 3$

$12 \div 3 = 4$

Figure 13.11 Meta-cognitive tasks explaining errors on Level I

Episode 5: Frank's Little Push

At the end of the second session, after working with the addition bar model as well
as the multiplication bar model, Frank worked on the task in Figure 13.11, which
asks students to verbalise the differences between both. At first glance, Frank does
not see any error in Max's writing. But looking closer, he describes:

76 Frank: Oh, the 3 is bigger than the 4.

77 Frank: [*Some minutes later while looking at the task*] Ah. I would see a plus
there [*points at the addition bar*].

78 DE leader: How do you see that?

79 Frank: Because there's only one 3 and one 4. For me that makes 7 and not
12. But if there's a 3 twice, or how do you calculate it now? 3 times 4
at the most. Or... I would see a plus. But I don't know.

80 DE leader: Can you explain again why you see a plus?

81 Frank: Because the number isn't there several times like in the other tasks. In
the other tasks, there are several numbers. In the other exercises, when
there was a 12, there was a 3, four times, instead of a 3, once. But
because there is now a 3 and a 4, it only makes 7 theoretically. And
they are the same length as the 12, and that doesn't make any sense.

In Turn 76, Frank only refers to the size of the numbers in the addition bar, still
without focusing the operations. This changes some instances later in Turn 77, when
he realises that the drawing shows additive structures whereas the equations represent a multiplication. Although, in Turn 79, he cannot find the right words to
articulate what is wrong, in Turn 81 he speaks about 'a 3, four times', which is
missing in the bar model.

    This episode indicates a small nudge to push Frank towards a meaningful linking of
the underlying mathematical operation in both representations, scaffolded by the
teacher's repeated prompts to articulate more deeply. But Frank is still missing
adequate language means to describe more precisely which operation is suitable
and, especially, why. It confirms the need of scaffolding language means for expressing the additive and multiplicative structures as planned in the revised teaching–
learning arrangement. It has also motivated us to start producing instructional videos
in the research project MuM-Video in order to provide models for good, meaning-
related explanations.

13.6   Conclusion and Outlook

We started our paper by reporting about the ambitious goals of mathematical literacy (OECD, 2007), which aim to foster an individual's capacities to use algebra for describing and organising phenomena (e.g. by structuring context situations so that the mathematical structure underlying the situation can be captured). However, these ambitious goals had to be confronted with the reality of low-achieving students for whom the school system has failed to provide access to these capacities. We worked with 18-year-old students who were not able to use algebra as a powerful language for organising phenomena and exploring their mathematical structures (Bednarz, Kieran & Lee, 1996).

Investigating these low-achieving students' learning pathways provided deep insights into the role of disciplinary literacy as needed for a deeper learning algebra. Of particular use has been the observation of how they struggle to explain the meaning of algebraic equations and argue how they can be connected to graphical or contextual situations. Episodes 1–3 illustrated how students compensate missing conceptual understanding by surface strategies in connecting representations in a superficial way and allowed us researchers to identify the language means for a deeper engagement in the discourse practices of *explaining meaning* and *arguing.* Episodes 1–3 also showed that multiple representations are not a self-contained learning medium with immediate effects, because low-achieving students tend to use them with surface strategies as well. In order to initiate deeper learning, the additive or multiplicative structures inherent in the representations must be explicitly articulated; only then can students learn to use the graphical representations in the intended way.

The detailed analysis of potential obstacles and required language means allows us, as design researchers, to design learning opportunities in which students can develop their mathematical thinking and the necessary language for learning at the same time.[1] Episode 4 and 5 provided first insights into the necessary nudges and scaffolding processes on these learning trajectories.

---

[1] What was exemplified here with excerpts from an ongoing design research project on algebraic equations has already been accomplished for other mathematical topics, such as fractions (Prediger & Wessel, 2013), percentages (Pöhler & Prediger, 2015), functions (Prediger & Zindel, 2017) and proving (Prediger & Hein, 2017). These publications do not use the framework of pluriliteracies but work in a similar approach and with language-responsive design principles, which become increasingly established in the mathematics education subcommunity dealing with enhancing language in mathematics classrooms (Erath et al., 2021). For German-speaking readers, we also refer a teacher book in which the approaches are presented (Prediger, 2020) and the website *sima.dzlm.de/um*, which has open educational resources for language-responsive teaching units on the different mathematics concepts.

13.7 What Can We Learn about Designing Deeper Learning Opportunities in Subject-Matter Classrooms in Language-Responsive Ways?

Even if developed and investigated for mathematical concepts, we believe that the language-responsive design principles might be of use in every subject-matter classroom where deeper learning involves the development of conceptual understanding for abstract, deep concepts. For these classrooms, four design principles are key:

(0) Focus on a deep and robust conceptual understanding of the abstract concepts and provide targeted learning opportunities for students' individual and collective meaning-making processes, starting from imaginable (possibly everyday) contexts.

(1) Engage all students in rich discourse practices (individually and collectively), such as

- *explaining* meanings of subject-specific concepts and representations
- *arguing* how symbolic and graphical or contextual representations are connected to each other.

To achieve equitable participation in these collective discourse practices, their realisation of such activities should be supported by written sentence frames and oral micro-scaffolding.

(2) Connect multiple representations and languaging options with increasing degrees of integration and explicit articulation:

- only juxtaposing the representations
- only identifying the numbers in each representation
- identifying the relevant subject-specific structures in each representation
- arguing how the relevant subject-specific structures correspond between the representations.

(3) Implement macro-scaffolding by systematically sequencing and combining content and language learning opportunities in a dual learning trajectory. Within this dual trajectory (see Figure 13.12 for a generalised version of the levels), the construction of meanings with a meaning-related language is the key linguistic step. It is prepared on Level I by introducing new ideas in a well-known context where students can discover and describe subject-related structures, initially in their own language. On Level II, these preparatory experiences build the ground for introducing or reinventing the abstract concepts and connecting them to the early experiences. On this level, establishing a joint meaning-related language in the classroom is crucial because this guarantees more equitable participation also for students with a still-limited repertoire. Once the conceptual understanding of the new abstract concepts is well established, then formal connections (principles) and procedures are derived, and a technical language is introduced and explicitly

	Content trajectory towards the abstract subject-matter concept	Language learning trajectory for different discourse practices
Level I	Introducing a new idea in a well-known context and getting to know the inherent subject-related structures	Telling stories from context situations and describing subject-specific structures, first in students' own language
Level II	Meaning-making for new abstract concepts by explicitly relating them to structures discovered in contexts	Explaining the meanings in collectively established meaning-related (academic, but not yet technical) language
Level III	Deriving formal connections, principles or procedures from the concepts	Generally describing formal connections or principles and reporting procedures in a technical subject-specific language
Level IV	Applying the learned concepts, connections, principles and procedures in rich and authentic context problems	Multiple discourse practices combining the three earlier levels and flexibly connecting different language varieties

Figure 13.12 Macro-scaffolding principle with generalised dual learning trajectory for combining conceptual and language-related trajectory

connected to the joint meaning-related language (Level III). This technical language is optimised for communicating technical details efficiently and concisely, but not for deeper learning of conceptual understanding. Finally, on Level IV, the learning trajectory comes to the applications of the learnt concepts, connections, principles and procedures in rich and authentic context problems. On this level, the authentic and holistic literacy projects that are described in other chapters of this book can take place. In some cases, the same context as on Levels I and II can be used, but the problems are much more complex once the abstract ideas are learnt. Only this complexity, which was not demonstrated in this paper, can guarantee authenticity, whereas for the first acquisition of deep abstract concepts, the complexity can be an avoidable obstacle.

Each of the language-responsive design principles (1)–(3) serves the main subject-matter education principle (0) in a functional way. In each realisation, the discourse practices are the key language unit on which to reflect during the teaching unit planning process, in particular for:

- *specifying the language learning content* (on each level of the trajectory, first the content goal is specified, then the discourse practices needed to learn the context goal, and only then the lexical and syntactical means to enact the discourse practice)
- *sequencing the language learning content* in a language trajectory
- *selecting subject-specific activities* and enriching them with respect to the language
- *noticing students'* states of learning
- *providing support.*

Acknowledgement. The reported design research study is a part of the project 'MuM-Video – Instructional videos for content- and language-integrated mathematics classrooms' (funded 2020–2024 by the German Ministry for Education and Research, BMBF grant 01JD2001A to S. Prediger and M. Altieri).

REFERENCES

Amit, M., & Fried, M. N. (2005). Multiple Representations in 8th Grade Algebra Lessons: Are Learners Really Getting It? *Proceedings of the 29th Conference of the International Group for the Psychology of Mathematics Education, 2*, 57–64.

Bednarz, N., Kieran, C., & Lee, L. (Eds.). (1996). *Approaches to Algebra: Perspectives for Research and Teaching*. Kluwer Academic Publishers.

Blum, W., & Borromeo Ferri, R. (2009). Mathematical Modelling: Can It Be Taught and Learnt? *Journal of Mathematical Modelling and Application, 1*(1), 45–58.

Cobb, P., Confrey, J., diSessa, A., Lehrer, R., & Schauble, L. (2003). Design Experiments in Educational Research. *Educational Researcher, 32*(1), 9–13. https://doi.org/10.3102/0013189X032001009

Coyle, D., & Meyer, O. (2021). *Beyond CLIL: Pluriliteracies Teaching for Deeper Learning*. Cambridge University Press.

Erath, K., Ingram, J., Moschkovich, J., & Prediger, S. (2021). Designing and Enacting Instruction that Enhances Language for Mathematics Learning: A Review of the State of Development and Research. *ZDM – Mathematics Education, 53*(2), 245–262. https://doi.org/10.1007/s11858-020-01213-2

Fong Ng, S., & Lee, K. (2009). The Model Method: Singapore Children's Tool for Representing and Solving Algebraic Word Problems. *Journal for Research in Mathematics Education, 40*(3), 282–313. https://doi.org/10.5951/jresematheduc.40.3.0282

Friedlander, A., & Talbach, M. (2001). Promoting Multiple Representations in Algebra. In A. A. Cuoco (Ed.), *The Roles of Representation in School Mathematics: 2001 Yearbook of the National Council of the Teachers of Mathematics*. NCTM, pp. 173–185.

Gibbons, P. (2002). *Scaffolding Language, Scaffolding Learning: Teaching Second Language Learners in the Mainstream Classroom*. Heinemann.

Götze, D., & Baiker, A. (2021). Language-Responsive Support for Multiplicative Thinking as Unitizing: Results of an Intervention Study in the Second Grade. *ZDM – Mathematics Education, 53*(2), 263–275. https://doi.org/10.1007/s11858-020-01206-1

Gravemeijer, K. (1998). Developmental Research as a Research Method. In J. Kilpatrick & A. Sierpinska (Eds.), *What is Research in Mathematics Education and What Are Its Results?* Kluwer.

Gravemeijer, K., & Cobb, P. (2006). Design Research from a Learning Design Perspective. In J. van den Akker, K. Gravemeijer, S. McKenney, & N. Nieveen (Eds.), *Educational Design Research*. Routledge, pp. 17–51.

Grünkorn, J., Klieme, E., Praetorius, A.-K., & Schreyer, P., eds. (2020). *Mathematikunterricht im internationalen Vergleich: Ergebnisse aus der TALIS-Videostudie Deutschland*. DIPF | Leibniz-Institut für Bildungsforschung und Bildungsinformation.

Hiebert, J., & Carpenter, T. P. (1992). Learning and Teaching with Understanding. In D. A. Grouws (Ed.), *Handbook of Research on Mathematics Teaching and Learning.* Macmillan, pp. 65–97.

Jablonka, E. (2003). Mathematical Literacy. In A. Bishop, M. A. Clements, C. Keitel, J. Kilpatrick, & F. K. S. Leung (Eds.), *Second International Handbook of Mathematics Education.* Kluwer, pp. 77–104.

Kaput, J. J. (1998). Representations, Inscriptions, Descriptions and Learning: A Kaleidoscope of Windows. *The Journal of Mathematical Behavior, 17*(2), 265–281. https://doi.org/10.1016/S0364-0213(99)80062-7

Kieran, C. (2004). The Core of Algebra: Reflections on Its Main Activities. In K. Stacey, H. Chick, & M. Kendal (Eds.), *The Future of the Teaching and Learning of Algebra: The 12th ICMI Study*, vol. 8. Kluwer Academic Publishers, pp. 21–33. https://doi.org/10.1007/1-4020-8131-6_2

Kuhnke, K. (2013). *Vorgehensweisen von Grundschulkindern beim Darstellungswechsel: Eine Untersuchung am Beispiel der Multiplikation im 2. Schuljahr.* Springer.

Malle, G. (1993). *Didaktische Probleme der elementaren Algebra.* Vieweg.

McConachie, S. M., Petrosky, A. R., & Resnick, L. B. (Eds.). (2016). *Content Matters: A Disciplinary Literacy Approach to Improving Student Learning.* Jossey-Bass.

Moschkovich, J. (Ed.). (2010). *Language and Mathematics Education.* Information Age.

Moschkovich, J. (2013). Principles and Guidelines for Equitable Mathematics Teaching Practices and Materials for English Language Learners. *Journal of Urban Mathematics Education, 6*(1), 45–57.

Moschkovich, J. (2015). Academic Literacy in Mathematics for English Learners. *The Journal of Mathematical Behavior, 40*(A), 43–62. https://doi.org/10.1016/j.jmathb.2015.01.005

OECD. (2007). *PISA 2006: Science Competencies for Tomorrow's World: Volume 1: Analysis.* OECD. https://doi.org/10.1787/9789264040014-en

Pimm, D. (1987). *Speaking Mathematically: Communication in Mathematics Classrooms.* Routledge.

Pöhler, B., & Prediger, S. (2015). Intertwining Lexical and Conceptual Learning Trajectories – A Design Research Study on Dual Macro-Scaffolding towards Percentages. *EURASIA Journal of Mathematics, Science and Technology Education, 11*(6), 1697–1722. https://doi.org/10.12973/eurasia.2015.1497a

Polias, J. (2016). *Apprenticing Students into Science: Doing, Talking & Writing Scientifically.* Lexis Education.

Prediger, S. (2019a). Mathematische und sprachliche Lernschwierigkeiten: Empirische Befunde und Förderansätze am Beispiel des Multiplikationskonzepts. *Lernen und Lernstörungen, 8*(4), 247–260. https://doi.org/10.1024/2235-0977/a000268

Prediger, S. (2019b). Welche Forschung kann Sprachbildung im Fachunterricht empirisch fundieren? Ein Überblick zu mathematikspezifischen Studien und ihre forschungsstrategische Einordnung. In B. Ahrenholz, S. Jeuk, B. Lütke, J. Paetsch, & H. Roll (Eds.), *Fachunterricht, Sprachbildung und Sprachkompetenzen.* De Gruyter, pp. 19–38. https://doi.org/10.1515/9783110570380-002

Prediger, S. (2020). *Sprachbildender Mathematikunterricht in der Sekundarstufe – Ein forschungsbasiertes Praxisbuch.* Cornelsen.

Prediger, S., & Hein, K. (2017). Learning to Meet Language Demands in Multi-Step Mathematical Argumentations: Design Research on a Subject-Specific Genre. *European Journal of Applied Linguistics*, *5*(2), 309–335. https://doi.org/10.1515/eujal-2017-0010

Prediger, S., & Krägeloh, N. (2016). 'X-Arbitrary Means Any Number, but You Do Not Know Which One': The Epistemic Role of Languages while Constructing Meaning for the Variable as Generalizers. In A. Halai & P. Clarkson (Eds.), *Teaching and Learning Mathematics in Multilingual Classrooms*. SensePublishers, pp. 89–108. https://doi.org/10.1007/978-94-6300-229-5_7

Prediger, S., & Wessel, L. (2013). Fostering German Language Learners' Constructions of Meanings for Fractions – Design and Effects of a Language- and Mathematics-Integrated Intervention. *Mathematics Education Research Journal*, *25*(3), 435–456. https://doi.org/10.1007/s13394-013-0079-2

Prediger, S., & Zindel, C. (2017). School Academic Language Demands for Understanding Functional Relationships: A Design Research Project on the Role of Language in Reading and Learning. *EURASIA Journal of Mathematics, Science and Technology Education*, *13*(7b), 4157–4188. https://doi.org/10.12973/eurasia.2017.00804a

Prediger, S., Erath, K., & Opitz, E. M. (2019). The Language Dimension of Mathematical Difficulties. In A. Fritz, V. G. Haase, & P. Räsänen (Eds.), *International Handbook of Mathematical Learning Difficulties: From the Laboratory to the Classroom*. Springer, pp. 437–455. https://doi.org/10.1007/978-3-319-97148-3_27

Usiskin, Z. (1988). Conceptions of School Algebra and Uses of Variables. In A. F. Coxford & A. P. Shulte (Eds.), *The Ideas of Algebra, K-12*. NCTM, pp. 8–19.

Warren, E. (2003). The Role of Arithmetic Structure in the Transition from Arithmetic to Algebra. *Mathematics Education Research Journal*, *15*(2), 122–137. https://doi.org/10.1007/BF03217374

Conclusion: Moving beyond First Steps by Using PTDL for Whole-School Development and Transformation

The pedagogic considerations and practical ideas presented in this volume offer, we believe, a compelling rationale for exploring the potential of deeper learning across a wide range of subjects through an explicit focus on subject literacies that:

- Promote the prioritisation of deeper understanding of subject-specific concepts alongside subject-specific ways of constructing and communicating that understanding.
- Illustrate how a continuous focus on meaning-making and languaging of understanding will not only support and facilitate conceptual understanding of subject content but will also render learning more transparent by making subject-specific thinking and processing visible and thus more accessible and easier to grasp for learners.
- Emphasise that using more than one language in subject lessons to highlight subject-specific ways of meaning-making across languages can be a powerful learning catalyst. This is because a focus on **PLURI**-literacies will create synergies that will increase our learners' meaning-making potential by empowering them to successfully communicate across subjects and languages, purposefully using a wide variety of genres, modes and styles.
- Show that the concept of *deeper learning episodes* (DLEs) is compatible with a wide range of subjects. At the same time, the experts report that our suggested template for designing such episodes, along with the guiding questions we developed, constitute useful planning tools that offer practitioners effective, systematic and adaptable guidance in designing DLEs.

We hope that readers will be inspired to adapt their approach to learning by moving from focusing on 'teaching students' to *mentoring* their learners' personal growth in explicit ways. PTDL suggests novel ways of rethinking and adapting teaching strategies by providing opportunities for building, applying and transferring understanding as it evolves. This will facilitate deeper learning and foster engagement, commitment and mastery orientation.

However, it would be naïve to think that these ambitious goals are achievable by occasional experiments with DLEs. While we acknowledge that first steps are crucial, the challenge ultimately lies in moving beyond these and exploring ways of designing trajectories for deeper learning in the classroom. These require longer-term planning, encouragement and investment.

In addition, we believe that teachers exploring and embracing PTDL might reach out to their colleagues in co-creating active learning communities. When teachers and school leaders are ready to jointly prioritise pluriliteracies development in their learners through building a shared understanding of educational goals, values and practices across subjects and disciplines, this will open novel and unprecedented ways for transdisciplinary whole-school development.

The pluriliteracies approach does not intend for school subjects to lose their specific character and their unique ways of constructing and communicating knowledge and understanding. On the contrary, highlighting the core constructs of school subjects and aligning them with the mechanics and drivers of deeper learning will allow teachers to increase task fidelity. Higher task fidelity will lead to a more holistic, authentic and engaging learning experience. It also offers a way for teachers to design performance and learning tasks that are meaningful and relevant by reflecting the challenges of real-world problems.

Digitisation has created an opportunity to design learning spaces that enable plurimodal and pluriliterate co-constructive learning and mentoring. Learning ecologies can evolve far beyond the individual classroom, allowing for more autonomous learning experiences with the help of appropriate scaffolding, feedback and assessment. But while the use of digital tools and strengthening the digital infrastructure are considered essential, professional development is crucial for pedagogic innovation.

However, it must be emphasised that coherent goals and ideas for transforming classrooms into digital learnscapes are still emerging. In this chapter we would like to outline a more holistic vision for whole-school development at different stages of implementation.

Table 14.1 offers an initial framework for whole-school development using the values and visions promoted by schools to steer classroom practices underpinned by PTDL principles. The framework encourages self-evaluation for schools in terms of educational goals and aspirations through a series of questions that ultimately focus on classroom practices.

Pluriliteracies principles relating to these questions are intended to guide an evaluation that offers possible repositioning and new directions for school developers building on and connecting with existing strengths and identities.

Table 14.2 offers ways of implementing PTDL, ranging from steps taken by individual teachers to collaborative short- and medium-term projects by groups of teachers, leading to and informing whole-school moves for curriculum development and transformative pedagogies. Moving along the continuum offers learners increasingly purposeful opportunities for literacies progression that support deeper understanding, deep practice and transfer of learning.

Table 14.1 PTDL guiding framework for whole-school development

Values	Vision	Principles to Practise
What are the values underpinning learning in our school in terms of:	How do we articulate/define our vision?	How can PTDL principles guide us in shaping and implementing our vision?
Educational Goals	How do we raise confident individuals and responsible citizens?	• *Responsible global citizenship*
Knowledge Building	How do we enable learners to become effective contributors?	• *Deeper understanding*
	What do we want learners in our school to know, do and value?	• *Deep practice* • *Sustainability of learning* • *Critical literacies*
Role of Languages in Learning	How can we enable our learners to become effective communicators?	• *Disciplinary literacies* • *Textual fluency*
	1. How can we help them communicate understanding adequately and respectfully across languages, cultures and subjects?	• *Pluriliterate language use* • *Intercultural meaning-making*
	2. How do we include other languages, such as heritage/regional languages?	
Assessment	How will learners in our school demonstrate deep understanding?	• *Transfer of learning* • *Demonstrating deep understanding*
Curriculum	How do we envision and sustain learning progressions for pluriliteracies development?	• *Disciplinary literacies/ pluriliteracies* • *Learning progressions*
Role of the Teachers	How can we, as teachers, mentor learning and personal growth?	• *Mentoring learning*
Role of the Learners	How can we generate and sustain learner commitment and achievement?	• *Deeper learning partnerships* • *Learner engagement* • *Growth mindset* • *Well-being* • *Self-efficacy*

Ultimately, our vision for a PTDL school is one where deeper learning and personal growth are transparently foregrounded. We realise that changing classroom practices takes time and investment by teachers and school leaders. However, while we know there are no panaceas in education, the subject practitioners contributing to this volume have shared their own understanding, interpretation and explorative practices embedded in PTDL, and in so doing provide readers with examples of what has inspired them and their learners to experience pluriliteracies spaces for deeper learning. The examples in this volume therefore illustrate evolving

Table 14.2 PTDL whole-school development continuum

PTDL Whole-School Development Continuum

Organisational Factors	PTDL for Individual Subject Lesson Planning	PTDL for Short-Term Transdisciplinary Projects	PTDL for Longer-Term Transdisciplinary Projects	PTDL For Whole-School Curricular Development
Professional Development	Individual teachers explore and evaluate PTDL principles with learners, supported by professional development opportunities.	Groups of teachers collaborate and share PTDL classroom practices and learner experiences supported by professional development opportunities.		Regular PTDL professional development events strengthen whole-school and cross-school collaboration.
Course Design	Subject *learning objectives* are enhanced by exploring and emphasising subject literacy development.	PTDL principles inform project design, implementation, assessment and course evaluation.		PTDL principles inform design, implementation, assessment and evaluation across courses.
Role of Languages of Schooling	Subjects are taught mostly in the language of schooling. Additional languages are explored for synergies in academic language/literacy development.	Additional languages are further explored for increasing synergies in academic language/literacy development.		The potential of additional languages for promoting PTDL development is fully recognised and reflected in course design across a range of subjects.
Learning Tasks and Materials	Subject-specific learning materials and tasks are designed to focus on disciplinary literacies development.	Subject-specific learning materials and task are designed for pluriliteracies development.		Learning materials offer multi-dimensional, dynamic and interrelated scaffolding for literacies development in more than one language.
Integration of Digital Media	Digital media is used occasionally to promote critical literacies development within the classroom.	Digital media is used systematically to explore the potential for pluriliteracies development inside and outside the classroom.		Digital media is used systematically for pluriliteracies development inside and outside the classroom to create integrated learning ecologies or *learnscapes*.
Resources	Professional development of pioneer teachers cascades PTDL practices across the school.	Sustainable investment over time for whole-school development includes: • regular professional development events • allocation of time resources for teacher collaboration (development of teaching and evaluation strategies, resources, assessment guidelines) • financial resources for hardware/software/learning materials and architectural redesigning of learning spaces.		

principles of pluriliteracies practices that can be used to inform design, implementation, assessment and evaluation across courses and the curriculum. At the same time, the value of investing in and sustaining professional learning communities should not be underestimated.

From the very beginning, PTDL has been about collaboration between researchers, curriculum developers and educators. We hope that this volume continues to inspire those partnerships to flourish and action future directions for research in and shared practices for deeper learning and teaching.